Stories of
Oprah

Stories of Oprah

The Oprahfication of American Culture

EDITED BY
TRYSTAN T. COTTEN
AND
KIMBERLY SPRINGER

UNIVERSITY PRESS OF MISSISSIPPI
JACKSON

www.upress.state.ms.us

The University Press of Mississippi is a member of the Association of
    American University Presses.

First printing 2010
∞
Library of Congress Cataloging-in-Publication Data

Stories of Oprah : the Oprahfication of American culture / edited by
    Trystan T. Cotten and Kimberly Springer.
      p. cm.
  Includes bibliographical references and index.
  ISBN 978-1-60473-407-2 (cloth : alk. paper) 1. United States—
    Civilization—1970- 2. Winfrey, Oprah—Influence. I. Cotten,
    Trystan T., 1986– II. Springer, Kimberly, 1970–
  E169.12.S842 2010
  973.924—dc22   2009022458

British Library Cataloging-in-Publication Data available

Contents

VII Introduction
Delineating the Contours of the Oprah Culture Industry
KIMBERLY SPRINGER

Part I. Oprah the Woman, Oprah the Empire

3 Chapter 1. Beginnings with O
JOHN HOWARD

19 Chapter 2. "I'm Everywoman"
Oprah Winfrey and Feminist Identification
JENNIFER L. REXROAT

33 Chapter 3. New Age Soul
The Gendered Translation of New Age Spirituality on The Oprah Winfrey Show
KARLYN CROWLEY

Part II. Contesting the Oprah Experts

51 Chapter 4. Post[ed]structuralism?
Oprah's Message Boards, Soul Stories, *and the Everyday Lives of Women*
SHERRA SCHICK

65 Chapter 5. Oprah para Mujeres Chicanas
A Survey of the Impact of Oprah's Message on Chicanas
ADRIANA KATZEW AND LILIA DE KATZEW

85   Chapter 6. Confessions from At-Risk Teens
     Abstinence, the Social Construction of Promiscuity, and
     The Oprah Winfrey Show
     KATHERINE GREGORY

99   Chapter 7. Oprah Goes to Africa
     Philanthropic Consumption and Political (Dis)Engagement
     HEATHER LAINE TALLEY AND MONICA J. CASPER

Part III. The Oprahfication of Media

115   Chapter 8. Oprah and the New News
      KATHLEEN DIXON AND KACIE JOSSART

131   Chapter 9. The Oprahfication of 9/11
      September 11, the War in Iraq, and The Oprah Winfrey Show
      JAAP KOOIJMAN

145   Chapter 10. From the Nobel to Oprah
      Toni Morrison, Body Politics, and Oprah's Book Club
      EDITH FRAMPTON

161   Chapter 11. Lost in Translation
      Irony and Contradiction in Harpo's Production of Zora Neale Hurston's
      Their Eyes Were Watching God
      TRYSTAN T. COTTEN

179   Contributors

183   Index

Introduction

Delineating the Contours of the Oprah Culture Industry

KIMBERLY SPRINGER

What Would Oprah Do? That is what actress Robin Okrant set out to discover on January 1, 2008. She launched her blog, LivingOprah.com, to detail her attempt to "live the [her] best life." More than a riff, Okrant set out to use Oprah Winfrey's tips, admonishments, and claims to expert knowledge for how she should shop, dress, behave, and think. Adopting the name LO (Living Oprah), she wrote in her mission statement, "I am performing an experiment: for one year, I will live as Oprah advises on her television show, on her website and in the pages of her magazines. The tagline to LivingOprah.com is 'Live Your Best Life' and I wonder, will I truly find bliss if I commit wholeheartedly to her lifestyle suggestions?"

At the seventh-month mark, in an interview with National Public Radio's Michele Norris, Okrant admits that her preliminary finding is that she is *not* living her best life. She is, frankly, living an exhausted existence. In acquiring Oprah's Favorite Things (white jeans), eating the way Oprah and her trainer Bob Greene says she should (by savoring every meal), and carrying herself in the world as Oprah and her spiritual gurus mandate (constant contentment), Okrant accumulates emotional, physical, psychic, and most of all, financial expenses.

She does not factor in writing about her experiences on LivingOprah.com nor participating in press interviews as increasing her living-like-Oprah work-load. Often journalists and fellow bloggers question Okrant's motive and sanity, not for the clearly expensive lifestyle her experiment entails. Instead, the main question is, what person in their right mind would criticize Oprah publicly? After noting the extensive disclaimer on LivingOprah.com (the trademark assertions lifted almost word-for-word from Oprah.com), Norris asks, "Are you at all aware that she's looking over your shoulder?" Note Norris's question does not inquire about the possibility of Oprah surveillance but assumes Winfrey's watchful eye ("Are you at all aware . . ."). Oprah is veritably omniscient in both Norris's query and Okrant's response. Okrant issues the seemingly obligatory denials and qualifiers one must when offering any critique of Oprah: she is not making fun of Oprah. In fact, Okrant says gravely, "Nooo . . . I actually admire her quite a bit and I think that there's actually a lot to learn from her" (NPR, 2008). Ultimately, she professes to be engaged in one of the central aims of cultural criticism: to critique cultural "products" and challenge our engagement with that product.

Okrant's blog and her experience attempting to live according to an Oprah template neatly bring together media synergies, cultural trends, economic shifts, movements for social change, and ideological imperatives. Okrant is a white woman using a relatively new electronic medium to explore what it is like to live her life according to the religious and capitalist edicts of a black woman who is successful (whether she acknowledges it or not) owing to the gains of the civil rights and women's movements in an era alternatively called "post-civil rights," "postfeminist," and neoliberal. Oprah's directives are delivered using the same new medium that Okrant employs (the internet and world wide web), as well as television and print.

Okrant is not alone in asking, "What Would Oprah Do?" Millions of women (and some men) worldwide consume brand Oprah economically, culturally, and politically.[1] Oprah's economics, both those of the individual and her corporate holdings, tell us about America's spending priorities, aspirations, and shortcomings. Oprah Winfrey's net worth, according to *Forbes* magazine, is $1.5 billion. The philanthropic arm of Winfrey's enterprise, Oprah's Angel Network, has raised $50 million on behalf of nonprofits worldwide to date. On her ABC primetime television show, *Oprah's Big Give*, contestants must give away hundreds of thousands of dollars in order to demonstrate empathy for others . . . and win $1 million.

Too, Oprah was named one of *Time Magazine's* 100 Most Influential People in the World for four consecutive years in a row. This influence is often measured in terms of economic impact. For example, aside from Jonathan Franzen,[2] most contemporary authors would sell their souls for Oprah to pick their novels for Oprah's Book Club. *Business Week* opines, "Publishers estimate that [Oprah's] power to sell a book is anywhere from 20 to 100 times that of any other media personality" (2005). Commenting on how much money Winfrey is worth, how much she gives away to charity, and how much ancillary experts make as part of the Oprah brand are the usual topics broached when discussing Winfrey.

Winfrey is a political entity, yet, as John Howard and Jennifer Rexroat outline in this volume, Winfrey credits neither the civil rights nor women's movement activism with contributing to her successful rise from news anchor to media giant. Instead she credits inner strength and spirituality. As contributors Karlyn Crowley and Sherra Schick unmask in their respective chapters in this volume, this spirituality has political ramifications.

Thus, if we take one topic that Winfrey chooses to speak out on in her television show—sexual abuse of children—we find politics present despite the personal nature of abuse. Drawing on sexual abuse as a child and in her adolescence, Winfrey started a number of initiatives designed to stop sexual abuse. Problematically, she seeks to redefine abuse as "sexual seduction" but is successful in marshalling her audience members and local law enforcement agencies to support the establishment of a national database listing convicted pedophiles (Winfrey, 2005). Winfrey testified before the Senate Judiciary Committee on behalf of the bill that later came to be called "Oprah's Bill," and President Bill Clinton signed the National Child Protection Act into law in 1993. Whether in print, on television, or on radio, any discussions of power relations (for example, in sexuality, race, disability, or gender issues) are inherently political whether those initiating those conversations wish to acknowledge this fact or not.

The appearances of presidential candidates Al Gore and George W. Bush can seem apolitical or at least nonpartisan on *The Oprah Winfrey Show* (*TOWS*). Winfrey's discussions with the presidential candidates about children, family, past drinking problems, and spiritual/religious dedication evoke commitment to, as Janice Peck defines it in her book *The Age of Oprah*, "the 'enchanted self' exalted by Oprah Winfrey and the 'enterprising self' championed by neoliberalism" (Peck 2008, 220).

Even when Winfrey finally makes an overt political move, such as throwing her support behind Democratic presidential candidate Barack Obama, her reasons are seemingly apolitical. Interviewed May 2, 2007, on *CNN Larry King Live*, Oprah claims to simply like Obama as a person and his stand on significant sociopolitical issues. The areas with which Oprah finds agreement (foreign policy? domestic security?) with Obama remain obscured. Much like an item on her list of product endorsements, Obama joins the litany of Oprah's Favorite Things ("He's my favorite Senator") with little information regarding the rationale behind her choices.[3] Contrary to avoiding politics, Peck finds that is it precisely this appearance of being apolitical that makes Oprah and her cultural spin-offs politically dangerous in a time of neoliberal hegemony (222).

Most obviously, the sphere in which Winfrey's influence crosses a number of boundaries is in the cultural. *TOWS* entered national syndication in 1986,

quickly surpassed its only competitor, *Donahue*, and spawned a host of imita-
tors. Forty-six million viewers watch the show in 134 countries each week. The
recipient of numerous Daytime Emmy Awards, Winfrey decided 40 awards
were plenty and removed herself from the running for host honors in 1999
and the show in 2000. The cultural impact of *TOWS* leaves both audiences
and television industry insiders wanting more.

This something more manifests itself in the diversification of Winfrey's
production company, Harpo, Inc., and her media holdings, which include print,
internet, television, radio, and film interests. In addition to her long-running
television show, Winfrey is a cofounder of Oxygen Media and the Oxygen
Network, a cable television channel dedicated to reruns and reality television
shows.[4] Oprah's Book Club is widely credited with a resurgence in American
reading habits, but this impact is measured in terms of book *sales* not those
actually read. *O, the Oprah Magazine* has a circulation of 2.7 million readers,
despite a 10 percent decline in sales between 2005 and 2008 (Kuczybski 2000).
Until it folded in Winter 2008, *O at Home*, an interior design magazine, helped
Winfrey's fans manifest their spiritual growth in home decorating makeovers.
Oprah.com emerges as a formidable entity with, according to the site's statistics,
92 million page views, 6 million users per month and 1.8 million+ newsletter
subscribers. The XFM Satellite Radio channel *Oprah & Friends*, launched in
2006, features well-known Oprah experts dispensing Oprah-certified health,
spirituality, finance, and relationship advice. Less than a year after its debut
in 2007, Oprah YouTube videos have more than 1 million views, and, starting
in 2009, the premier of the appropriately named *OWN*, or Oprah Winfrey
Network (a media venture with Discovery Communications), returns Winfrey
to television just before *TOWS* concludes its run in 2011.

Finally, it does not take a great deal of attentiveness to note, and be over-
whelmed by, the proliferation of Oprah references in popular culture. Un-
solicited promotion perpetuates the Oprah brand at no cost to Harpo, Inc.
What might have begun as disdain for her particular brand of confessional
television in the 1980s has evolved into a mixture of reverence, fear, and con-
flicted emotions today. Television shows (*The Boondocks, 30 Rock, South
Park, The Man Show, Grey's Anatomy, The War at Home, Chappelle's Show,
Fresh Prince of Bel-Air, Ellen, Married with Children, The Colbert Report, The
Daily Show, Noah's Arc, Roseanne, Scrubs, Stargate SG-1, The X Files*), films
(*Talladega Nights: The Ballad of Ricky Bobby, Miss Congeniality 2: Armed
and Fabulous, Austin Powers: International Man of Mystery* and *The Spy Who
Shagged Me, Barbershop, Ocean's Thirteen*), the music industry (Notorious
B.I.G.'s posthumous video "Nasty Girl," Missy Elliott's *The Cookbook*), and
internet websites (D-listed, TMZ, Glitterati Gossip) reference Oprah as an

omnipotent but beneficent goddess to be courted or a power-hungry demon to be mocked and taken down. It is difficult to tell whether popular culture generates or merely reiterates culture-at-large's love/hate relationship with Oprah Winfrey, but most certainly "Oprah" is shorthand for any number of emotional responses screenwriters wish to convey.

In a sense, the divisions I have drawn among the cultural, economic, and political are meaningless owing to the overlap in Winfrey's cultural productions. Where does Oprah the woman end and Oprah the brand begin? Attention to specificity becomes crucial in answering this question. One must be constantly and consistently vigilant to specify *which Oprah* is under examination.

Oprah the dieter was a staple of America's self-obsessed 1980s fitness craze. We also have Oprah the media empire with Oprah as founder, producer, programmer, and host for television show, radio, and cable networks. Oprah the philanthropist wades through flooded New Orleans and builds a girls' school in South Africa. There are also Oprah the actor in films and television appearances, such as *The Women of Brewster Place*, *Native Son*, and Steven Spielberg's *The Color Purple*, and Oprah the Broadway producer of *The Color Purple*. Oprah, the editorial director of *O, the Oprah Magazine*, made the decision to feature Oprah the cover girl on each monthly issue. And as already noted, the newest Oprah, Oprah the politico, entered into the fray of American politics by endorsing Senator Barack Obama's candidacy for president, staging fundraisers, and attending town hall meetings on his behalf.

Yet, there are also unspoken, uninvestigated Oprahs. Oprah the civil rights leader or black liberation activist is not a persona that readily comes to mind. Oprah the feminist is a debatable aspect of her ideology as reflected in her perspectives on such topics as relationships, sex, work, and home. "Feminist" is not an identity she claims. The unmarried and child-free Oprah is surprisingly unremarked upon, a strange elision given her audience demographic (women, mothers) and the amount of expert advice dispensed regarding child-rearing and protection of children. Indeed, Oprah as a sexual being is a persona mitigated and glossed over through her permanent engagement to her fiancé Stedman Graham: she is heterosexual and monogamous, but that is all the public needs to know for reassurance. The Oprah she chooses to offer us and the Oprah we choose to engage provide historical and political information about American culture and its anxieties from the late 1980s through today. Despite popular culture paranoia or consumer wishful thinking, as the Oprahs I have outlined show, there is no universal Oprah.

If we revisit Theodor Adorno and Max Horkheimer's culture industry thesis as posited in *Dialectic of Enlightenment* (1947), we find cogent points of entry into making distinctions amongst the many variations on an Oprah theme. Drawing on Marxist themes of alienated workers' pacification through ideology, Horkheimer and Adorno turned that lens onto mass culture and offered a lasting, if persistently pessimistic, view of the ideology of cultural work. Through standardization and claims to providing guidance in confusing, complex times, the culture industry exerts hegemonic control that appears as consumer choice but is, in fact, the perpetuation of the status quo.

Oprah Winfrey's embodiment, her cultural productions, her actions, and her ideology constitute *The Oprah Culture Industry* (TOCI). The sheer number of productions and enterprises indicates TOCI's extensive reach into American lives, media, and culture. TOCI ranges across a variety of media forms and uses tactics from the psychological to the material to gain a following in the millions and garner consensus for her projects. Despite the plurality of TOCI's media and influences, given the monolithic nature with which popular culture and audiences reference Oprah, it is apropos to speak of a singular Oprah Culture Industry.

What then is the Oprah Culture Industry's project? Is it a political endeavor to influence public policy on social issues such as violence and poverty? Is the central aim of TOCI to, as Peck asserts, turn material structural inequities into personal deficiencies (220)? Does TOCI assume a spiritual mantle and seek to provide solace to a traumatized American public's post-9/11 psyche? Where outside the United States does TOCI make its mark and by what means is its message disseminated? How well does TOCI convey this message to audiences of different ethnicities and cultural backgrounds?

The Oprah Winfrey Show's stated goal is "to transform people's lives, to make viewers see themselves differently and to bring happiness and a sense of fulfillment into every home" (Winfrey 2007). Winfrey the television show host and magazine editor drives this agenda, in part, by referencing her own and others' personal struggles and methods of triumph. But by turning her rags-to-riches biography into hagiography and disseminating it through her television show, radio program, and magazine, TOCI perpetuates a mythology about an already tenuous ideal: the American Dream.

Winfrey is not unlike other celebrities or cultural icons today who are keen marketers of their most prized product: themselves. She evinces a self-awareness that must successfully translate across numerous media formats in which consumer choice demands constantly new information about famous people. The difference, however, between Winfrey and other celebrities is the hegemonic project that TOCI advances. It's all about Oprah.

But what is that elusive "it"? *It* is how academics, audiences, culture producers, fans, critics, and a number of other constituencies interact with TOCI. Perceptions of Oprah the Woman directly impact our consumption of the cultural products bearing her name or production mark. *The Oprah Winfrey Show* and its descendants enter, or intrude, into our homes, workplaces, therapists' offices, courts of law, schools, and places of worship/spirituality by changing the terms of our collective discourse in the more than twenty years since the first talk show episode aired. So, while there is no universal Oprah, there is a coherent Oprah ideology.

This volume provides theories and hypotheses that address the questions that drive the Oprah Culture Industry. To date, writing on Oprah Winfrey falls into three broad categories: pop biography, media and communications, and critical cultural analysis, with the latter two constituting the bulk of academic research. At this stage, there is only one published anthology on Winfrey and four books of critical analysis focusing predominantly on Oprah's Book Club (Peck 2008; Harris and Watson 2007; Rooney 2005; Farr 2004; Illouz 2003). Journal articles and chapters in other edited volumes make up the remainder of academic investigations of Winfrey. It would not be far off, given the wealth of material yet to be investigated, to situate *Stories of Oprah* within a field of Oprah Studies. TOCI is both shaped by and helps shape a new era and values concurrent with another stage of capitalism. This is particularly the case as Winfrey continues to expand beyond the original genre of the television talk show and adapts to media and economic developments.

   Love, hate, or ambivalence (which is also still an assertion of opinion), TOCI inspires discussion across a wide range of topics. Keeping up with the Joneses might be marginally easier than keeping up with Oprah. The pioneering explorations of *TOWS* and Oprah's Book Club, starting in the 1990s, aimed to decipher the subtext of this cultural phenomenon and place them in context (Epstein and Steinberg 1998, 1996; Peck 1994; Haag 1993; Masciarotte 1991). The next decade's scholarly inquiry should examine the far-reaching impact of TOCI in all its dimensions, particularly as its influence coincides with and epitomizes globalizing forces of transnational capitalism. Both in its avocation of a global (media and human) village and in its permeation of international, cultural, and media boundaries, TOCI dictates a number of important cultural, political, social, economic, and spiritual discourses.

   Interdisciplinary methods and interpretive frameworks are crucial to thinking through the complexity, density, and impact of TOCI. *Stories of Oprah* contributors write across a number of disciplines and fields of research, including African American studies, women's/gender/sexuality studies, sociology, Southern studies, English, psychology, media studies, religious studies, philosophy, communication studies, political science, queer studies, and cultural studies. At the same time, three main sections guide our exploration of

Oprah's impact on our public and private spheres: Oprah the Woman, Oprah the Empire; Contesting the Oprah Experts; and the Oprahfication of Media.

Part I, "Oprah the Woman, Oprah the Empire," starts from a point that many analyses of Oprah Winfrey accept at face value: her solitary and impoverished background growing up in rural Mississippi. Or at least that is the narrative that John Howard skillfully deconstructs for its manipulation of an individualist Horatio Alger trajectory in chapter 1, "Beginnings with O." He interrogates Winfrey's own words as disseminated in popular press interviews and situates a highly constructive biography in the historical realities of 1950s Mississippi, 1960s Nashville and Milwaukee, and 1980s Chicago. Howard finds in this hagiography a queer turn: a repurposing of the American Dream trope for a multicultural America. In doing so, Howard reveals the subtle nuances of the progress narrative and its evacuation of political radicalism that dance at the edges of TOCI.

While Howard notes the disjuncture between Winfrey's individualized success story and the social movements that enabled that success, Jennifer Rexroat tackles a question brought to the fore by the successes of the women's and civil rights movements: is Oprah Winfrey a feminist? *TOWS* features episodes that confront formerly personal but, until relatively recently, political issues such as sexual assault, child abuse, and battering. What kind of feminist consciousness, if any, does Winfrey bring to the predominantly middle-class, white women who watch her show? Similarly, Rexroat shows in her chapter, "'I'm Everywoman': Oprah Winfrey and Feminist Identification," that while claiming to be the anthemic Everywoman, Winfrey does not claim feminist identity for herself or for her talk show. She does, however, Rexroat argues, occupy the position of the premier de facto feminist: "Oprah promotes feminist ideology and practice without explicitly acknowledging the fact that she is endorsing either feminism or the United States women's movement." Once Rexroat establishes this position, it is up to the reader to decide: does Winfrey's stance on significant sociopolitical issues support or undermine feminism's objectives? Once intent and consequence are weighed, can feminists meaningfully include Winfrey's de facto feminism as the logical outcome of decades of struggle for gender equality? Is that enough? Does situating Oprah as a de facto feminist actually offer us a critique of feminism's limits?

Turning from the subtly political questions of biography, Karlyn Crowley's chapter, "New Age Soul," teases out Oprah's take on spirituality and the personal style that makes her, in effect, the lead minister in a church of her own making. Membership in any of Oprah's enterprises is as easy as turning on the television, reading a Book Club selection, subscribing to her magazine, listening to the radio, or giving a donation to her Angel Network. In this sense, Oprah plays Svengali to her chosen experts by handing them an audience but also is the ultimate arbiter of taste and morals as conveyed via the experts. Both therapeutic and evangelical about everything from overcoming sexual abuse to what one should do if one's home décor fails to live up to standard, Oprah, Crowley suggests, is the leader of a New Age feminist spirituality that seeks to heal her parishioners/audience from trauma but fails to address systematic and institutionalized oppression.

The chapters in part II, "Contesting the Oprah Experts," build on the previous chapters' focus on biography, spiritualism, and social change politics to delve into TOCI's extension beyond the bounds of Oprah's original television talk show. Sherra Schick's chapter, "Post[ed]structuralism? Oprah's Message Boards, *Soul Stories*, and the Everyday Lives of Women," begins the next section of this book by asking about optimistic hopes for the internet as a new public sphere or a truly networked society. What kind of community is created online by and for *The Oprah Winfrey Show* viewers? Schick finds that, as one would expect, on Oprah.com Winfrey's mission is at the center of the topics presented for discussion on her message boards. But, similar to the existing literature's argument for Oprah's Book Club as politicizing, Schick maintains that, in fact, Oprah.com message board users claim agency for themselves and talk back to Oprah's experts. Often they ignore the experts who are purported to know best about their lives. This may be the unexpected side effect of a genre (the talk show) that sought to establish all personal experience and opinion as valid. Regardless, even in privileging their experience, Schick finds that Oprah.com message board participants create their own meaning but only do so once that experience is filtered through Oprah-approved ideological constructs. Just as it conveys her Favorite Things, the Oprah.com message boards drive home TOCI's Favorite Ideas. Schick raises compelling questions about conducting research on the world wide web and message boards and whether users can effectively maneuver on corporate-mediated websites.

In "Oprah para Mujeres Chicanas," Adriana Katzew and Lilia de Katzew undertake an important cross-cultural analysis of Chicana viewer reception of *The Oprah Winfrey Show* in order to ascertain Oprah's impact on Chicana/Mexicana viewers. They find several interesting contradictions that show the cross-cultural limits of Oprahfication. Not least among them is that, while Chicana viewers embrace Oprah's message of love-thyself and self-actualization, they did not feel that her show addressed important "issues, problems, culture, or life situations" affecting Chicanas. In fact, many subjects point to *TOWS*'s limitations in reaching out to other ethnicities and races besides white and black Americans, even though the Chicana respondents enjoy *TOWS*. Many respondents feel that she caters to African Americans' issues but "doesn't relate to other ethnicities with the same level of interest." In another vein, while Chicanas see themselves within the general category of "universal woman" (touted by Oprah) and view women's independence as a vital factor in their own lives, they are also turned off by the underlying emphasis on individualism of Oprah's message, which conflicts with the mores of their Mexican and Chicano cultures rooted in family and community connections. Oprah's individualism stands in contrast to a female identity that is anchored in familial roles and relations and that measures achievement in terms of contributions to the family's welfare.

Katherine Gregory continues to delineate TOCI's limits in her chapter "Confessions from At-Risk Teens." Through content analysis of *The Oprah Winfrey Show's* coverage of teen sexuality, she interrogates the "regime of abstinence," or *TOWS's* prescription for teens and their parents, around promiscuity. A moral panic ensues and results in the normalization of parental fear-as-control that far exceeds what public health officials deem necessary according to empirical research. In heightening parental paranoia, Gregory finds *TOWS's* approach to public health issues makes teens' allegedly deviant behavior hypervisible, thus shifting the focus from fostering healthy teen sexuality to reasserting hegemonic sexuality.

The Oprah Culture Industry's hegemonic reach does not stop at the borders of the United States and, in fact, has ramifications for people worldwide and for American perceptions of the world. "Oprah Goes to Africa," focuses on her widely distributed "Christmas Kindness" episode. Heather Laine Talley and Monica Casper coin the term "philanthropic consumption" to describe the celebrity-centric impulses behind Winfrey's giving and the motives for non-profit organizations seeking celebrity endorsement. Connecting her charitable endeavors with the (Red) Campaign that is centered on shopping as charitable giving, Casper and Talley skillfully argue that, "while Oprah is 'doing good,' she is simultaneously displacing political engagement on the part of viewers/consumers with a weak and ultimately ineffective version of action."

The Oprah Winfrey Show's presentation of its topics speaks to the increasingly blurry line between entertainment and information. Oprahfication, or Oprahization, denotes here the simultaneous opening of discourse to traditionally marginalized communities and the sensationalizing of those voices. As contributor Crowley observes, Oprah, in addition to being a person and a culture industry, has become a verb. While Crowley defines being "Oprahed" as the moment "when someone gets something emotional and personal out of you," *Stories of Oprah* shows how U.S. institutions, cultures, and spaces, too, have been Oprahed. The personalization of politics and the milquetoast politicization of the personal marks Oprah's impact on media beyond talk shows, notably in literature, film, and the news. Our book's final section, "The

Oprahfication of Media," queries the national and international impact of TOCI as it shapes rhetoric and discourse in shifting historical, geographical, and political terrain.

Discussing the *TOWS*'s hybridization of the news and talk show conventions, Kathleen Dixon and Kacie Jossart's chapter, "Oprah and the New News," reveals the conventions that we accept as commonplace as having significant roots in *TOWS*'s particular style of melodrama. Using the show's coverage of Hurricane Katrina's aftermath as their case study, Jossart and Dixon show how an Oprahfied brand of "soft" news characterizes the devolution of mainstream broadcast news under the guise of advocacy journalism.

As Jaap Kooijman demonstrates, after the tragic events of September 11, 2001, and the start of the Iraq War, Oprahfication became synonymous with Americanization of the global political atmosphere. In "The Oprahfication of 9/11," Kooijman finds that the show's discourse on terrorism and war "transform[ed] possible feelings of fear, anger, anxiety, and grief into acts of American patriotism," turning "9/11 into a personal yet collective experience of the political." Episodes that focused on translating international politics and expert opinion rest on assumptions about American exceptionalism masquerading as universalism. Oprah and America's positioning as Everywoman/Everycountry reveal both entities as distinct new millennium Empires with decision-making powers that define national and international discourses of what it means to be political in times of war, poverty, and terrorism.

Edith Frampton, in "From the Nobel to Oprah," returns to the topic of Oprah's most written-about cultural contribution. Previous studies examined the foundations of the Book Club and its impact on readership more generally. Moving on from these initial findings, Frampton investigates whether it is the text, the author, the reader, or, in this case, the host who carries the most influence in determining textual reception and perceptions. Frampton finds that, beyond merely reaping the extreme financial benefits from Oprah's seal of approval, authors, such as the Nobel Prize winner Toni Morrison, must reckon with the politicization of readers as they claim agency according to Winfrey's edicts and apply that agency to their literary works in both expected and perhaps unintended ways.

Our volume concludes with Trystan T. Cotten's exploration of a dimension of TOCI that has received very little critical attention by scholars: Harpo, Inc.'s 2005 film production of Zora Neale Hurston's novel, *Their Eyes Were Watching God* (1937). What happens to race and gender realities when a text is Oprahfied? Who benefits from separating a book, in this case Zora Neale Hurston's revelatory novel *Their Eyes Were Watching God*, from the author's original insights into racism and sexism? Cotten shows how Harpo producers deracialize the novel and mute Hurston's black feminist voice, thus glossing America's social consciousness of racial, class, and gender inequalities. One effect, Cotten maintains, has been the whitewashing of black feminine subjectivity via Harpo's over-romanticization of plot and wholesale gutting of Hurston's vision of African American women's struggles. Another has been the loss of Hurston's love and appreciation for rural Negro culture, including her literary ingenuity in rendering its creative innovation. Cotten also explores how the politics of media ratings intersect with the nation's will to forget its sordid racial past as the context for Harpo, Inc.'s thorough erasure of sticky social issues that the film might have productively portrayed. Drawing on a critical framework of contradiction and irony, moreover, he theorizes why Oprah chooses texts that highlight such politically charged topics like structural inequality and then goes to great lengths to minimize their social critique.

Critically engaging the Oprah Culture Industry is imperative, not merely because of the longevity of *The Oprah Winfrey Show* or, indeed, Winfrey's career, which appears to go from strength to strength. Nor is her extreme wealth and how she wields her power the deciding factor in determining the value of a collection of criticism. Few public figures traverse the cultural, political, economic, and media boundaries with as much savvy and success as Oprah Winfrey. Her story is one of rags-to-billion, and she has achieved international fame through her media productions, philanthropy, and global networking. There is probably no one in America who has not heard of Oprah. Winfrey's influence is felt throughout the world, and everyone has an opinion about her, but not everyone can articulate his or her passion for or reservations about her. *Stories of Oprah* aims to change that by showing that it is possible to admire and even envy the accomplishments of an American cultural icon while maintaining a critical perspective that asks for more than what is presented on the surface by the Oprah Culture Industry, its adherents or its detractors.

Notes

The editors would like to thank Ishtla Singh for graciously and skillfully lending her copyediting skills to this project, as well as thanks to Tammy O. Rastoder. We're immensely grateful to them both. We would also like to thank Cecilia Konchar Farr for her careful attention and insightful feedback on the manuscript.

1. All figures except estimated wealth from "Oprah Winfrey's Biography," http://www.oprah.com/article/pressroom/oprahsbio/20080602_orig_oprahsbio (accessed July 24, 2008).
2. Jonathan Franzen, author of the novel *The Corrections*, famously expressed to the media apprehension about his book carrying The Oprah Book Club seal. He sparked debates about boundaries between high and low culture, as well as the gendered nature of books in the United States.

3. What is clear, or what was hoped, was that Oprah's endorsement would mean a clear choice for her middle-class female viewers. Subsequent polls claimed that, in fact, Oprah's political endorsement, though relatively benign in substance, hurt *her* brand rather than improved the Obama brand.

4. According to a November 20, 1997, NBC Universal press release, NBC Universal purchased Oxygen for $925 million in 1997. http://tinyurl.com/6l34m2 (accessed July 31, 2008).

Works Cited

"Actress chronicles year following Oprah's advice." 2008. *All Things Considered*, National Public Radio, July 16. http://www.npr.org/templates/story/story.php?storyId=92602017 (accessed July 22, 2008).

Carr, David. 2007. "Oprah puts her brand on the line," *New York Times*, December 24. http://tinyurl.com/5g6xeh (accessed July 31, 2008).

Epstein, D., and D. L. Steinberg. 1998. "American Dreamin': Discoursing Liberally on *The Oprah Winfrey Show*," *Women's Studies International Forum* 21, no. 1: 77–94.

———. 1996. "All Het Up! Rescuing Heterosexuality on *The Oprah Winfrey Show*," *Feminist Review* no. 54: 88–115.

Haag, L. L. 1993. "Oprah Winfrey: The Construction of Intimacy in the Talk Show Setting." *The Journal of Popular Culture* 26, no. 4: 115–22.

Harris, Jennifer, and Elwood Watson. 2007. *The Oprah Phenomenon*. University Press of Kentucky.

Illouz, Eva. 2003. *Oprah Winfrey and the Glamour of Misery: An Essay on Popular Culture*. Columbia University Press.

Konchar Farr, Cecilia. 2004. *Reading Oprah: How Oprah's Book Club Changed the Way America Reads*. State University of New York Press.

Kuczybski, Alex. 2000. "Winfrey breaks new ground with magazine," *New York Times*, April 3. http://tinyurl.com/6ldvwj (accessed July 31, 2008).

Manly, Lorne. 2006. "For Oprah Winfrey, Satellite Radio Is the Newest Frontier," *New York Times*, February 10. http://tinyurl.com/6j7xqx (accessed July 31, 2008).

Masciarotte, G. J. 1991. "C'mon Girl: Oprah Winfrey and the Discourse of Feminine Talk." *Genders* 11: 81–110.

The Oprah Winfrey Show, "Fact Sheet." 2007. http://www.oprah.com/about/press/about_press_ows-faq.jhtml (accessed 9 October 2007).

Peck, Janice. 2008. *The Age of Oprah: Cultural Icon for the Neoliberal Age* (Boulder, Colo.: Paradigm Publishers).

———. 1994. "Talk About Racism: Framing a Popular Discourse of Race on *Oprah Winfrey*," *Cultural Critique*, Spring: 89–126.

Rooney, Kathleen. 2005. *Reading With Oprah: The Book Club That Changed America*. University of Arkansas Press.

"Why Oprah opens readers' wallets." 2005. *Business Week*, October 10. http://www.businessweek.com/magazine/content/05_41/b3954059.htm (accessed July 24, 2008).

Winfrey, Oprah. 2005. "Heartprints," *The Oprah Winfrey Show: 20th Anniversary DVD Collection*.

Wyatt, Edward. 2008. "A Few Tremors in Oprahland," *New York Times*, May 2. http://tinyurl.com/6mmu46 (accessed July 31, 2008).

Part I

Oprah the Woman, Oprah the Empire

CHAPTER ONE

Beginnings with O

JOHN HOWARD

> I've gathered the women like talismans, one
> by one.[. . .] I used them. I used
> the significance
> of each card to uphold the dream [. . .]
> —OLGA BROUMA (1977, 20)

A new century's rags-to-riches narrative features not a street-smart white shoeshine boy with moxy but a bookish black farm girl with a painful secret. A fictional account, perfected by a defrocked minister accused of "unnatural" acts with his young male charges, the older model emphasized gumption, virtue, and—above all—hard work: *Shine your shoes, mister?* (Trachtenberg 1990, vi). At the feet of his superiors, the resourceful bootblack overheard and absorbed the lessons of the robber barons, helping him to master the diction and get a leg up. A "true" story, by contrast, told about one of its real-life inheritors, the new paradigm takes eavesdropping to new heights, charting the rise of the very media mogul in question: *Listen to your trauma, ma'am?* In the information age, the wealthy gobble up the tales of the woe-begone, reflect them back (*My story's just like yours*—no matter how odd), and put them all on display to be consumed by the masses.[1]

To call Oprah Winfrey's life history a "Horatio Alger story" is to overstate the similarities and overlook—as she often does—the important differences (McAlister 2000). For her rise to prominence, whether she chooses to describe it in these terms or not, is a testament to the distinctive efforts and challenges of black women and black institutions. Like Alger's, however, her story is also one given to queer insinuations.

A Small Pig Farm in Mississippi

Watch Oprah Winfrey's daytime talk show for a month or so and you're likely to catch just a few snippets of her personal history, brief moments from her past meant to help illuminate the topic under discussion on any given day. Winfrey uses these moments, in part, as a means of building rapport with guests: comparing or contrasting elements in their life stories—as revealed in informal interviews and depicted in short slick films by the Harpo production team—with those of her own. Pieced together by journalists, Winfrey's life fragments achieve a certain coherence. And ideological significance. Avid fans may feel that they're getting the full picture in exposés from weekly magazines such as *People* or *Time,* women's monthlies like *Elle* or *McCall's,* or even state-wide or local newspapers. But through tactics of selection and emphasis, rising and falling action, these popular biographies provide both less and more. They follow aspects of an individual tale or yarn; they also weave and refashion the fabric of the American dream. They tell us a familiar, if somewhat altered, American success narrative.

Oprah Gail Winfrey was born on a farm in rural Attala County, Missis-sippi, on 29 January 1954, her first name purportedly a misspelling of Ophra, from the Old Testament book of Ruth (Gates 2000, 18). In brief accounts, she is said to have been raised in a "broken home," simply put (Scott 1986, n.p.). Longer accounts demonstrate that she grew up in a succession of homes, no-tably three: her maternal grandparents' in Mississippi (until roughly the age of six), her mother's in Milwaukee (until about thirteen), and her father's in Nashville (through her college years), with considerable movement back and forth among them all. The first and third are characterized as stable households of solid values, the second as disruptive and traumatic, representing the nadir of our heroine's journey. Though the chance result of "a one-day fling under an oak tree" between eighteen-year-old Vernita Lee and twenty-year-old soldier Vernon Winfrey (Richman 1987, 50), the "illegitimate" young Oprah got off on the right foot thanks to grandmother Hattie Mae Lee, who modeled hard work and enforced strict discipline during those crucial first six years when—as Winfrey later cautioned a Head Start audience—"your whole brain is set for either achieving or not achieving" (Edwards 1986).

"I called my grandmother 'Momma,'" Winfrey has told *Woman's Day* (Torn-abene 1986, 48). "I slept with my grandmother. In the big featherbed. There was an outhouse in the back. . . . I was a *really* likeable child and loved to kiss people and talk to them. But I couldn't because my grandmother's philoso-phy was children should be seen and not heard. Company would come and I would be ordered to sit in the corner and keep my mouth shut" (50). When she misbehaved, Oprah had to go cut her own switch, which Hattie Mae Lee then used to administer a whipping. Even so, Winfrey has said, "I am what I am because of my grandmother: my strength, my sense of reasoning, everything" (56). Lee instilled the notion "somewhere in my spirit, that I could be, I could do, I could go wherever I wanted to" (Skipper 1988). Winfrey concludes that grandmothers are the "bridges we have crossed over on" (*Jackson Daily News* 1987c).

Though *Biography Magazine* has called it a "small pig farm"—no doubt to accentuate squalid poverty and thereby augment the subsequent socioeconomic ascent, as Lee's neighbors and relatives have charged of Winfrey—the Lee farm was, more accurately, a diversified, virtually self-sufficient operation, a part of the little community of Buffalo, between the town of Ethel and the county seat of Kosciusko (Peterson 1999, 42). "My grandmother owned the farm, and she did [almost] everything herself. She made my clothes; I never had a store-bought dress" (Tornabene 1986, 52). Even as a small child, Oprah had chores of her own too. She fetched water from the well each morning, helped make lye soap, washed clothes and bed and bath linens, and hung them on the line to dry. After Bessie the cow was milked, Oprah took her out to pasture, then churned butter on the back porch. Family members "grew everything we ate," including a range of fruits and vegetables (52). They raised chickens and sold their eggs to generate cash for staples they couldn't cultivate in the sand-clay soil, such as rice and sugar and the more faraway necessities such as coffee and tea. Though they cured their own hams, they likely sold at least some of their hogs, perhaps to agents of Bryan Foods, whose president—West Point, Mississippi-native John Bryan—later became chairman of Sara Lee Corporation and joined with Winfrey in charitable fundraising activities.[2]

In describing her Mississippi upbringing to reporters, Winfrey has repeatedly called up two events meant to demonstrate her promise, drive, and initiative. Like so many biographical constructions, they are assertions of individual achievement and potential greatness, the beginning of a trajectory toward notoriety, aspects of the early life retrospectively narrated as predictors of later success. It is worth noting, however, that although both episodes attest to the power of literacy, they were a part of Winfrey's self-revelatory repertoire long before the launch of the Oprah Book Club. They were not created or embellished in order to plug that venture. Unsurprisingly, they involve the central institutions of rural childhood socialization: churchgoing and schooling.

As recounted for the *New York Times* and *USA Today*, *TV Guide* and *Ladies Home Journal*, Oprah could read by the time she was two and a half years old. From the age of three, she remembers with pride, she was called upon to read passages of Scripture and deliver short speeches from the pulpit of the

Buffalo United Methodist Church.[3] On special occasions such as Christmas and Easter, she delighted members of the congregation with her oratory. By the time she reached kindergarten, it was apparent to Oprah that her great talents outstripped those of her classmates. Frustrated with the simple games and lessons in sharing, the young upstart penned a letter to her teacher. "Dear Miss New, I don't think I belong here," she wrote. "Could I please go to the first grade?" (Kolson 1986). Then, using an advanced placement technique common in underfunded public schools, the principal let Oprah skip kindergarten and start classes immediately in the first grade.

It is obvious and perhaps unnecessary to note that in late-1950s Mississippi, hers was a segregated black farming community, a segregated black church, a segregated black school. But when these racial dynamics go unremarked, it makes it easier for Winfrey to narrate her childhood as one of individual development rather than of budding collective consciousness—not to mention, mutual aid. Surely soothing for her overwhelmingly white, self-help-oriented audiences, Winfrey foregrounds only one mentor from this period, rooted firmly within the family: her grandmother. Though she was surrounded by relatives young and old—those brought up with her and those who looked after them—she describes a lonely, barren existence: "No one ever told me I was loved. Ever, ever, ever. Reading and being a 'smart girl' was my only sense of value, and it was the only time I felt loved" (Anon. 1997a). As she has said on numerous occasions, her books were her best friends. While others "sat in a circle and spit all day," she was resolutely situated—by choice or by design—outside the circle (Tornabene 1986, 48).

Such rhetorical tropes of individualistic, idiosyncratic achievement foreclose other possible interpretations of the early years. What if Winfrey's handlers chose to circulate representations of Attala County as a place of strong African American institutions, of nascent black empowerment? "You know," we can imagine her reading from a script, "that little farming community was *filled* with industrious black folk, who grew all their own food, sustained a lively black church, and built a meager but vibrant black school. I felt safe, protected, and supported by them all." What if, in addition to Hattie Mae Lee, Winfrey gave a consistent shout-out to the other women who recognized and nurtured her talents, promoting a feminist reading of events? For Miss New was undoubtedly in league with other teachers who guided the young standout. And who would have extended those invitations to recite Scripture and give speeches, if not the very church ladies who make the occasional cameo in Winfrey's recollections? When these local people do feature, however, implicitly or explicitly, it is with a cool remove, a clear sense that moving on and moving up means moving away.

Competing versions of Winfrey's beginnings emerged when she made a rare return trip to Kosciusko in 1998. A reminder that her early years were rooted not just in family but also in community, Winfrey was presented not with the key to the city but with "a large vegetable," a locally grown rutabaga (*Greenwood Commonwealth* 1998a). Leaders had long since renamed a red-clay, graveled road after her, the one that ran alongside the farm of Hattie Mae Lee, long since dead. Still, the savvy Winfrey couldn't help but offend some of the women and men, black and white, who turned out to see her at the Attala County Coliseum. As a journalist noted, though she readily claimed her Mississippi ancestry, Winfrey mostly "tout[ed] the importance of self-esteem and spirituality." Onstage in a rocking chair, amidst plants and flowers, underneath a sign reading "KOSCIUSKO, MISSISSIPPI Welcomes Home Oprah"—gesturing grandly and sometimes standing up to stress a point—the celebrity associated this place with nothingness and described it only as a launching pad to greater things: "I'm from Kosciusko, Mississippi. Mississippi, Mississippi, Mississippi. There ain't nothing there but corn. [Not people?] So that means you can do anything" (Miller 1998). Indeed, what she had already done—left—was subtly reiterated by her curious distancing reference to this place, underneath her very feet, as "there," not here. In this way, a subject of so-called small talk, one's background, a story rehearsed and repeated in her adoptive home of Chicago—and probably told at countless cocktail parties around the world—at least did not contain the hollow phrase, much more damning (for both the signified and the signifying): nothing here.

Similarly, the anecdote about her Scripture readings—recounted to this particular audience—had embedded within it a disregard for former friends and neighbors. "My grandmother, Hattie Mae, taught me to believe in myself," she said, for what was maybe the thousandth time. "The women at church used to say, 'Hattie Mae, this child sure can talk. This is the talkingest child.'" Then Winfrey delivered her punch line: "But that talking has paid off" (ibid.).

Told for comic value, the tale could conceivably be construed as an homage to the church ladies at Buffalo United Methodist. Notably undifferentiated by name, however, they could also be seen to come off as a group of meddlers, attempting to squelch the uppity child, who responds with an "I'll show them" mentality. The punch line cinches it. By contrast to poor old Mississippi—number fifty on almost every state ranking scale—Winfrey is now spectacularly successful in the traditional American sense. She's rich. Keeping tabs in 1998, *Essence* ranked her among "America's richest sisters" (Chapelle and Gambles 1998, 109); *Fortune* dubbed her the second most powerful of all women in the United States (*Jet* 1998b, 61). Spinning hallowed words into cold hard cash, Winfrey's gift of gab, she points out for the folks back home, had truly "paid off."

Many in the audience found it "an inspiring message" (Miller 1998). *Woman's Day*, quoting Winfrey in another context, refers to it as "the Great American Message: 'You have the power to make a difference in your life regardless of who you are and where you come from. You are responsible for yourself'" (Tornabene 1986, 48). And yourself alone, one might ask? Oprah's cheery façade of optimism seems to crack only when angered or distressed by those less successful people she's left behind, the great gulf between what she has and what they need. As she further confided about another reunion, "I went to dinner at my mother's house and there were cousins and uncles and friends and they're bringing friends I don't even know who want me to help them with their careers. . . . I was so stressed. . . . Everyone's so needy. They *need* so much. And I'll give them whatever I can; it's no skin off my back" (60). And yet it *does* seem to get under her skin. If I can make it, she nearly lets slip, then why the hell can't y'all?[4]

"Tradition has it," according to historian Richard Weiss, "that every American child receives, as part of his birthright, the freedom to mold his own life [regardless of] the limitations that circumstances impose. . . . The belief that all men, in accordance with certain rules, but exclusively by their own efforts, can make of their lives what they will has been popularized" since at least the nineteenth century (Weiss 1988, 3). This "American myth of success" may have originated as a gendered ideology of *male* autonomy—as Weiss makes evident with reference to the "birthright" of "men"—but Winfrey's narrative seems to suggest that it now applies to women as well. If her story thereby modifies the old success myth formula, it nonetheless holds tight to one of its supernatural Puritan corollaries, "link[ing] virtue with success and sin with failure" (6). Thus, "the 'rags-to-riches' tradition, by creating an illusion of opportunity, served as a social pacifier inimical to reform. Furthermore, by equating failure with sin and personal inadequacy, self-help popularizers obscured the objective causes of social injustice" (7).

In Mississippi—with the lowest percentage of doctors and dentists, the lowest percentage of high school and college graduates, and the lowest per capita income in the nation—the failures of American capitalism are most acutely in evidence. The problems seem insurmountable, beyond redress. These problems are more structural than personal, more systemic than psychological. Still, ask Winfrey to pinpoint "the greatest threat to African- Americans," and she won't hesitate to reply: "It's the loss of our spiritual self. I believe every social ill has resulted from a spiritual deficit. We have lost memory of who we are, that is that we are spiritual people. If you are one of these people who sit in church all day and then go home and worry about how you are going to pay your light bill, you need to check on that. The same God that can move planets can move your light bill" (Stringfellow 1998). Such is the faith of the individual who has succeeded—confident that a higher power has taken a special interest in her life, assured that her riches are her just reward.

Oprah's Dashiki

Narratives of Oprah Winfrey's early life construct a dark period from age six to thirteen. Now living with her irresponsible, unmarried mother in "the North," Oprah was raped by a cousin and was "molested," as she puts it, by an uncle as well as "a family friend"—demonstrating once again that campaigns like Oprah's Child Predator Watch List, designed to track "pedophiles [who] seek employment where they will be in contact with children," misdirect our attention away from the site and the perpetrators of most childhood sexual assault: the family (Farrell et al. 1991, 69). Buried deep within her for years, Winfrey's own secret was revealed spontaneously to another victim of incestuous attacks on the talk show. Once out, the episode helped Winfrey interpret other aspects of her past. "I became a sexually promiscuous teenager," she forewarned a black female high school student in Mississippi, "and got myself into a lot of trouble" (Johnson 2006). That is, until another important family member stepped in and straightened her out.

Winfrey characterizes her father, a black barbershop operator, in much the way she does her grandmother: a person with a stern moral code and high expectations. When she joined him in Tennessee, he set the rules, and she obeyed, turning in a book report to him once a week, among other duties. And as before, she distinguished herself—was set apart—at school. "In Nashville," as a Knight-Ridder reporter surmised, "Winfrey flourished. She always knew the answers and earned the best grades, for which the other kids hated her. 'Everyone went through the black-power phase. All the other black kids were fist-raising, dashiki-wearing folks, and I knew I was not a dashiki kind of girl'" (Kolson 1986). Far from it, Oprah had imbibed fantasies through the years of being white. "I used to sleep with a clothespin on my nose, and two cotton balls. And I couldn't breathe and all I would do is wake up with two clothespin prints on the side of my nose, trying to get it to turn up. I wanted Shirley Temple curls; that's what I prayed for all the time" (Tornabene 1986, 56). In Milwaukee, her prayers had been partially answered. Unlike her younger, light-complected, half-sister Patricia, who "got all the attention," Oprah was sent twenty-five miles outside the "ghetto" to an elite suburban school "where everyone else was white" (56, 59). Oprah commuted by bus, alongside black domestics who worked in white homes. But it was a step in the right direction, as she saw it, like skipping kindergarten and the second grade.

If Winfrey failed to get along with black classmates in her Nashville high school, then just across town at Tennessee State University—founded as "an agricultural and industrial state normal school for Negroes"—she was downright hostile (Tennessee State University 2007). As *People Weekly* discerned it:

College was trying for a young black girl uninterested in the compelling black issues of the day. Winfrey says she retains neither fond memories nor good friends from college. "They all hated me—no, they resented me. I refused to conform to the militant thinking of the time. I hated, hated, hated college. Now I bristle when somebody comes up and says they went to Tennessee State with me. Everybody was angry for four years. It was an all-black college, and it was in to be angry."

As she adds, "Whenever there was any conversation on race, I was on the other side, maybe because I never felt the kind of repression other black people are exposed to. I think I was called 'nigger' once, when I was in fifth grade"—surely evidence, if true, of the extent to which her community was racially segregated and she was successfully sheltered in racist Mississippi. The lessons of college, at least the (a)political ones learned outside the classroom, apparently stuck. "Whenever I hear the words 'community organization' or 'task force,' I know I'm in deep trouble." As she elaborates, "People feel you have to lead a civil rights movement every day of your life, that you have to be a spokeswoman and represent *the race*. . . . Blackness is something I just am. I'm black. I'm a woman. I wear a size 10 shoe. It's all the same to me" (Richman 1987, 56).

And yet, once again, black community institutions, including those of black women, presented the key opportunities for Winfrey at this stage of her life. Educated in speech and drama at the historically black college, Winfrey received vital on-the-job training as a newsreader at a local soul radio station newly staffed by black disc jockeys and programmers. At the same time, she participated with other women in black beauty pageants, winning the Miss Black Nashville and Miss Black Tennessee titles and finishing as a runner-up at the Miss Black America contest. Experience and exposure in these African American ventures led directly to her appointment as the first black female reporter and then news anchor in mainstream white Nashville television. She would go on to Baltimore, where she launched her first talk show, and then to Chicago, eventually overtaking Phil Donahue in the local as well as national ratings.

From the time she left Nashville in 1976, Winfrey was repeatedly characterized as a college graduate. But she wasn't actually awarded a diploma until over a decade later, when she returned to Tennessee State as commencement speaker. As newspaper coverage made clear, "Winfrey left the university . . . with one senior-year project unfinished and only recently completed the course work" (Jackson Daily News 1987b). Remembering soul station WVOL, *The Oprah Winfrey Show* addressed not, in the words of historian Brian Ward, the "direct action protests designed to challenge discriminatory employment practices" there at the very time of Winfrey's hiring but rather—in the episode's title—"The Man Who Discovered Oprah" (Ward 1998, 432). There was, the video preview asserted, just "one man [who] gave a sixteen-year-old girl a chance," showing but not telling viewers that both were black (Oprah.com 2004). Similarly, in saluting others who helped or inspired her on the road to success, Winfrey cannot identify with the collective of foot soldiers in the struggle for racial equality, those who adopted the uniform that was the dashiki. Though she frequently references black female historical figures (for example, Fannie Lou Hamer), they are decontextualized from the groups and organizations they joined or led. Each is understood as an individual, an admirable role model of personal fortitude and striving. A handful of important contemporary writers (for example, Maya Angelou, Toni Morrison, Gloria Naylor) likewise are individuated, cast in the singular, as collaborator, friend, or mentor to Winfrey. Thus, not only does Winfrey gather together female viewers, one by one, from an atomized position at home in front of the TV set, into a potentially empowering national and international collectivity that nonetheless falls back onto individualistic self-help techniques; so too she assembles an ancestral lineage of African American heroines, herself included, all of whom seem autonomous and isolated, somehow going it alone, self-made.

As scholar Dana L. Cloud has perceptively noted, whether crafted by Winfrey or, more commonly, by journalists, such "tokenist biography . . . resonates with and reinforces the ideology of the American Dream, implying the accessibility of this dream to black Americans despite the structural economic and political obstacles to achievement and survival in a racist society." These kinds of popular narratives "authorize a person from a marginalized or oppressed group to speak as a culture hero *on the condition* that the person's life story be framed in liberal capitalist terms," especially so as to incorporate "the exhortation to transcend racial or cultural conflict" (Cloud 1996, 116). "It's not skin color that people look at on TV," Winfrey told *Elle*. "If you're good, you can transcend racial barriers" (Guzman 1985, n.p.). Though later in her career Winfrey would acknowledge the sustaining, character-building significance of all-black educational institutions, making substantial contributions to historically black high schools and universities such as the Piney Woods School in Mississippi and Morehouse College in Georgia, such giving would act as a "celebration of philanthropy as an appropriate means of social change (in contradistinction to political activism)" (Cloud 1996, 124). Thus, social priorities are established through the high-minded beneficence and individual decision-making of the wealthy—like Bill Cosby and Oprah Winfrey—as opposed to the more democratic but reviled task force or community organization.

Oprah's dark period—her interval away from the South, from 1960 to 1967—coincided with the region's key battles in the African American civil rights movement, a subject rarely scrutinized on *The Oprah Winfrey Show*. Instead, the daily program gestures toward the complex dynamics of gender and sexuality, race and responsibility, within a reassuring framework of individual makeover more than collective struggle, of recovery more than resistance. Winfrey appeals to the family values of her predominantly white audience with talk of her father and grandmother's wisdom, not racially marked, even as her very real victimization by other relatives authenticates her role as the arbiter of cultures of healing. Also downplayed are the self-governing—some say, separatist—black institutions that helped improve her odds of success. Hailing from America's blackest state, with an African American population of 35 percent and with an almost unparalleled history of vicious white supremacy and racist violence, Winfrey and her commentators mobilize select aspects of her past to forward a wholesome agenda of bootstrap assimilation, racial integration (if not deflection), and middle-class respectability.

Yet Another Mama-on-the-Couch Play

Dependent, in part, upon her famously fluctuating body weight, Winfrey is often represented either as her white female audience members' "beloved girlfriend" or as their mother substitute (Decker 2006, 170). Though the latter inevitably calls up the resilient Mammy stereotype—the hefty black nurse, maid, and cook of movies, whose own family is eclipsed by the demands of "her" white family—also evoked is the long-suffering African American mother of Christian virtues and middle-class aspirations, made palatable over the years for white theatergoing audiences. Playwright George Wolfe both honors and satirizes such representational lineages in his sweeping, audacious stage piece, *The Colored Museum,* from 1986. In one of eleven scenarios, entitled "The Last Mama-on-the-Couch Play," Wolfe—through a tuxedoed, Oscar-toting NARRATOR—presents a "well worn" widow MAMA on a couch "reading a large, oversized Bible" and generally looking after her ne'er-do-well SON, daughter-in-law, and daughter, all patterned after figures from classic twentieth-century African American theater (Wolfe 1998, 24). Caricaturing and transcending the work of Lorraine Hansberry, Ntozake Shange, and Adrienne Kennedy—"searing domestic drama that tears at the very fabric of racist America"—these characters eventually find themselves in a depoliticized "all-black musical," where they must "dance with zombie-like frozen smiles" to stay alive: "DON'T SHAKE A FIST," MAMA sings, "JUST SHAKE A LEG" (31–32).

From her daily televisual perch atop her own sofa, Winfrey transforms both the Mammy and the Mama, adopting agreeable attributes of each. Of the Mama, she foregrounds religiosity, recognizing that her competitors are not just a too-serious Phil Donahue and, later, a too-frivolous, too-outlandish Jerry Springer but also the too-earnest, too-obviously-money-grubbing cable televangelists Jimmy Swaggart, Pat Robertson, Joyce Meyer, and—most of all—feel-good, success-oriented Jim and Tammy Faye Bakker, whose tagline mimicked the implicit central message of almost every *Oprah* episode: "You Can Make It!" "I am a woman of God," Winfrey has said. "You come from a power source and therefore you have great power. And the moment you recognize that power, you will recognize the power is God" (*Clarion Ledger* 1987a). Her TV program she has referred to as "a ministry"; guests' tales of surviving life-threatening events are regularly described as "miracles," with assertions of direct, divine intervention; Winfrey's charitable partners are lauded as "angels" (Rickey 1998). Of the Mammy, Winfrey channels a chief concern for the needs of whites. This new Mammy on the couch knows her audience members are, like her, physically on the couch, at home—if not simultaneously cleaning up the home—but also symbolically "on the couch," in this pseudo-psychotherapeutic sanctum that is talk television.

This latter dynamic was brilliantly highlighted on primetime television by the production team around Ellen DeGeneres (who would go on to host her own daytime talk show). For their legendary 1997 coming-out episode, producers of the sitcom *Ellen* cast Winfrey as the lesbian protagonist's shrink, the two together thinking through the implications of self-discovery and outness. But Winfrey's decision to accept this literalized therapist's role exacerbated the lesbian rumors that had been circulating around her too. Indeed, so concerned was Winfrey about audience reception and interpretation that she, in the words of a *Dallas Morning News* reporter, "felt compelled to issue a statement to media outlets across the country": "I am not in the closet," it read. "I am not coming out of the closet. I am not gay." Indeed, she had said as much on *The Oprah Winfrey Show*. Alas, Winfrey lamented, "the rumor mill still churns" (Mendoza 1997).

Representations of the old Mammy show us little of her home life, her husband, and her children. And Winfrey has often asked that reporters respect her privacy when it comes to her intimate associations. Whereas early in her career she confessed botched relationships and professed a desire for normative marital union—such that failing to find a husband by thirty-eight would represent failure in life—she began to disclose less about her boyfriends. In this sense, her life history was marked by a narrative disconnect from those of her viewers. For although the TV show regularly addresses dating and relationship-building, featuring authors of such tomes as the *Sex and the City*-inspired *He's Just Not That Into You,* Winfrey's love life is now infrequently elaborated. Nonetheless, devoted fans know from the magazines that she has dated a black executive named Stedman Graham—indeed, continues to date him, her steady Stedy, two decades on. Winfrey has described their sleeping "in separate bedrooms" when visiting her father (Littwin 1990, 6). Graham "calmly" loves her, she has said; she "sweetly" loves him (Rensin 1992, 12).

Indeed, in this regard and others, Winfrey's tale takes a queer turn, in the sense of its nonnormative, nonconforming properties. Judging from the show's content alone, viewers respond to dominant white middle-class assumptions about gender and sexuality. Women date men, usually sequentially, in order to find one true love, a potential spouse; once married, they expect to raise children. Realistically, they may marry and divorce more than once, but lengthy periods without a spouse are to be avoided. A woman is either coupled or in search of the next male partner. Winfrey defies these audience assumptions. Less frequently revealed in the popular biographies, at age fourteen Winfrey became that most castigated of American scapegoats, the unwed teenage black mother, before suffering the death of her prematurely born child. She has never married, and increasingly it seems she never will. Queer rumors therefore have circulated not only around her but also around Graham. The two sued one supermarket tabloid for $300 million for "publishing a false and defamatory story claiming Graham had an affair with a male cousin" (*Clarion Ledger* 1992).

The Oprah Winfrey Show further suggests that to be labeled gay is to be defamed, to be on dubious moral ground. As one scholar notes, episodes on lesbian and gay issues are characterized by "edginess" (Squire 1994, 64), with Winfrey's "lesbian and gay guests . . . required to defend themselves," in the words of another two scholars (Epstein and Steinberg 1996, 94). Not long after lesbian couple Brenda and Wanda Henson founded Camp Sister Spirit, a "feminist educational and cultural retreat" in Winfrey's home state of Mississippi, she invited them onto the show to describe their experiences of hate crimes— the killing of their dog, shotgun blasts over the compound, and the like. But Winfrey also interviewed local "opponents" of the camp, such that the episode became a "free-for-all," as Wanda Henson called it, airing the views of "a small rabid group" denouncing lesbian "recruitment" (Remwolt 1993). Unlike her idol Barbara Walters, who promised on the television newsmagazine *20/20* to join the boycott of the Tennessee-headquartered Cracker Barrel Restaurants, which had adopted a formal policy of firing lesbian and gay employees, Winfrey hosted boycott leaders, including the terminated Cheryl Summerville, without explicitly offering support for their cause. Quite the contrary, Winfrey has been filmed eating at Cracker Barrel (Oprah.com 2006). In these early episodes on queer topics especially, Winfrey takes up the position of therapeutic detached observer or above-the-fray moral arbiter, appearing equally bemused with, if not repelled by, both sides of the polarizing debate. She seems condescendingly to pity such guests even as she showcases them. They are, to her, disturbing and dispiriting.

Indeed, for years, Winfrey has threatened to cease production of the very program that established and solidified her reputation and prosperity. She has said she feels that her heart is in acting, with references to *The Color Purple, Native Son, The Women of Brewster Place,* and *Beloved* as more serious, worthy endeavors. In a revealing interview in 1999, outside the United States, with *The Sunday Times* of London, Winfrey confided her growing sense of disappointment and frustration. Daytime television was "a vulgarity circus," she said. "Coming off that wonderful film [*Beloved*] to be just interviewing more dysfunctional people was a letdown" (*Clarion Ledger* 1999). Such are the resentments of the individual who has succeeded—convinced of her own importance, her superior yet thwarted vision, as compared to the petty concerns of those from whom she has profited.

Even as her own life story differs so markedly from the traditional American success narrative—in which a poor but industrious white boy, with the advice of powerful white men, makes his way upward—Oprah Winfrey upholds its central tenets. Even as black women and black institutions have enabled her ascent, she and her biographers narrate a life of individual striving informed by individual role models and mentors, all constituting a lesson for her self-help audiences. Even as the racial subordination of her early years and the spectacular wealth of her later years make her utterly unlike her mostly white middle-class female viewers, they feel an affinity with her, experts tell us, as "someone like themselves": "a nonthreatening person they can identify with" (Maddec 1998, 11). The more threatening aspects of her past Winfrey's handlers play down; her racial positioning, in particular, must be characterized as irrelevant, such that the American Dream becomes depoliticized and deracialized. Thus, when she hints at it, it seems almost as ludicrous, almost as impossible as when, in the 1979 rags-to-riches send-up *The Jerk*, white comedian Steve Martin says it: "I was born a poor black child."

Notes

1. In its eighth annual "Power Issue," listing "the 101 most powerful people in entertainment," *Entertainment Weekly* ranked Oprah Winfrey in the top five, along with Michael Eisner, Rupert Murdoch, Steven Spielberg, and Ted Turner (*Entertainment Weekly* 1997b, 25). Winfrey reached the top of the list the next year, "the first woman and the first Black" to do so (*Jet* 1998b, 61).

2. As reported in the *National Enquirer*, Winfrey's relatives were far from the lowest rung on the social ladder. According to second cousin Malena Winfrey Dow, an instructor at historically black Tougaloo College, "There was a family rule that no Winfrey women were allowed to work in the homes of white families. They could work in the fields, but it was a point of honor that they didn't do maid work." As another second cousin, Laura Henson, stated, "All the Winfreys were prosperous and hardworking. Everyone owned their own property and sent their kids to school" (Nelson et al. 1994, 33). If the Lees likewise owned their farm, as Oprah Winfrey states, then they were indeed comparatively well-off. As historians have shown, black farm ownership in the mid-century South was rare, owing to economic disadvantage and systemic governmental racism (Daniel 2007).

3. One Knight Ridder reporter suggests Winfrey attended a Baptist church in Kosciusko (Rickey 1998). Of course, it is possible she attended both.

4. To be fair, Winfrey contributed large sums of money around the time of this trip—and before and after—to Habitat for Humanity, in Kosciusko and elsewhere. But even these aid efforts deliver the credo of individualism, constructing *single-family detached* homes instead of more efficient row houses or apartment blocks, apparently too reminiscent of the projects and too given to "broken" householding arrangements like her own. Further, ostentatious giving—as when Winfrey turns up with a camera crew to record the completion of a house she has funded, in a subdivision named after her—highlights recipients' indebtedness to the donor. That recipients are chosen from a pool of applicants suggests that, as in the Victorian era, distinctions are drawn between the deserving and undeserving poor. For further discussion of Winfrey's impact on philanthropy, see "Oprah Goes to Africa," by Talley and Casper in this volume.

Works Cited

1987a. Oprah Winfrey says she's a woman of god. *Clarion Ledger*, April 22.

1987b. Winfrey awarded diploma. *Jackson Daily News*, May 4.

1987c. Winfrey praises grandmas. *Jackson Daily News*, June 8.

1992. Winfrey wins lawsuit vs. tabloid. *Clarion Ledger*, May 3.

1997a. Oprah Winfrey. *Clarion-Ledger*, August 15.

1997b. Oprah Winfrey, talk-show host/actress. *Entertainment Weekly*, October 31.

1998a. City hopes landmark draws tourists. *Greenwood Commonwealth*, November 16.

1998b. Oprah to continue her show through year 2002. *Jet*, November 9.

1999. Oprah leaving show when contract is up. *Clarion Ledger*, February 10.

2004. The man who discovered Oprah. http://www.oprah.com/tows/pastshows/200401/tows_past_20040127.jhtml.

2006. The home stretch. http://www.oprah.com/presents/2006/rtrip/slide/20061017/rtrip_20061017_350_105.jhtml.

2007. A brief history of Tennessee State University. http://www.tnstate.edu/interior.asp?ptid=1&mid=399.

Broumas, Olga. 1977. Calypso. In *Beginning with O*. New Haven, CT: Yale University Press.

Chapelle, Tony, and Jeffrey Gambles. 1998. The 20 wealthiest African-American women. *Essence,* October.

Cloud, Dana L. 1996. Hegemony or concordance? The rhetoric of tokenism in "Oprah" Winfrey's rags-to-riches biography. *Critical Studies in Mass Communication* 13: 115–37.

Daniel, Pete. 2007. African American farmers and civil rights. *Journal of Southern History* 73: 3–38.

Decker, Jeffrey Louis. 2006. Saint Oprah. *MFS: Modern Fiction Studies,* 52: 169–78.

Edwards, Jeff. 1986. It's a long way from Mississippi to Michigan Avenue. *Jackson Daily News,* November 24.

Epstein, Debbie, and Deborah Lynn Steinberg. 1996. All het up!: rescuing heterosexuality on the *Oprah Winfrey Show. Feminist Review* 54: 88–115.

Farrell, Mary H.J., Katy Kelly, and Barbara Kleban Mills. 1991. Oprah's crusade. *People,* December 2.

Gates, Anita. 2000. Unstoppable Oprah. *McCall's,* February.

Guzman, Teri. 1985. Grand ol' Oprah. *Elle,* September.

Johnson, Gwendolyn. 2006. Interview with Oprah Winfrey. http://shs.starkville.k12.ms.us/mswm/MSWritersAndMusicians/writers/WinfreyOprah/winfrey.html.

Kolson, Ann. 1986. Winfrey has come a long way since her days in Kosciusko. *Jackson Daily News,* January 21.

Littwin, Susan. 1990. Oprah opens up. *TV Guide,* May 5.

Maddec, Bobby. 1998. In Oprah we trust. *Gadfly,* December.

Mendoza, Manuel. 1997. Oprah assures fans she's not gay. *Clarion Ledger,* June 5.

McAlister, Nancy. 2000. "Biography" details Oprah Winfrey's life Sunday on A&E. *Vicksburg Post,* January 16.

Miller, Hanna. 1998. An American dream: Oprah comes home. *Columbus Commercial Dispatch,* November 16.

Nelson, Jim, David Wright, and Donna Barr. 1994. Oprah's amazing roots. *National Enquirer,* March 8.

Peterson, Linda. 1999. Oprah: she came, she talked, she conquered. *Biography Magazine,* March.

Remwolt, Lisa. 1993. Oprah to air talk show on gays in state. *Biloxi Sun-Herald,* December 18.

Rensin, David. 1992. The prime time of Ms. Oprah Winfrey. *TV Guide,* May 16.

Richman, Alan. 1987. Oprah: TV's queen of talk has a hit show, a new man and a peeve. *People Weekly,* January 12.

Rickey, Carrie. 1998. Winfrey learns pain of slavery in "Beloved" role. *Clarion Ledger,* October 13.

Scott, Walter. 1986. Q&A. *Parade Magazine,* April 27.

Skipper, Deborah. Attala welcomes Oprah Winfrey home. *Clarion-Ledger/Jackson Daily News,* June 5.

Squire, Corinne. 1994. Empowering women? the Oprah Winfrey show. *Feminism & Psychology* 4: 63–79.

Stringfellow, Eric. 1998. Oprah: I was once young, poor and from Mississippi. *Clarion Ledger,* November 17.

Tornabene, Lyn. 1986. Here's Oprah. *Woman's Day,* October 1.

Trachtenberg, Alan. 1990. Introduction to *Ragged Dick; Or, Street Life in New York with the Bootblacks,* by Horatio Alger. New York: Signet Classic.

Ward, Brian. 1998. *Just My Soul Responding: Rhythm and Blues, Black Consciousness, and Race Relations.* Berkeley: University of California Press.

Weiss, Richard. 1988. *The American Myth of Success: From Horatio Alger to Norman Vincent Peale.* Urbana: University of Illinois Press.

Wolfe, George C. 1988. *The Colored Museum.* New York: Grove.

CHAPTER TWO

"I'm Everywoman"

Oprah Winfrey and Feminist Identification

JENNIFER L. REXROAT

Although Oprah Winfrey is not a publicly identified feminist, her comprehensive societal influence can be extrapolated to the United States women's movement. To borrow a term from Patricia Misciagno, she is the nation's foremost de facto feminist (Misciagno 1997). In the alternative, discursive social and political space created for women by *The Oprah Winfrey Show*, Oprah promotes feminist ideology and practice without explicitly acknowledging the fact that she is endorsing either feminism or the United States women's movement; in doing so, Oprah promotes de facto feminism on a regular basis in the homes of millions of "everywomen" in the United States, all the while without directly acknowledging her own feminist identity. Consequently, Oprah becomes a living embodiment of the contradictions of de facto feminism.

An emerging body of scholarship exists that analyzes the relationship between Oprah, her television show, and feminism. A primary theme of this burgeoning literature is the notion that *The Oprah Winfrey Show* blurs the boundaries of public and private, personal and political. Sujata Moorti states that "*Oprah* blurs our understandings of public and private issues, public and private spaces, and the characteristics differentiating the guests from the host and the participants . . . On daytime talk shows the personal is, indeed, political" (Moorti 1998, 86–87, italics in the original). Gloria-Jean Masciarotte continues this thread with her assertion that "in a real sense, then, on *The*

Oprah Winfrey Show, there is no area of politics that is not personal and no space where the personal is exempt from politics" (Masciarotte 1991, 96). In its convergence of the personal and the political, *The Oprah Winfrey Show* shares a major tenet with the contemporary United States women's movement.

Oprah succeeds in blurring these boundaries in large part because she makes women feel as though she is their friend. Deborah Tannen claims that women, in particular, listen to Oprah because, in opposition to the early style of the talk show founded by Phil Donahue, whom she says relied on "report-talk," or the basic exchange of information typified by men's conversation, Oprah utilizes a method of "rapport-talk," which, in its focus upon confessional, intimate, personal conversation, is unique to women's relationships (Tannen 1998, 198). In her discussion of Oprah's personal exchanges with her audience members, Corinne Squire concurs that these examples of expressiveness "signify an empathy that is traditionally feminine, but also feminist in its insistence on the 'personal'" (Squire 1997, 101).

A second dominant theme of the recent scholarly literature about Oprah is that her television show is rooted in the feminist tradition of consciousness raising. Masciarotte claims that Oprah gives a voice to the mass subject—those who have been Othered in society—including women, working- or lower-class people, and people of color (Masciarotte 1991, 103). *The Oprah Winfrey Show*, like talk shows in general, enables women to overcome their alienation as a result of talking about their specific experiences as women in society; by privileging the voice of women's experiences and struggles over the "learned" voice of the expert, the talk show continues the traditions of consciousness raising formulated within the liberal American women's movement (89–90).

Recent scholarly literature about Oprah has also focused upon the ways in which her show creates an alternative social and political space for women. Moorti suggests that *The Oprah Winfrey Show* creates both a "protofeminist discursive space" and a "feminist counter public sphere" (Moorti 1998, 83, 93, 97). Resultantly, *The Oprah Winfrey Show* functions as a discursive site for women publicly to share their stories, by and for women, forming bonds with others who have had similar life experiences.

Another thread binding emerging feminist scholarship about Oprah is the thesis that her show promotes the empowerment of women. Debbie Epstein and Deborah Lynn Steinberg remark that "Oprah's stated intention for her show is, at least in part, to challenge prejudice and foster empowerment, particularly, for women" (1998, 81). Squire observes that feminism is most explicit on *The Oprah Winfrey Show* in its "often-declared commitment to empowering women . . . the show's aim is to empower this shared womanhood," creating a "televisual feminism" in the process (1997, 102).

Some scholarly assessments of the treatment of racial issues on *The Oprah Winfrey Show* suggest that Oprah has managed to transcend race, a principal reason for her show's success. In transcending race, Oprah "has been described as a comforting, nonthreatening bridge between black and white cultures"; she is successful at presenting racially charged issues precisely because she vacillates between "sometimes embracing, sometimes minimizing her blackness," thus managing to depoliticize her race (Peck 1994, 90–91). Other academics, however, including Squire, argue against the notion that Oprah transcends race, suggesting instead that *The Oprah Winfrey Show* is as "permeated with 'race' as much as it is with gender," and that "black feminism seems, as much as woman-centered feminism, to define the show" (Squire 1997, 104–6).

The relatively modest amount of recent scholarship about Oprah has begun to address the ways in which issues of race, class, gender, and feminist identification are treated within the Oprah Winfrey enterprise. In this chapter, it is my desire to build upon this extant literature by utilizing Patricia Misciagno's theory of de facto feminism as a framework through which to view Oprah's feminist identification.

The De Facto Feminist Persona of Oprah Winfrey

In *Rethinking Feminist Identification*, Patricia Misciagno calls attention to what she identifies as the "paradox of feminism": "Many women who agree with (and, in many cases, actively support) the goals of modern feminism refuse to identify themselves *as* feminists" (1997, xvii, italics in the original). Misciagno characterizes these women as de facto feminists (xix).

Misciagno asserts that de facto feminists have often been omitted from view within the political landscape owing to narrowly defined constructs of feminism based solely upon feminist consciousness, at the expense of feminist praxis. In order to broaden the conceptualization of feminist identification to include the presence of de facto feminists, Misciagno argues for the importance of examining "the *actions* of de facto feminists, or what feminism has accomplished through and in history . . . It is for this reason that emphasis needs to be placed instead on women's agency, or on what they in fact *do*" (85, italics in the original). If this examination occurs, Misciagno contends, then "the group of women 'doing feminist things' far surpasses women who consider themselves feminists and thus supports the notion of the existence of a large number of de facto feminists" (69–70).

Oprah, in her personal statements about women's issues and through the medium of her television show, exhibits behavior that qualifies her as a de facto feminist. Oprah's de facto feminist approach fosters de facto feminism in her audience, transplanting feminist ideology and practice from the academy to the daily lives of "everywomen."

Biographical information reveals the presence of an early feminist influence in Oprah's life. Oprah's childhood role models include such historic black women as Sojourner Truth, Harriet Tubman, Ida B. Wells, and Madame C. J. Walker. As a young child, these were the women whom Oprah wanted to emulate; she often performed award-winning dramatic readings of their writings and speeches as a teenager. As Oprah became famous, she continued to exhibit feminist tendencies. When she opened Harpo Studios, her production company, in 1989, Oprah became the first African American and only the third woman in history to own a major film studio (Wooten 1999, 85); she became a prominent example of a woman who successfully broke through the glass ceiling of the television business world. In January 1989, Oprah was given the *Ms.* Magazine Woman of the Year award by Gloria Steinem "for being a role model showing women they can achieve whatever they dream of achieving" (Mair 1998, photo insert).[1]

Oprah has, over the years, made vast numbers of public statements about women's issues, including (among many others) violence against women, lesbianism, women's independence from men, and her own leadership responsibility to women, particularly African American women. Oprah once commented, with respect to the issue of violence against women, that she wished she "could just get black women connected to this whole abuse issue . . . I hear it all the time from black women who say, 'Well, he slapped me around a few times, but he doesn't really beat me.' We are so accustomed to being treated badly that we don't know that love is supposed to feel really good" (Oprah Winfrey, quoted in Adler 1997, 68). Oprah has also spoken about her ability to use her show as a forum to expose America to the issue of violence against women. In a 1998 interview, she stated that "there is a body of work—about the neglect and abuse of children, about women and the way they treat themselves and allow other people to mistreat them, about alcoholism and dysfunction in families and its effect on the way we live our lives today—that I'm immensely proud of" (Oprah Winfrey, quoted in Borden 1998, A77).

Oprah has also been guardedly supportive of lesbianism, even in the face of rumors about her own sexuality. Oprah appeared as a psychiatrist on the 1997 *Ellen* television show's "coming out" episode. Later, Ellen DeGeneres was a guest on *The Oprah Winfrey Show*, and during that episode several audience members were vehemently opposed to Ellen's character coming out on the *Ellen* show. Oprah responded to this controversy by stating that "a lot of people said me being on your show . . . was me promoting lesbianism. I simply wanted to support you in being what you believe was the truth for yourself" (Oprah Winfrey, quoted in Borden 1998, A77). This sentiment suggests that Oprah's greater concern is not the promotion or endorsement of lesbianism, per se, but rather the advancement of women's independence and freedom, no matter what their sexual orientations may be.

Oprah has voiced her feelings many times over the years about women's relationships with men, namely, her desire for women to form their own identities independent of the male figures in their lives. She reveals her views in this regard in the following: "I'll tell you what frustrates me the most. What frustrates me the most is these women who still live their lives for men. I want to just shake them sometimes! But I've been one of those women, so I understand. I understand that you have to come to it in your own time, and that it just takes some of us longer than others. And so you may have six children and three husbands before you figure it out" (Oprah Winfrey, quoted in Adler 1997, 194). Oprah is following the advice she gives to other women; she has stated that "I no longer feel . . . that I have to have a man in order to make myself whole—I feel there are important discoveries yet to be made" (Oprah Winfrey, quoted in Adler 1997, 194). Oprah is on the road to living her own life, confidently, independently, and by and for herself; in 1990, she resolved that, "from now on I'm living this life for Oprah, not for some man. Women diet to keep their men, everybody knows that. But I've decided men can go to blazes. Why should I spend the rest of my existence worrying about some man? If he doesn't want me the way I am, he can take a hike. The charade is over. I'm going to be the Oprah I always wanted to be: fat and sassy!" (quoted in Adler 1997, 193).

Oprah continues to practice what she preaches about the possibilities of egalitarian, autonomous relationships between men and women. During a 2001 interview with CNN's Larry King, Oprah maintained that marriage is not in her future; when asked the direct question of whether she and longtime beau Stedman Graham would marry, Oprah replied, "For the past 15, 16 years the answer has been no" (CNN 2001a). Oprah reaffirmed this answer in a 2003 interview with *Essence* magazine, remarking that "the truth of the matter is, had we gotten married we wouldn't be together now . . . because in no way is this a traditional relationship. Stedman's a traditional Black man, but I'm in no way a traditional woman, so to take on that role just doesn't fit" (Oprah Winfrey, quoted in Edwards 2003, 246). In a 2003 interview with *TV Guide*, Oprah noted that "Stedman and I have a great relationship that allows me to be me in the fullest sense, with no expectations of wifedom and all that would mean" (Oprah Winfrey, quoted in Logan 2003, 39). Oprah most recently re-iterated this opinion during a 2004 interview with ABC's Barbara Walters, commenting that "not being married works for us" (Oprah Winfrey, quoted on ABC 2004). Clearly, Oprah feels that marriage is not a necessary condition for a meaningful, rewarding partnership with a man.

Over time, Oprah has more explicitly dedicated herself to her position as a role model for women. In 1988, she stated that "the greatest contribution you can make to women's rights, to civil rights, is to be the absolute . . . best at what you do" (Oprah Winfrey, quoted in Lowe 1998, 25). Oprah's early commitment to working on behalf of women remains true today, as her multimedia ventures continue to expand and she is able to reach women in a variety of media formats. Regarding her 1999 cofounding of Oxygen Media, a female-oriented cable television channel, Oprah commented that "it will be an avenue for me to continue to influence women to better themselves" (Russell and Dampier 1999, 144). At the first anniversary party for *O, The Oprah Magazine* in 2001, Oprah proclaimed that "this has been one of the most joy-filled years of my life because I did exactly what I intended to do: create a magazine that would help women see themselves differently" (Oprah.com 2001). In a 2001 interview with CNN's Larry King, Oprah emphasized that she wants to use her fortune to educate and empower women and girls.

To this end, Oprah has donated $40 million to build the Oprah Winfrey Leadership Academy for Girls South Africa, which admitted its first students in 2007 (Samuels 2007). At the 2002 groundbreaking ceremony for the academy, Oprah said, "We are looking for strong, brave girls with heart. I believe girls are going to take over the world. Men have been in control long enough. But don't worry, we're prepared to share power" (Oprah Winfrey, quoted in Miller 2003, 54). This is the first of twelve such schools that Oprah plans to build on the African continent because she feels that "women are going to save Africa . . . And this will be my legacy" (Oprah Winfrey, quoted in Edwards 2003, 180).

Oprah's philanthropic initiatives in Africa were the subject of a 2003 episode of *Prime Time Live,* hosted by Diane Sawyer. During the interview, Oprah expounded further about her motivations for choosing Africa and, primarily, African women as the recipients of many of her recent charitable endeavors:

So I thought, "Well, what can I do?" So, for me, education has been the road to success. To me, education is freedom, and I believe the future of this country—of Africa—will depend upon the leadership of its women. And that's just not a—a feminist rhetoric—it really is the truth as I see it, and as do a lot of the other leaders of Africa see it. When you're driving out in the morning, it's the women who are going to get the water to bake the morning's porridge; it's the women who have to gather the wood to heat the water; it's the women who farm the fields. In my lifetime, we're not gonna change the patriarchal system there, but you can—I have seen—where you just, just the slightest word of encouragement, um, empowers women. I mean, the very idea that you can take care of yourself (Oprah Winfrey, quoted on ABC 2003).

It is noteworthy that, in this statement, Oprah specifically and purposively distances herself from an overtly "feminist rhetoric," choosing to liken her rationale for empowering Africa's women to that of "other leaders of Africa" who have not adopted a decidedly feminist framework for their actions. Oprah does, however, center women's empowerment as the primary reason for her work in Africa, imbuing her remarks with a de facto feminist connotation.

In addition, Oprah has used her magazine as a vehicle through which to encourage American women to exercise their voting rights. In a 2004 *O, The Oprah Magazine* column, Oprah soundly reminds women of the sacrifices their suffragist foremothers made for their benefit, and of the potentially disastrous consequences of women's electoral apathy:

I cast a ballot for everybody who came before me and gave their life's energy so that yours and mine could be a force that matters today. Emancipated slave and civil rights activist Sojourner Truth, speaking at the Women's Rights Convention in Akron in 1851, said, "If the first woman God ever made was strong enough to turn the world upside down all alone, these women together ought to be able to turn it back, and get it right side up again!" . . . The most recent statistics are embarrassing and disrespectful to our female heritage—to every suffragette, to every woman who didn't have a voice but hoped someday her daughters might be heard . . . We owe more—we ought to do better and respect ourselves enough to be counted. Vote. (Winfrey 2004, 324)

Oprah's poignant call to action is clearly informed by and sympathetic to feminist history, but she refers to "our female heritage" instead of an overtly feminist one, again suggesting that her desire to inspire American women to vote in increased numbers stems from her de facto feminist tendencies.

Oprah is extraordinarily committed to the advancement of women in society, but she seems even more acutely aware of her responsibility toward continuing the legacy of black women. In a 1987 interview, Oprah stated that "I wouldn't say I feel an obligation to speak 'for all blacks,' but I do feel myself as part of a tradition. I carry with me the voices of the women who have gone before me. When I speak for me, I also speak for them" (Oprah Winfrey, quoted in Lowe 1998, 28). In this same vein, Oprah elaborated upon her sense of responsibility to black women in a 1995 interview, disclosing that "the greatest responsibility I feel is to my creator and what I try to fulfill for myself is to honor the creation. The fact that I was created a black woman in this lifetime, everything in my life is built around honoring that. I feel a sense of reverence to that. I hold it sacred. And so I am always asking the question, 'What do I owe in service having been created a black woman?'" (Oprah Winfrey, quoted in Adler 1997, 75). Oprah's loyalty to the legacy of the black women who preceded her is a primary reason why she continues to produce *The Oprah Winfrey Show*. She revealed in 1998 that she has come "very close to quitting. I thought I was going to quit in 1997. But I woke up one morning and I was making coffee when it just connected . . . that I am a descendant of slaves and what does that mean? You're an African-American woman, you have this show and now you're thinking about giving it up? What would the ancestors say? You have created power, credibility for yourself and you have nothing to say? So, that's why I decided to continue" (Oprah Winfrey, quoted in Borden 1998, A77).

Oprah's most recent celebration of the legacy of pioneering African American women occurred in 2005, when she hosted a gala weekend at her California mansion honoring African American women in the arts, entertainment, and civil rights fields (*People Weekly* 2005, 59). Oprah stated that the commemoration was inspired because she wanted to thank her ancestors and "rejoice in the spirit" of those who came before her (Winfrey 2005, 178). She considers herself to be an inspiration for black women, in particular, because, like the legendary African American women who preceded her, she is living proof that "you can be born poor and black and female and make it to the top" (Oprah Winfrey, quoted in Adler 1997, 278).[2]

In her words and actions, Oprah has given a voice to women's issues in a way that few women, and even fewer black women, have been able to do throughout American history. The fact that she regularly provides a sympathetic platform for the discussion of women's issues through the forum of her television show, combined with her show's stated objective of "raising consciousness" (Oprah Winfrey, quoted in Adler 1997, 78) begs the question of whether Oprah is, herself, a feminist. Oprah's public statements thus far, however, appear to negate an explicit identification with feminism. In fact, over the years, Oprah has shied away from being labeled a political "activist" of any kind.[3] Oprah has expressed her aversion to an activist identity several times in various interviews; she has stated, "I have a great sense of heritage. I feel a strong sense of legacy. But I'm not a flag-waving activist" (Oprah Winfrey, quoted in Adler 1997, 273). Statements in which Oprah implicitly links activism to "radical" politics characterize the definition of an "activist" as her polar opposite. Oprah, thereby, maintains a de facto feminist identity because she implicitly and explicitly rejects any association with radicalized activist politics, be it in relation to the struggle for civil rights or women's rights.

Oprah appears, on the surface, to eschew an activist identity. But how, then, can we reconcile her public aversion to activism with her repeated efforts to advance the status of women in society? The theory of de facto feminism helps us to explain this tension. Oprah has demonstrated an implicit commitment to fostering a pro-women agenda, yet she refuses to pigeonhole herself as an explicitly identified feminist because of the many problematic and, often, pejorative associations made by numerous Americans with the feminist label.[4] Rather than tout herself or her show as an extension of organized feminism, Oprah has declared her goal to be "to empower women" (Oprah Winfrey, quoted in Harrison 1989, 46). Oprah has made several public statements to this effect; in particular, she commented that she considers her television show to be "a way of being a voice to the world, a way of allowing whatever I felt and the people I surrounded myself with felt, to empower, uplift, enlighten, encourage, and if we can entertain you, we're glad to do that too" (Oprah Winfrey, quoted in Adler 1997, 103).

Oprah has elected, in de facto feminist fashion, to call her efforts to advance the status of women in society the "empowerment of women" because, instead of branding her as a politicized "feminist" who alienates de facto feminists opposed to the feminist label, this tactic allows her to be "everywoman," enabling her to bond with both self-avowed feminists and de facto feminists alike. It is far easier to oppose a "feminist," with all of the loaded and radicalized political connotations that the term itself carries in American society, than to oppose someone who is benevolently working for "women's empowerment," a relatively controversy-free rallying cry. Oprah has knowingly pitched her appeal for the advancement of a pro-women agenda in the United States, not within the parameters of the politically charged women's movement but rather completely beneath the political radar screen by calling it something else: women's empowerment, a concept that is much less likely to be rejected by her mainstream audience than feminism.[5]

On one hand, Oprah cannot afford to explicitly identify as a feminist in today's society, where feminism is still so taboo in certain circles that it has been nicknamed the "f-word." If one subscribes solely to this argument, it follows that doing so would likely cost her everything: her television show, her media empire, and the legacy she has worked so hard to build on behalf of all women, especially black women. In order to promote a pro-women agenda on her show, she has to do so under the auspices of de facto feminism, due to the extremely high costs of establishing her feminist identity. *The Oprah Winfrey Show* needs to "please its audience, maintain its 'advertiser friendly' reputation, and not jeopardize Winfrey's mass appeal" (Peck 1994, 91); "the voicing of feminist understandings of women's oppression in society is thus tempered by the need to not alienate viewers" (Moorti 1998, 90). Oprah believes in her "everywoman" status so much that, for several seasons, even the theme song of her television show was the Whitney Houston version of "I'm Every Woman"; she remarked that she chose it "because I think my life is more like other people's, in spite of all the fame that has come to me" (Moorti 1998, 116). Consequently, Oprah must seek to bridge or erase gender divisions among viewers and participants, even as she tackles profoundly divisive gender issues. By adopting a de facto feminist strategy, she can still deliver feminist messages but without radicalizing herself as an overt feminist and thereby risking the alienation of her audience, advertisers, and the mass public. Dana Cloud writes that "one can hardly fault Winfrey as an individual for hedging (her refusal of collective identification has earned her millions of dollars)" (1996, 128). While Oprah's refusal to acknowledge her feminist identification is partially responsible for her mass appeal, it also has its tradeoffs; "she can never admit the need for systematic structural change and collective political activity" (129). Oprah deals with gendered, feminist issues on her television show, but due to social pressure to appeal to and empathize with women without making explicitly feminist calls to abate women's oppression, Oprah is left with little choice but to opt for a de facto feminist strategy if she is to balance her competing interests of improving women's social condition and cultivating her media empire.

On the other hand, it is precisely Oprah's massive wealth, seemingly boundless power, and pervasive social influence that should afford her every ability to out herself as a feminist, if she so desired. At this point in her career, Oprah has achieved such a high level of success and financial security that it would appear she should no longer be hampered by any social, professional, and financial pressures that might have previously encouraged her to hide an allegiance to organized feminism.

Why, then, does Oprah refuse to explicitly acknowledge a feminist identity? It is a contention of this analysis that Oprah's rationale for this refusal is more complicated than a monetary cost/benefit analysis alone. Oprah's de facto feminist behavior is not merely strategic—it is real. This study suggests that Oprah is not a publicly identified feminist who is carefully screening her identity to avoid detection; instead she, like many of the women in her audience, is a de facto feminist who may very well consider an established feminist identification and/or an overt relationship to organized feminism to be unimportant. Oprah, herself, is a living embodiment of the de facto feminist contradiction. If she wanted to explicitly identify herself as a feminist, she could, because at this stage of her career it is no longer solely the need for high ratings, loyal advertisers, or social acceptance that is stopping her; that Oprah repeatedly refuses to publicly establish a feminist identity is telling, however, as it suggests that, for various and perhaps more complex reasons, she simply may not wish to do so.

Oprah's very power lies in her ambiguity as "everywoman"; she is a mirror in which, under certain conditions, American women see themselves. Today, perhaps the most pressing danger that Oprah faces in explicitly identifying herself as a feminist is the potential alienation of much of her female audience, many of whom are also de facto feminists. Introducing overt feminism to her largely female audience—women with whom Oprah has built a deep, solid connection over the past twenty years—would potentially defy the "girlfriend" solidarity and homogeneity that Oprah has worked so diligently to cultivate between herself and her audience by pitting women against each other on the basis of fundamentally divisive political views. No longer would Oprah and her audience be a homogeneous community of women; instead, they could become adversaries opposed on the basis of their acceptance or rejection of an explicitly feminist political identity. Oprah would no longer be a mirror in which American women see themselves; rather, she would become a distorted reflection of the politics of only some women. Rather than risk this possible outcome, Oprah generally avoids politics and activism, and particularly an allegiance to organized feminism, altogether. Because of the polarizing connotations of "feminists" and "feminism," Oprah embraces de facto feminism not only as her own identity, but also as a means of safeguarding her "everywoman" status, reinforcing her similarities to her audience, and protecting the integrity of the community of women she seeks to empower.

Oprah seems to want women to believe that she is just like them; she wants to be perceived as the television equivalent of their next-door-neighbors, a "woman in progress" (Oprah Winfrey, quoted in Smolowe and Steptoe 2001, 52) with the same struggles, challenges, and joys as every other woman. Oprah's quest to be "everywoman," however, is fraught with contradictions. She is "everywoman" and an anomaly at the same time. Oprah's loyal followers "know that the life of the multimillionaire in the couture gowns is nothing like theirs. Yet they believe that her inner goals and aspirations mirror their own" (Clemetson 2001, 48). Oprah touts herself as "everywoman," but her boundless affluence and luxurious lifestyle, unthinkable for most women, render Oprah an antithesis to the "everywoman" title she espouses. Why, then, do women love her anyway and follow her lead as though she were the Pied Piper with a Midas touch? Because she balances her extravagant lifestyle with a down-home persona that resonates with her audience. We know she is *not* like us, but we simultaneously want to believe that she *is*, for if that is true, then not only is it possible for Oprah the "everywoman" to be just like us, but it is also possible for us to be just like her. It is a relationship of mutual convenience—Oprah gives women the friendship, solidarity, and hope they crave, and they forgive her fortune.

As one of the most prominent media figures in the history of the United States, Oprah carries unprecedented clout with her viewers. Oprah is acutely aware of the enormous amount of power she possesses: "It's a powerful medium [television] . . . I think a politician would want to be me. If you really want to change people's lives, have an hour platform every day to go into their homes and say what you want to say" (Oprah Winfrey, quoted in Adler 1997, 246–47). Oprah's pervasive influence upon her audience extends to de facto feminism as well. Just as she endorses products and lifestyle advice on *The Oprah Winfrey Show*, Oprah also promotes the ideology and praxis of de facto feminism among her viewers. If we subscribe to Masciarotte's notion that "the cultural importance of '*The Oprah Winfrey Show*' for the viewer is . . . in being subject to Oprah" (Masciarotte 1991, 93), then the previous examination of the de facto feminist persona of Oprah Winfrey reveals the extent to which Oprah subjects her audience to de facto feminism.

This analysis contends that Oprah's feminist and "everywoman" identities are fundamentally at odds with each other; she cannot be both at the same time. Oprah, as "everywoman," is a figurative site for the projection of women's identities, whatever they may be; her power lies in her ability to reflect this ambiguity. If Oprah were openly to establish herself as a feminist, she would both marginalize and isolate herself from the de facto feminist and antifeminist women in her audience, effectively nullifying her appeal to all women. This would result in Oprah's abandonment of her implicit contract with her viewers, in which she proclaims to bond with them as "just another one of the girls." To avoid this tension, Oprah promotes the empowerment of women in a de facto feminist fashion. Oprah's de facto feminist identity is not, however, merely strategic; Oprah is an embodiment of the de facto feminist contradiction. Oprah has stated that her show reflects her personal beliefs; she asserts that "we offer what we offer because that's what I believe. I mean, this show, on a daily basis, reflects my personal beliefs and standards" (Oprah Winfrey, quoted on CNN 2001a). Oprah reiterated this view in her 2005 declaration that "where I am on the show is always where I am personally" (quoted in MSNBC 2005). Consequently, the ambivalence about feminism and activism of any kind that Oprah regularly expresses on her television show, in her personal statements, and throughout her media enterprise—coupled with her simultaneous promotion of women's empowerment—lends credence to this chapter's claim that, because de facto feminism accurately reflects her own political beliefs, Oprah's allegiance to de facto feminism is her sincere personal choice.

Notes

1. Despite her apparent lack of an "official" feminist identity, Oprah Winfrey has been interviewed and featured several times in recent years by the iconic feminist publication, *Ms.* magazine (Barthel 1986; Gillespie 1988; Angelou 1999). Whether or not Oprah considers herself to be a feminist role model, it is clear that *Ms.* magazine does. I posit that Oprah would not agree to be featured in and interviewed by one of the leading feminist publications in the United States if she, herself, were not sympathetic to feminist goals and objectives.

2. This assertion should not be taken to mean that the level of Oprah's personal, individual success can easily be generalized to the lives of all black women, for there are structural and institutional forces, including racism and poverty, which complicate the ability of black women to easily emulate Oprah's achievements. Oprah's groundbreaking success as a black woman, however, can be considered an inspiration for others to follow her lead in their daily lives.

3. For further discussion of Winfrey's aversion to overt political engagement, please see Howard, "Beginnings with O," in this volume.

4. See Misciagno (1997) for an explanation of the negative associations that women often make with the feminist label. While it is a valid assertion that Oprah and many other women of color may reject feminism because of its negative stereotypes, a lack of interest in feminist objectives, and/or a scarcity of time, energy, and desire to do feminist activist work, it is critically important to note that women of color are not a monolith (Mohanty 1998) and, consequently, their reasons for the rejection of feminism might be broader and, perhaps, more complicated than previously suggested by feminist research in this area conducted by white, western women. As Mohanty suggests, it is imperative that we remain conscious of—and make every effort to avoid—the western feminist tendency to ascribe overly generalized theoretical principles of feminism (and, vis-à-vis this analysis, of feminist identification) to women of color who, in practice, make individualized and often highly specific decisions about their rejection or adoption of a feminist identity (including a de facto feminist identity) based upon a complex personal calculus involving numerous combinations and permutations of the intersections of race, class, and gender in their lives.

5. In her efforts to promote women's empowerment in American society, Oprah often advances a substantive, issue-based agenda that illustrates the ways in which women are oppressed. While Oprah does spend a fair amount of time on her television show and in her other media endeavors discussing "lighter" lifestyle issues (e.g., cosmetic makeovers, diets and recipes, fashion, relationship advice, interviews with celebrities), Oprah also devotes a significant amount of time and energy to the examination of more serious, politicized issues that adversely affect women (e.g., rape, incest, domestic violence, sexism, racial discrimination, body image, women's health).

Works Cited

ABC. 2004. *Barbara Walters Presents: The 10 Most Fascinating People of 2004*. December 8.

ABC. 2003. *Prime Time Live*. December 17.

Adler, Bill, ed. 1997, *The Uncommon Wisdom of Oprah Winfrey: A Portrait in her Own Words*. Secaucus, N.J.: Citadel Press.

Angelou, Maya. 1989. "Oprah Winfrey." *Ms.* 17: 88–89.

Barthel, Joan. 1986. "Here Comes Oprah! From 'The Color Purple' to TV Talk Queen." *Ms.* 15: 46–50, 88.

Borden, Jeff. 1998. "Next, On Oprah." *Crain's Chicago Business* 21, no. 22: A76–77.

Clemetson, Lynette. 2001. "Oprah on Oprah." *Newsweek*, January 8: 38–48.

Cloud, Dana L. 1996. "Hegemony or Concordance? The Rhetoric of Tokenism in 'Oprah' Winfrey's Rags-to-Riches Biography." *Critical Studies in Mass Communication* 13: 115–37.

CNN. 2001a. *Larry King Live.* September 4.

CNN. 2001b. "Oprah: No Wedding Plans for Now." *CNN.com*, September 5. http://www.cnn .com/2001/SHOWBIZ/TV/09/05/oprah.lkl/index.html?related.

Edwards, Audrey. 2003. "The O Factor." *Essence* 34, no. 6: 176–80, 246.

Epstein, Debbie, and Deborah Lynn Steinberg. 1998. "American Dreamin': Discoursing Liberally on the *Oprah Winfrey Show." Women's Studies International Forum* 21, no. 1: 77–94.

Gillespie, Marcia Ann. 1988. "Winfrey Takes All." *Ms.* 17: 50–54.

Harrison, Barbara Grizzuti. "The Importance of Being Oprah." 1989. *New York Times Magazine* (June 11): 28–30.

Logan, Michael. 2003. "The Power of One." *TV Guide* 51, no. 40: 36–40.

Lowe, Janet. 1998. *Oprah Winfrey Speaks: Insight From the World's Most Influential Voice.* New York: John Wiley & Sons, Inc.

Mair, George. 1998. *Oprah Winfrey: The Real Story.* Secaucus, N.J.: Citadel Stars.

Masciarotte, Gloria-Jean. 1991. "C'mon, Girl: Oprah Winfrey and the Discourse of Feminine Talk." *Genders* 11: 81–110.

Miller, Samantha. 2003. "Earn, Baby, Earn." *People Weekly* 59, no. 10: 54.

Misciagno, Patricia S. 1997. *Rethinking Feminist Identification.* Westport, Conn.: Praeger Publishers.

Mohanty, Chandra Talpade. 1988. "Under Western Eyes: Feminist Scholarship and Colonial Discourses." *Feminist Review* 30: 61–88.

Moorti, Sujata. 1998. "Cathartic Confessions or Emancipatory Texts? Rape Narratives on *The Oprah Winfrey Show." Social Text* 57, no. 4: 83–102.

MSNBC. 2005. "How I Got There." *MSNBC.com*, October 25. http://www.msnbc.msn.com/ id/9712069/site/newsweek/print/1/displaymode/1098/.

Oprah.com. 2001. "*O Magazine's* First Anniversary Party." *Oprah.com*, May. http://oprah.oxygen .com/omagazine/200105/omag_200105_party.html.

Peck, Janice. 1994. "Talk About Racism: Framing a Popular Discourse of Race on *Oprah Winfrey." Cultural Critique* 27: 89–126.

People Weekly. 2005. "Oprah's Big Weekend Bash." *People Weekly* 63, no. 20: 59.

Russell, Lisa, and Cindy Dampier. 1999. "Oprah Winfrey." *People Weekly* (March 15–22): 143–44.

Samuels, Allison. 2007. "Oprah Winfrey's Lavish South African School." *MSNBC.com*, January 8. http://www.msnbc.msn.com/id/16396343/site/newsweek/page/3/print/1/displaymode/1098/.

Sellers, Patricia. 1998. "The 50 Most Powerful Women in American Business." *Fortune* 138, no. 7: 76–81.

Smolowe, Jill, and Sonja Steptoe. 2001. "O On the Go." *People Weekly* 56, no. 3: 50–54.

Squire, Corinne. 1997. "Empowering Women? The *Oprah Winfrey Show." In Feminist Television Criticism*, edited by Charlotte Brunsdon, Julie D'Acci, and Lynn Spiegel, 98–113. New York: Oxford University Press, Inc.

Tannen, Deborah. 1998. "Oprah Winfrey." *Time* 151, no. 22: 196–98.

Winfrey, Oprah. 2004. "What I Know for Sure." *O, The Oprah Magazine* (October): 324.

———. 2005. "Heaven in My Living Room." *O, The Oprah Magazine* (August): 178.

Wooten, Sara McIntosh. 1999. *Oprah Winfrey: Talk Show Legend.* Berkeley Heights, N.J.: Enslow Publishers, Inc.

CHAPTER THREE

New Age Soul

The Gendered Translation of New Age Spirituality on
The Oprah Winfrey Show

KARLYN CROWLEY

Recently Oprah Winfrey held a web seminar on the New Age guru, Eckart Tolle, and his 2008 book, *A New Earth: Awakening to Your Life's Potential.* Tolle is a German-born, Cambridge-educated spiritual leader, who writes about the "spiritual awakening" that he feels is the "next step in human evolution" (Oprah's Book Club 2008a). Oprah touted his book as "her boldest choice yet" and raved about the book's ability to awaken readers to "the possibilities of their lives" (Oprah's Book Club 2008c). She began the seminar by talking about Tolle's ideas and their central importance in her life: "The one thing I know for sure is that you cannot even begin to live your best life without being connected to your spirit" (Oprah's Book Club 2008c). When Oprah opened the field for audience participation, she received a question from an audience member who asked how she should reconcile her religious faith with her spiritual seeking. What interests me about this question is less its content than its intended recipient; it is not a question fielded by Oprah for Tolle. Instead, the woman in the audience posed the question directly to the real guru on the set: Oprah.

This seeming confusion about who, exactly, the spiritual authority is here highlights how increasingly Oprah has become not just a widely loved talk show host but a spiritual leader in her own right. This essay shows how Oprah Winfrey blends New Age culture with a racialized "sister sensibility" to create a unique female-centered ministry for her largely female audience. Critics have observed that Oprah is "a compelling and successful spiritual teacher" who promotes her own "gospel" and others have noticed that she popularizes New Age spirituality by focusing on "spiritual uplift, individual will, personal responsibility, and grand cosmic design" (McGrath 2007, 127; Nelson, 2005, xv). I am interested in how Oprah manages to engender her translation of New Age spirituality and make it authentic and appealing through race. Oprah's autobiography is a testimony of hardship, racism, and institutional poverty that establishes her credentials as "black enough" and, therefore, gives her authority to preach New Age spirituality. By analyzing the appearances of white, New Age experts on her talk show, I demonstrate how Oprah positions women at the center of her church by translating a New Age vision authenticated by African American struggle. Women's spiritual experiences are central on *The Oprah Winfrey Show (TOWS)*, not secondary or peripheral. I argue that Oprah's appeal to women, white women in particular, is her ability to filter white, New Age ideas in gendered terms that are legitimized through race.

Oprah explains her own transition to New Age spirituality from the traditional black Baptist church where she grew up as a transition from the oppressive to the liberatory. Oprah reports that she adored church until the day the minister said, "God is a jealous God." Somehow the idea of a "jealous God" just "didn't feel right" to Oprah and she began on a journey to take "God out of a box" (Oprah's Book Club 2008b). A rigid hierarchy characterizes this traditional church order of a "jealous God" with power located only at the top. Oprah calls this "old spirituality" and summarizes Elizabeth Lesser's definition of it this way:

The hierarchy has the authority. Church authorities tell you how to worship in church and how to behave outside of church . . . 2) God, and the path to worship Him, have already been defined. All you need to do is follow the directions . . . 3) There is only one path. It is the right way and all other ways are wrong . . . 4) Parts of yourself—like the body, or ego, or emotions—are evil . . . 5) The truth is like a rock. Your understanding of it should never waver (2000, 51–52).

This is no longer how Oprah views power; her belief system has evolved to one in which power is diffuse and located within us, a system ostensibly more empowering to women who may rarely get to the top of the hierarchy but can experience some power within.

Oprah believes in "new spirituality" and again draws on Lesser's definition, in which "You are your own best authority . . . You listen within for your own definition of spirituality . . . Many paths lead to spiritual freedom and peace . . . Everything is sacred—your body, mind, psyche, heart, and soul. The truth is like the horizon—forever ahead of you, forever changing its shape and color"

(Oprah's Book Club 2008b). Winfrey validates the personal, which for many women means listening to one's own experience and intuition. Oprah suggests that if we recognize, confess, and become "intentional" about our problems, then we can have greater control over our destiny, which is a significant tenet of New Age spirituality, where mind and thought control are central. Oprah's altar call uplifts audiences rather than punishing and admonishing them for their sins. By emphasizing women's agency in taking care of themselves, Oprah creates a kinder, gentler "confession booth."

The *Oprah Winfrey Show* is no ordinary talk show. It is a carefully orchestrated ministry that makes use of the techniques of "old school" religion to enhance Oprah's personal message geared toward women. Her rhetorical strategies and emotional rapport with audiences effectively establish her as an authority of self-help gospel. Corrine Squire suggests that on *TOWS*, "the stress on communication recalls a religious commitment to testifying" (1997, 108). For example, Oprah punctuates the ideas of others on her show as the "testifier": the one who attests to the importance of her invited guests. But Oprah is neither distant nor ethereal in this role like the saints or a "jealous God" have been—although, as with the faithful and saints historically, her audiences do often want to touch her clothing or get close to her. Rather Oprah balances her charismatic authority as a larger-than-life persona with a performance of emotional intimacy and personal disclosure. By moving among speech registers of the black vernacular, "girl talk," and spiritual advice, she makes audiences feel familiar, as if she knows them and they know her. Oprah is astoundingly good at appearing genuine, accessible, and open. She marries the intimacy and individuality of the New Age movement with the adulation and power of a *700 Club*–like ministry.

Oprah and the Female Godhead

Scholars have explored Oprah's ability to captivate viewers' attention and her use of communication modes that are considered more feminine in dynamics to engage audiences. Laurie Haag (1993) observes, for example, that Oprah, "reacts, no holds barred, laughing, screaming, even crying at the appropriate times, and allows us to do the same" (119). Oprah is not an emotionally distant commentator like her early 1980s and 1990s rivals, Phil Donahue and Geraldo Rivera, but expresses a broad range of emotions on her show. The "Give-Away" episode, where every audience member received a new car, is a good example. Oprah jumped up and down in excitement and joy with them, and the audience moved to near mass hysteria. It is this open emotionality that allows female viewers to feel that she is just like them, that, indeed, she is "every woman," and that she empathizes on all levels of human experience. New Age author Kathy Freston reinforces this connection on Oprah's *Soul Series:* "Oprah you are so empathic, that is why everyone loves you" (*Oprah's Soul Series* 2008). A Saudi woman viewer felt that "Oprah truly understands me" (Zoepf 2008). Oprah's ability to be eminently available makes her one of the ordinary "folk," or one of the girls, by narrowing the gap between herself as a high-profile celebrity and her audience.

Oprah's "ministry" meets the needs of a female-centered audience that has become dissatisfied with mainstream religions but still hungers for a spiritual outlet. Her audience looks to her for spiritual truths, and in return they receive a unique experience that is more than the typical Sunday television evangelist offers. Oprah's dramatic entrance on *TOWS*, the theme song, her regal clothing, and her focus on personal spiritual transformation make it nearly a complete Sunday service. She also projects characteristics from the black preaching tradition like charisma, vocal intonation, and a certain physical presence that enhances her spiritual authority. For example, her *Soul Series* radio show opens with a jazzy, gospel score and rhythm and with Oprah's voice: "It's uplifting, enlightening, truly powerful—welcome to *Soul Series*" (*Oprah's Soul Series* 2008). Oprah also racializes spirituality through her choice of speech, music, guest roster, and general "sister" sensibility. She includes guests of color, ranging from author Maya Angelou to motivational speaker Dr. Robin Smith to gospel stars, such as BeBe and CeCe Winans, Yolanda Adams, Kirk Franklin, Oleta Adams, and Joshua Nelson, all of whom cite a higher power in their work and further foreground the racialization of spirituality. These features all converge to frame Oprah as the quintessential minister of self-help backed by racial authenticity.

Oprah is, however, more than just talk. Like any good congregation leader, her 2005 "Change Your Life TV" campaign was dedicated to self-improvement through good works. She is famous not only for her "random acts of kindness" but also for her Angel Network, founded in 1997. Oprah states that the "Angel Network works around the globe to give people the chance to live their best lives" (Oprah's Angel Network 2008). This description conjoins evangelical missions of reaching out to unenlightened others together with the New Age goal of helping people achieve more spiritual depth and better lives in this lifetime—aided by angels to be sure. In addition to its name and vision are the Angel Network's praxis of helping children at risk, and especially young girls and poor children of color. Oprah built a school for girls in South Africa under her "Oprah Winfrey Leadership Academy Foundation," for example, and helped draft and lobby for the 1991 National Child Protection Act. Her philanthropy is a kind of ministry that resembles the outreach of churches dealing with human and social needs. Oprah tends to mobilize philanthropy around gender and race in ways that shore up her New Age feminist church. Her donations are "good works" that are usually women-centered, which draws in women viewers.

Oprah creates her own brand of New Age feminism that expresses feminist desires without overt feminist claims. Scholar Kathryn Lofton notes that Oprah has invented her own "ritual of behaviors for helping others achieve personal goals. She urges fans to read, keep personal journals and purchase self-indulgent gifts" (Deggans 2003). Through her Book Club she frequently chooses plots that function liturgically for her afternoon show, or "service," moving from abuse to recovery. For example, Oprah's 1998 Book Club selection, Edwidge Danticat's *Breath, Eyes, Memory* (1994), follows a Haitian protagonist from sexual abuse to recovery through both therapy and reconciliation with her abuser. The book has a feel of redemption about it, as it moves the heroine from victim to agent, but it is a redemption that resonates chiefly with women, as the story centers around women's relationships with other women and deals with body and weight issues in addition to sexual abuse. These are all issues that are especially important to women and are also issues that are present in many of Oprah's book choices. One guest reiterates on the "Letters to Oprah's Book Club" show: "I could be the poster child for your Book Club at this point. I've read over 400 books since you started your Book Club" (2007). Through her Book Club choices and the magazine, Oprah creates a home liturgy founded in "the spiritual practice of soulful reading" to empower women (Driedger 2000). It seems that Oprah is selling deliverance through these rituals. The Bible is not Oprah's primary text however; her Book Club choices and the *Ur*-text of her own life story (from trial to triumph) constitute the inspirational resources for her afternoon "service."

Oprah makes women feel like they have an intimate relationship with her, akin to a "personal Jesus." She offers women a different home spiritual practice: she is a fan of personal space, altars, and special baths—all ways to encourage women toward self-love and better self-care.[1] Jane Shattuc notes that talk shows can reframe women's personal, private experiences as important, not frivolous. She suggests that talk shows "elicit common sense and everyday experience as a mark of truth that has been a central tenet of feminist claims of the personal being political and a mantra of its standpoint epistemology in particular" (1999, 169). In this forum, women grapple with issues that are important to them and that are reflected in the show's program (or liturgy), while being largely absent from mainstream churches.[2] By eliciting women's daily, and sometimes mundane, experiences and legitimizing them, Oprah provides a public forum for the invisible, privatized lives of many women.

White women do not gravitate to Oprah as simply another woman. Their attraction to her is always informed by racial difference and ideology. Oprah models a strong black female spirituality that appeals to followers of New Age culture and religions. Historically, white women have found solace in the spiritual practices and religions of people of color. In this sense, Oprah provides the "love" for which many whites long. Barbara Grizzuti Harrison notes: "[T]he oppressor wants to believe he's loved by the oppressed. The 'majority' seeks proof that they are loved by the minority whom they have so long been accustomed to oppress, to fear exaggeratedly, or to treat with real or assumed disdain. They need that love, and they need that love in return in order to believe that they are good" (1989, 6). Many white viewers—perhaps unwittingly—read Oprah's black female body as a sign of suffering and redemption, which her autobiography reinforces. As the figure of the black female minister who has cultivated upper-class speech patterns and tastes in clothing, food, and material objects, as reflected in her Favorite Things lists, Oprah is both the woman whom white women want to emulate and the "Earth Mother" of suffering and deep feeling who knows their pain. White women, in particular, feel her forgiveness and kindness with a profound intensity based on racist assumptions. Tammy Johnson suggests that Oprah "plays the wise black matriarch who redeems white people from their misdeeds and foibles by helping them embrace love and realize their true, good selves. Oprah seems to take on the role of new-age mammy for suburban soccer moms. In the process, she safely reduces all things racial to the personal, sidestepping the hard questions of institutionalized racial oppression and white privilege" (2001–2). Johnson's identification of Oprah as "new-age mammy" is fitting for the ways in which Oprah refracts New Age spirituality and culture through her own subjectivity as a black woman. Thus New Age spiritualities take on another level of authenticity on *TOWS*, as Oprah resignifies them through the black vernacular. She often uses the black vernacular and her own experiences to re-present New Age authors and gurus on her show, refracting and overlaying their beliefs and practices with a black (feminist?) narrative of struggle and triumph. As Nelson notes, "Oprah's roots in the black church experience lend the television personality some of her authority" (2002, 24).

The Soul, Humanism, and Girl Power

Oprah's talk show filters New Age ideas in gendered ways that translate them for her female audience. While Oprah does not use the term "New Age" or locate herself within the movement specifically, she is nonetheless one of its most visible proponents, and many of her productions endorse New Age philosophies. While Oprah's guests make grand spiritual claims that appear to transcend the everyday problems of ordinary lives, she takes those same generic religious ideas and makes them particular to women's experience and her own black female struggle.

We can best understand this "translation" by looking at how Oprah highlights and then transforms one New Age author's ideas—in this case author Gary Zukav, who has been one of Oprah's most frequent guests. In *The Seat of the Soul*, one of his most famous books, Zukav describes how there will be an emerging new order that will free us from past paradigms weighing on our souls. His apocalyptic tone is common in New Age writing, as is his belief that humans are not fundamentally flawed because of "original sin." He argues that by turning inward and becoming acquainted with our own emotions, intuition, and higher rational self, we can avoid being controlled by negative emotions like anger or fear. As humans, we can choose goodness at any moment, Zukav suggests. Zukav notes, "An angry personality, for example, will create unpleasant, even tragic situations, until its anger is faced and removed as a block to its compassion and love, to the energy of its soul" (1989, 79). Because Zukav locates goodness internally rather than externally as "works or faith" as in many mainstream faith traditions, he empowers readers and Oprah's viewers to transform their own psychology, not by asking for external help but by modifying one's inner emotional world.

Oprah reshapes New Age philosophies by modifying and refracting Zukav's ideas through her own black female voice and experience. In effect Zukav's book becomes a new one on her show, as Oprah uses his text to amplify her own beliefs. In a key *TOWS* episode entitled "On How to Get Your Power Back," Zukav articulates a different kind of metaphysical power, one advocating "authentic power" rather than a lack of anger (2000). Oprah draws on Zukav to reimagine power. As the description at Oprah.com details: "When something happens that leaves you powerless, how do you recover? How do you create a power that can never be taken away?" Oprah begins the episode with an alluring description that suggests that she has found the advice personally powerful and effective: "This is a really important show." She challenges the viewer to do the same "if you're ready for it." Bruce Robbins suggests that Oprah "mediates between the expert's knowledge and a lay audience, in effect putting across that knowledge to a public whose resistance can be assumed" (Robbins 2000).

In this episode, Oprah's gendered glossing of universal spiritual ideas is transparent. After Oprah's opening statement about the show, a young woman, Gina Cotroneo, discloses: "I was raped. It made me fearful, ashamed. I thought about committing suicide." Oprah then asks, "How do you recover?" and Cotroneo answers: "Rape was a power struggle between two souls. I am more powerful than he is." Confronting her attacker in court, Cotroneo states: "I told him that he had taken a piece of my soul and that I wanted it back. And I reached forward with my hand, and I kind of grabbed the air in front of him, in a symbolic gesture of taking my power . . . I felt like the rape was a power struggle between two souls. He may have been more forceful than I was, but I am more powerful than he is." It is important to note not only that Cotroneo's story is the center of this episode but that women's stories are the focus of most episodes. While occasionally there are men's stories featured and some male guests, everything about the show is geared toward women: the language, shared stories, advice, as well as the layout and tone of the program. Thus, highlighting the example of taking back your power after being raped is not coincidental but geared to addressing what many women might see as one of the most threatening and disempowering experiences: sexual violence. Cotroneo has succeeded in doing what Zukav teaches viewers: "Authentic power is building something inside of you that no one can take from you." Since rape has been viewed, historically, not only as a violation but also as stealing a woman's virginity or her supposed worth, it is notable that Zukav suggests that, while the body is ephemeral, the soul is not. The soul defines a woman's identity. Rape, however, is not simply a "power struggle between two souls," as Cotroneo notes, but clear and violent dominance of one soul over another in the material world (Zukav 2000). Interestingly, Oprah draws on examples from her own life to explore spiritual recovery from sexual trauma.

Oprah's repeated biographical narrative of suffering, redemption, and recovery (from sexual abuse, narrow ideas of God, weight management and feeling unattractive) genders Zukav's ideas about power. By drawing on her own experience, she personalizes her relationship with the audience, affecting a semblance of emotional intimacy and implied trust among herself, the New Age spiritual teachers, and her audience. Oprah's "church" is not about preaching or pointing fingers at sin. Such a ministry would feel alienating. Rather, Oprah's appeal recalls a fundamental tenet of black liberation theology in which suffering and hardship are not ends in themselves but occasions for the transformation and redemption of self and others.

To inspire her audience, Oprah must translate ideas about power. She continues to mold Zukav's notion of "authentic power" or "the alignment of your personality with your soul" by stating: "I love that definition. It's, actually, one of my favorite in the world." Oprah and Zukav play off of one another with Oprah personalizing and delighting over his philosophies. She goes on to explain to viewers that they must use their "personality to serve the energy of your soul . . . with what your sole purpose here is on earth, then that is authentic empowerment." Oprah's "ministry" emphasizes (Zukav's suggestion) that we are wholly in charge of our own empowerment to a) discern what we want in life; b) work through all negative emotions to free ourselves from them; and c) align our personality with positive energy. It is believed in much New Age spirituality and culture that focusing on negativity, especially loss, lack, and violence only wastes energy that could be better spent loving and empowering ourselves (Zukav 2000).

Oprah uses Controneo's rape story, a woman's story, to demonstrate her version of women's power; yet she also introduces race to negotiate this tension between hope and anger. For example, in regards to Cotroneo's personal agency, Zukav states: "[Controneo could have ended up] in an insane asylum consumed with grief; with anger or rage at men; with rage against the universe. That was an option. I heard a rap song once, and the young singer was . . ." (Zukav 2000). Then Oprah interrupts in surprise: "You heard a rap song?"

ZUKAV: Yeah.
OPRAH: Where were you?
ZUKAV: I heard part of a rap song.
OPRAH: OK. OK.
ZUKAV: And the part that I heard—the young man said, "I got a right to be angry."
    And I said, "Yes you got a right to be angry. You've got a right to be loving
    too." You have lots of rights. Which one are you going to take? (Zukav 2000)

This dialogue reminds viewers of the racial and cultural differences between Oprah and Zukav and simultaneously closes the gap through an exchange that resembles the vernacular of black women socializing. It has the effect of racializing Zukav's philosophy as a kind of "sister talk." Oprah asks Zukav to help audiences work through what she may also see as the difficulty of these moves: "['C]ause it's one thing to intellectually know it. It's another thing to work yourself through the process," thus further distinguishing Zukav's "intellectual" knowledge with her own lived "experience" (Zukav 2000). While Oprah calls out Zukav's cultural naiveté, positioning herself as authority on both rap and women's experience, she agrees with him that anger is ultimately ineffective.

Zukav needs Oprah to translate his otherwise abstract, naïve ideas gendered in white, male privilege, to make them meaningful to predominantly female audiences. When Zukav suggests a process by which someone can be free from this anger by listening to his or her intuition based on his or her "higher" self, Oprah responds that women often have a hard time listening to intuition because, in effect, they are conditioned to try to save what is failing around them rather than abandon it. Oprah confirms her authority once again by particularizing Zukav's claim, declaring, "'Cause a lot of women say, for ex—I—I refer to women a lot 'cause I talk to a lot of them, and I am one, so I know that experience very well" (Zukav 2000). Oprah's personalizing rhetoric establishes rapport and emotional intimacy with the audience and guests alike, and filters New Age beliefs through her popular cultural projection of black female uplift.

In describing Oprah's power and singular ability to translate New Age ideas, many viewers notably use affective language. June Mears Driedger, a viewer and minister, describes the uplifting experience of watching an episode of *Oprah*: "I found solace in Oprah. She comes across as a best girlfriend, someone with whom one can both cry and laugh" (Zukav 2000). Driedger discusses how she turned to Oprah and Zukav when she was depressed and "fighting to keep from drowning in feelings of uncertainty and powerlessness" (2000). She documents just how the relationship between Oprah and Zukav makes her *feel*, a feeling I would argue is based on Oprah's effective translation of Zukav:

I smile as I watch them interact. Despite their distinctly different personalities— Oprah is outgoing and gregarious while Zukav is quiet and thoughtful—their mutual respect and affection for one another is obvious. Their collaboration as host and guest began a few years ago when she sought him out like a student seeking a spiritual master, after she read *Seat of the Soul*. . . . Their relationship has evolved to friendship, and Oprah often translates Zukav's more obscure statements into plain language for the viewing audience. They laugh easily with one another (2000).

Driedger finds more comfort in watching Oprah and Zukav than in many religious services (2000). When Driedger, a minister herself, finds Oprah's "church of hope" more powerful than Sunday services, the extent to which Oprah garners people's trust and faith in her advice and how she performs a ministerial function is clear. My argument is built on Driedger's very observation that Oprah's ability to make women feel like a member of a new church is based on her translation of New Age ideas.

Obviously, there are limits to the power that Oprah endorses, even as she particularizes it. Zukav and Oprah call Controneo's moving story of her recovery from rape by overcoming her anger a "perfect example," suggesting that if a woman can recover from rape, then she has the ability (power) to recover from anything, thereby conflating personal with political empowerment. There is never any mention of political reform that allowed for Controneo to prosecute her rapist and, thus, have a powerful courtroom moment, perhaps unusual since many rape cases do not go to trial. Because Oprah and Zukav do not highlight this fact, it is taken for granted that women will have a fair trial, that the police will act in their favor, and that they will not be punished or blamed as victims and, thus, will be able to perform their empowerment publically, rather than hiding in secret shame. Critics Vicki Abt and Mel Seesholtz argue that responses to rape are always inadequate in the talk show medium and suggest that, rather than offering "scientific evidence for the efficacy" regarding good trauma responses to rape, they are "simply mouthing mantras of pop-therapy" (1994, 171). Franny Nudelman goes a step further in observing that Oprah's show may highlight one woman's story at the expense of many: "The injured woman becomes the representative speaker, while women, deprived of a listening audience, find their ability to influence public life radically curtailed" (1997, 311).

Indeed, Controneo, rather than drawing on public moments of activism and speech in the courtroom where she confronted her rapist, draws on private spiritual growth. She says: "during the rape, I was looking at a picture on my wall in my bedroom of a guardian angel. And I just kind of silently called out to my guardian angels to help me. My guardian angel did help me. I was able to be cool enough to get some evidence that would eventually catch this person." Controneo draws on another popular New Age belief: that angels are present and can help us. Her belief in angels helps her locate her rapist. Eventually, Controneo learns how to express her anger without dwelling in it, and uses it to find a better job where she is valued. Zukav responds that "the difference was the rape. Now where could she have been after that rape—spiraling downward in despondency in victimhood. Angry . . ." (Zukav 2000). In a frightening twist that flattens any distinctions between traumas, Zukav seems to imply, as do many New Age believers, that in the end everything is a "lesson" and for the "good"; the "rape" was ultimately beneficial. Though these sentiments play into the worst stereotypes of New Age culture as hopelessly naïve, dangerous even, Oprah, again, tries to navigate around them through her specific use of her life story of early oppression. While in New Age culture, these examples might stand as universal expressions, Oprah tries to humanize them to make them particular, and thereby debatably more political—even if through the personal, which makes for an interesting riff on the second-wave feminist slogan, "the personal is political."

Diva Spirituality and the Female Body Politic

Oprah's pattern of gendering New Age spiritual philosophies operates across the spectrum of her guests—for example, when she translates the New Age ideas of Caroline Myss. Myss first came on the show as a "medical intuitive," or someone who can telepathically diagnose medical diseases in others. Her life story, similar again to many Oprah Book Club selection plots, is a model of moving from being victimized and reveling in "woundology" to discovering her powers as an "intuitive." In Myss's work, *Sacred Contracts: Awakening Your Divine Potential* (2003), and on the episode of *TOWS* discussing the book, "On Discovering Why You Are Here," Myss suggests how to find your life purpose through archetypes. Oprah serves as translator and testifier who familiarizes New Age spiritual archetypes for her female audience and makes them meaningful to their lives.

While Myss argues that we all carry four basic archetypes (the child, the victim, the saboteur, and the prostitute) the ultimate goal, as Oprah translates it, is to find our purpose in the world. Once again, Oprah distills complex charts of chakra points, horoscopes, and archetypes to their most basic premise. She comments on Myss's traditional archetypes and suggest a new possibility for the archetypes even as she may not be able fully to recuperate Myss's notions, which are, ultimately, fundamentally limiting and conservative. It is not surprising, then, when Oprah says, "For example, are you a diva . . . If you're a diva, you would know it." With bravado Oprah claims her own positive archetype up front. By projecting a sassy, irreverent African American "sister" sensibility or a vulnerable, empathetic side ("I too have struggled with that"), Oprah formulates a new archetype founded on black feminine subjectivity, one not articulated in Myss's white model, which is supposedly universal. Myss argues that each archetype is complex, and again Oprah clarifies, "Each has a healthy form and a shadow form." Oprah goes on to say to the audience, "You're saying, OK, archetypes—I just want to know what my purpose is" ("Caroline Myss" 2002). Oprah anthropomorphizes the archetypes and even talks to them and asks them for help directly. If viewers had waded through Myss's book on the subject, they might have become dazed, but Oprah is there to mediate. Thus, Oprah reestablishes the classic frame of her show by turning to personal examples that translate to gendered communities: first she explains the philosophy or problem, and then she uses a personal example, almost always geared toward women. She uses this mode of "sister talk" to legitimize abstract concepts and archetypes and then filter them through her own experiences to imbue them with practical meaning and depth.

The classic female-empowerment-through-spirituality narrative of Oprah's show is usually manifested by several stories from women's lives that serve as an extension of Oprah's own interpretation of New Age ideas. On the Myss episode, her example is "Carrie." Carrie is sabotaging her life. Myss tells Carrie that she "folds up" and is a child, "the cute little girl, the baby, the little innocent girl," a negative archetype, and that she is actually afraid of her own success, an interesting dilemma for many women who have struggled historically to succeed working in the public sphere ("Caroline Myss" 2002). Notably, Myss and Oprah exchange interpretations of Carrie's struggle on equal footing. While Oprah has not created or written a new spiritual program as Myss does in her book, she can *read*—that is, gloss, interpret, and comment on—women's personal experiences in a way that legitimizes her interpretive power. Eventually Myss challenges Carrie to accept the fact of disappointing people and counsels her to leave her toxic marriage, which is a frequent occurrence on *TOWS* where women are supported in learning the basics of self-esteem.

But when Oprah says to Carrie, "As long as you need other people's approval, then you are owned by them . . . And slavery is dead, honey. It is way over," she hammers home the point in a way that Myss cannot ("Caroline Myss" 2002). Although Oprah makes the classic troubled analogue between gender and race (equating bad marriages and slavery), rhetorically, the metaphor legitimizes white female struggle with patriarchy and racializes Myss's archetypes. As with Zukav, Oprah connects and refracts Myss's New Age ideas through black feminine subjectivity to make them more meaningful and accessible to her audience.

Oprah's Church of "New Age Feminism"

Oprah's talk show is conceived as a women's space and as a spiritual space, but those spaces' complementary compatibility and the feminization of New Age messages on *TOWS* have yet to be articulated. Oprah's spirituality is one of translation. It involves reinterpreting and filtering New Age philosophies through a gendered framework of black women's experiences and the black church tradition, not to politicize them but to make them more accessible and meaningful to her audience. Oprah's modifications of New Age philosophies are the reason her guests are understood on *TOWS*. She enjoys a large following among women who, like herself, are looking for spiritual alternatives to the mainstream religions in which they grew up, for as Driedger puts it: "Oprah tells women they have value, that their words, their stories, are important. By contrast, the church's history of empowering women is brief, sporadic, and ambivalent, at best" (2000, 46). Because Oprah offers these meaningful, more uplifting liturgies, her New Age feminist congregation will continue growing in the twenty-first century.

Notes

1. Feminists critique Oprah's suggestion of personal solutions to political problems of oppression and inequality in the church. As Eric Deggans notes, "critics point to Winfrey's contradictions: She's a role model for mothers, but doesn't have children of her own; she's a seeming workaholic who encourages others to find fulfillment outside of their jobs; she talks constantly about marriage but hasn't wed longtime companion Stedman Graham." There is a feminist tension in Oprah's own life that if shared might truly highlight what so many women find difficult—finding agency and fulfillment in relationships, work, and children. See Deggans 2003.
2. Oprah may have more authority in her pop culture pastoral role than many black women ministers in the clerical hierarchy. Historically, women have been the backbone of the black church. They have always been present and powerful, though not always seen visually in the most publically prominent places like the pulpit or the clerical hierarchy. See Evelyn Brooks Higginbotham, *Righteous Discontent: The Women's Movement in the Black Baptist Church 1880–1920* (reprint, Boston: Harvard UP, 1994).

Works Cited

Abt, Vicki, and Mel Seesholtz. 1994. The Shameless World of Phil, Sally, and Oprah: Television Talk Shows and the Deconstructing of Society. *Journal of Popular Culture* 28, no. 1: 171–92.

Caroline Myss on Sacred Contracts. 2002. *The Oprah Winfrey Show* (August 15). http://www2.oprah .com/tows/pastshows/tows_2002/tows_past_20020125_c.jhtml (Accessed January 1 2007).

Deggans, Eric. 2003. Oprah Fans Get into the Spirit. *St. Petersburg Times on the Web*, June 21. http:// www.sptimes.com (Accessed January 1, 2007).

Driedger, June Mears. 2000. Spirituality According to Oprah. Fall. http://www.mennovision.org/ driedger.pdf (Accessed October 1, 2008).

Gary Zukav on How To Get Your Power Back. 2000. *The Oprah Winfrey Show* (September 13). http://www.oprah.com/article/spirit/knowyourself/ss_know_authentic_01 (Accessed January 1, 2007).

Haag, Laurie L. 1993. Oprah Winfrey: The Construction of Intimacy in the Talk Show Setting. *Journal of Popular Culture* 26: 115–21.

Harrison, Barbara Grizzuti. 1989. The Importance of Being Oprah. *New York Times Magazine*, June 11, 6.

Johnson, Tammy. 2001–2. It's Personal: Race and Oprah. *Color Lines* 4, no. 4. http://www.arc.org/C_ Lines/CLArchive/story4_4_04.html (Accessed January 1, 2007).

Lesser, Elizabeth. 2000. *The Seeker's Guide: Making Your Life a Spiritual Adventure*. New York: Villard Press. http://www.oprah.com/article/oprahsbookclub/anewearth/pkganewearthweb cast/20080130_obc_webcast_seekersguide/3 (Accessed October 1, 2008).

Letters to Oprah's Book Club. 2007. *Lexis-Nexis*, http://web.lexis-nexis.com/universe/document?_m =fd6c86dfocde9ca43944b260a7942134&_docnum=1&wchp=dGLzVlz-zSkVb&_md5=36076ab38 7ed573700f6f24ba305954b (Accessed January 1, 2007).

McGrath, Maria. 2007. Spiritual Talk: The Oprah Winfrey Show and the Popularization of the New Age. In *The Oprah Phenomenon*, edited by Jennifer Harris and Elwood Watson, 125–45. Lexington: University Press of Kentucky.

Nelson, Marcia Z. 2002. Oprah on a Mission: Dispensing a Gospel of Health and Happiness. *The Christian Century* (Sept. 25–Oct. 8): 20–25. http://www.christiancentury.org (Accessed October 1, 2008).

———. 2005. *The Gospel According to Oprah*. Louisville: John Knox Press.

Nudelman, Franny. 1997. Beyond the Talking Cure: Listening to Female Testimony on *The Oprah Winfrey Show*. In *Inventing the Psychological: Toward a Cultural History of Emotional Life in America*, edited by Joel Pfister and Nancy Schnog, 290–310. New Haven: Yale University Press.

Oprah's Angel Network. 2008. http://oprahsangelnetwork.org/ (Accessed October 1, 2008).

Oprah's Book Club. 2008a. "About Eckhart Tolle," http://www.oprah.com/article/oprahsbookclub/anewearth/20080130_obc_webcast_eckhartbio (Accessed October 1, 2008).

Oprah's Book Club. 2008b. "*A New Earth* Class." http://www.oprah.com/article/oprahsbookclub/anewearth/pkganewearthwebcast/20080130_obc_webcast_syllabus (Accessed October 1, 2008).

Oprah's Book Club. 2008c. "Awaken Your Spirit," http://www.oprah.com/slideshow/oprahshow/20080130_tows_webcast_anewearth (Accessed October 1, 2008).

Oprah's Soul Series. 2008. XM Radio, http://www.xmradio.com/oprah/index.xmc (Accessed October 1, 2008).

Peck, Janice. 1994. Talk about Race: Framing a Popular Discourse of Race on Oprah Winfrey. *Cultural Critique* 27: 89–126.

Robbins, Bruce. 1999. Celeb-Reliance: Intellectuals, Celebrity, and Upward Mobility. *Postmodern Culture* 9, no. 2. http://muse.jhu.edu/journals/pmc/ (accessed October 1, 2008).

Shattuc, Jane M. 1999. The Oprahfication of America: Talk Shows and the Public Sphere. In *Television, History, and American Culture: Feminist Critical Essays*, edited by Mary Beth Havalovich, 168–80. Durham: Duke University Press.

Squire, Corinne. 1997. Empowering Women? The Oprah Winfrey Show. In *Feminist Television Criticism: A Reader*, edited by Charlotte Brunsdon, Julie D'Acci, and Lynn Spigel, 98–113. Oxford: Clarendon Press.

Zoepf, Katharine. 2008. Dammam Journal: Saudi Women Find an Unlikely Role Model: Oprah. *The New York Times*, September 19, A1.

Zukav, Gary. 1989. *The Seat of the Soul*. New York: Simon & Schuster.

———. 2000. Gary Zukav on How To Get Your Power Back, *The Oprah Winfrey Show* (September 13, 2000), http://www.oprah.com/article/spirit/knowyourself/ss_know_authentic_01 (accessed January 1, 2007).

Part II

Contesting the Oprah Experts

CHAPTER FOUR

Post[ed]structuralism?

Oprah's Message Boards, Soul Stories, *and the Everyday Lives of Women*

SHERRA SCHICK

Fifty-eight-year-old Judy writes "I have tried suicide at least five or six times through the course of my life."[1] A young mother, Gail, questions life's lessons after the birth of her Down's Syndrome daughter. Peggy's "soul crys" because she feels that her nineteen-year-old son will soon die. A woman grieves the choice she made years ago, to divorce her husband, when she says, "My life has never been the same nor will ever be again. I think about him everyday and have wished a million trillion times that I had stayed, and fought . . . * The result has been a soul fragmentation that just never goes away." So raw, so intimate, so public. I sit here reading these online responses in an attempt to comprehend an online conversation that began following an episode of *The Oprah Winfrey Show* featuring Gary Zukav and his book *Soul Stories.*

I began this project as an attempt to understand how Oprah Winfrey's message of self-empowerment, intentionality, and spiritual transcendence were reflected in her message boards and how women's voices were represented. Perhaps not surprisingly, I found that the April 2000 online conversation that began with attempted suicide had evolved seven months later into "Today, again this Sunday we collectively gather our hearts in meditation and our voices in prayer, willing to listen, willing to be heard, seeking to understand and be understood. We are pinpoints of Light coming together to form a beacon of encouragement and healing." This move from hopelessness and despair into a spiritual community reflects the trajectory of the Winfrey message preached on *The Oprah Winfrey Show*—that we can all overcome hardships to achieve spiritual enlightenment.

As the interwoven and overarching concepts of Winfrey's "Change Your Life TV," these three spiritual directives—self-empowerment, intentionality, and spiritual transcendence—support an ideology that seems to contradict the early claim to empower women historically associated with Winfrey. Calling work her ministry, in recent years Winfrey's ideology of self-empowerment illustrates a changed register from her earlier claim to empower women enacted within a political frame. Winfrey's shift away from a category of women coming together in social activism toward self-empowerment rooted in spiritual principles raises any number of questions for those of us engaged in feminist cultural studies. What, for example, is the experience of these women and how do their communication practices inform our understanding of social formations, of subjectivities, of other cultural practices? This speaks to several of the tensions that cultural studies seeks to address and negotiate—the gulf between theory and practice, concepts of the "real," and inquiries into subjectivities, form, and power.

The value that these boards can offer is a glimpse into how power is understood and enacted in social networking. More specifically, Winfrey's boards can illuminate our understanding of power relations between what Michel De Certeau identifies as institutional strategies and the everyday practices, or tactics, of the user participants. With the reformation of Winfrey's concept of power, away from the political and toward the spiritual, the *Soul Stories* board also illustrates the negotiations that participants make within the structural mechanisms imposed by Harpo Inc. Additionally, the *Soul Stories* board demonstrates the manners in which women's websites are violated and minimized by outside intrusions represented as male.

With burgeoning communities of women on the Internet and rising social networking sites, it is crucial for cultural studies to turn its attention to new media practices and the political economy of these cultural forms. Do the models that Stuart Hall and others offer illuminate the cultural practices that the internet makes possible? Can we take models that are useful for approaching television studies and simply extend them to encompass corresponding web sites—where "real" people represent themselves? Do any of these models rooted in male experience apply to the communities of women growing on the internet, or do they replicate dominant forms of discourse? Do these communities suggest a growing separatism between male and female experiences? At stake are issues of power, representation, and experience. With these questions in mind, the *Soul Stories* board is a fruitful site to uncover how these kinds of boards may work within particular cultural regimes of power.

Ethnography of the *Soul Stories* Message Board

First introduced as a Spiritual Guide, Gary Zukav appeared over a dozen times on various episodes within the "Change Your Life TV" season, which launched in 1998. During Winfrey's 1999–2000 season, Oprah.com featured a link to "Guides and Teachers" that Winfrey had introduced on her television show. "Guides and Teachers" noted "Gary has been sharing his insights and knowledge with Oprah and us since the fall of 1998. Gary stresses he is not a therapist or a psychologist but his guidance has helped many of our viewers learn more about themselves and their spirits."

On April 26, 2000, Zukav appeared on *The Oprah Winfrey Show* to talk about his newly released book *Soul Stories,* to share with Oprah's audience three real-life stories in his book, and to share what he identified as finding authentic power. The first "soul story" was "Compassionate Universe," the story of a young woman, Laura, suffering from depression since she was fourteen years old. The second story, "Spiritual Partnership," was about Beth, married seventeen years, whose transformative experience reunited her with her separated husband. The third story was "The Power of Intention," which tells the story of Vicki and Mike and their six-year-old daughter Sarah who died from cancer. Sarah's life and death brought her parents to a deeper understanding of their own spirit and purpose in life. It was this presentation to which Oprah's audience was invited to respond in the message board "Gary Zukav and *Soul Stories.*"

Oprah.com took segments of this episode and featured them in an online magazine-style format. The website posted "Oprah and Gary talk to people who through soul searching have discovered the courage to lead authentic lives, and today share their *Soul Stories.*" Zukav also participated in a series of chat sessions, answering audience questions about a number of issues including love, spirituality, addiction, destiny, and passion. Additionally, there was a link posted somewhere on *The Oprah Winfrey Show* homepage directing the fan/viewer/reader to the *Soul Stories* message board; however, that homepage changed with every new show. With five shows a week, this means that any direct link to the *Soul Stories* message board was probably short-lived. Even when the board was active, the casual visitor had to spend time finding it. In other words, it was not that easy to find a particular post. The participants, on the other hand, could easily find it, and most of the participants posted more than one message. Of the 557 documented entries that I worked with primarily, 105 posted only once, with the bulk of the conversation contributed by approximately 15 women. When these women wanted a private conversation, they e-mailed each other. Even though the participants e-mailed each other their most personal messages, they also maintained a presence on this message board, open for those who seek a spiritual community, but not entirely public either.

From Conversation to Community

Shawn P. Wilbur asks those of us who examine these online communities to consider how we might

tell the difference . . . between a community and a market segment, or a culture of compatible consumption? What are the relations between the real and the virtual, between being and seeming, between "real life" and "net.life?" Are the structures and marks of class, race, gender and the like more or less deeply inscribed in these virtual spaces? Can these clearly mediated spaces provide a place for contesting "real world" powers? Or are many of these questions badly posed, as they assume a certain authenticity and lack of mediation in our everyday lives which is perhaps illusory? (Wilber 2000, 55)

Community is one of the most common tropes applied to internet forums, and it is the possibility of community that the *Soul Stories* participants seem to respond to. Several *Soul Stories* entries suggest, in fact, that the regular contributors not only saw themselves as a community but at one point discussed meeting physically. Moreover, the participants seem to identify as a community of women. The participants identify as female, primarily through their references to husbands, boyfriends, and so forth, and most identify as from the United States, with some from other countries. In their posts, the participants do not self-identify within a particular race or socioeconomic class. Community for the participants is based on shared experiences, shared narratives. The major recurring thematic elements in the narratives are of overcoming hardships as a way of validating the soul's purpose and sharing this process with others experiencing hardship.

In her article "Networking Women and Grrrls with Information/Communication Technology," Nina Wakeford argues for tropes that exhibit and establish women's presences on the web with more agency. Wakeford seeks to demonstrate the diverse social practices in the construction and maintenance of women's web sites. She offers "a modest intervention" as she explores gender issues within computer culture (2000, 350). Calling for metaphors elastic enough to embrace women's experiences of using the Web without essentializing them, Wakeford argues in opposition to the male-gendered and

Americanist surfing/frontier models. Comparisons with Donna Haraway's networking model and Sadie Plant's weaving model open the web to include practices familiar to women, such as "the historical association of weaving as 'the process so often said to be the quintessence of women's work'" (Wakeford 2000, 365). While Wakeford finds this weaving metaphor somewhat limited, she argues that "weaving describes the intimate connection which has emerged historically between women and computers . . . . [B]oth are sites of disguise or simulation which mediate between 'man and matter.'" Wakeford desires to work with the idea of weaving that Haraway suggests—as an analogy "to stress the process of networking" with multivalent dimensions (357).

Wakeford's invoking the "networking" trope can be problematic, however. As Lynn Joyrich demonstrates in her article "Networking: Interlacing Feminism, Postmodernism, and Television Studies," as a trope, "*networking* has attained a certain popular usage in feminist circles to describe a strategy for increasing women's power—one which has often come under attack for its practical emphasis on personal gain (on inserting women into, rather than challenging, the status quo). In other words . . . this strategy can be critiqued as a 'postfeminist,' rather than feminist, solution" (1996, 169).

Grrrl web sites advance the trope of resistance and opposition. Wakeford writes, "Women who might be grouped under this label have created sites with names such as Cybergrrl, geekgirl, as well as NerdGrrl and Homegurrrl. The words themselves are codes to explicitly subvert the easy appropriation of women, and to resist stereotypes" (355). While the grrrl sites invite a multidimensional understanding of women's experiences and interests in computer culture, many of these sites also erase an historical struggle grounded in women's desire to elevate all women to positions of agency.

Certainly agency is crucial for any discussion of power relations. Jane Shattuc writes that Winfrey, through *The Oprah Winfrey Show*, "enters the debate about the 'active' audience—the ideal viewers who enjoy but challenge the form and content of TV—that cultural studies has come to champion" (1997, 9). In this way, Shattuc agrees with Henry Jenkins, Ellen Seiter, and John Fiske, who all argue for the existence of an active audience.[2] At the time of Shattuc's study, Winfrey's television studio audience had opportunities actively to participate in the show. While changed formats of *The Oprah Winfrey Show* have eliminated the opportunities for Winfrey's studio audience to participate in an open forum, the message boards remain a site for audience participation. Additionally, they become a way to measure participation of Winfrey's audience. There is a difference, however, between participation and agency. The *Soul Stories* Message Board participants have limited agency within the context of the board. This is an important consideration since the ostensible impetus for the *Soul Stories* Message Board is women sharing their search for the authentic self. A central question then is "In what way does Winfrey's shift from active political engagement towards self-actualization through spiritual enlightenment call into question the concept of 'active,' especially since spiritual empowerment suggests that authenticity is now personal and resides within?" And does this mean that the personal is definitely not political after all?

Most of the entries to the *Soul Stories* board reflect a spiritual longing. There are very few entries that reflect an interest in the political arena. Moreover, there is one brief mention of the 2000 presidential election. PamelaSWOregon writes:

I pray that all of us (Americans and those from other countries as well) will remember in elections that we are ALL still God's children . . * whether we're Republicans or Democrats or Greens or whatever else . . * we're all still God's precious children . . * in politics may ALL of us remember to be God's children first and foremost and then do our political business from that centered peaceful place . . * May God's Will be done in our American presidential election and may each of us always remember to be love and light in our every moment, political and otherwise.

This entry suggests that the community sees its calling on an international level or—even higher—on a transcendent level: to be God's children first. What we do not know, and perhaps have no way of knowing, is whether or not other political references were posted and sanitized by the cyber-keepers and cyber-sweepers, those who monitor the boards, encourage conversations in particular directions, and sanitize unwanted posts.

Richard Johnson and others argue that "cultural studies is necessarily and deeply implicated in relations of power" (1986/87, 53). This is particularly significant since Zukav states that he wanted to guide his readers toward their authentic power. For Zukav, as for Winfrey, power in this context is removed from the public, social, political, and economic arena. While the *Soul Stories* participants use the message board as a site for spiritual seeking, there is little evidence of a conscious reappropriation, and no evidence of engaging power relations within a public setting. With no postings suggesting organized activities outside of the spiritual realm, how does *Soul Stories* work as a platform for authentic power?

Such a line of thinking lends itself to a discussion of how subjectivities are produced by the technology itself, and the hierarchies of power structured into the technology. As a structuring form, the internet is a linguistic structure operating from a double principle of language. Digital programming, possible only because of language as signification, is its own language. In a possible leap off of a "cultural theory," we can think of the internet as a structuralist form. The internet is possible because of a precise language that programs a computer to respond precisely to precise commands. If "A," then "B." Or, if not "A," then not "B." (In a Derridean manner, there are only differences, and the combination of these differences determines whether one can successfully program, access, and in some cases navigate, through the web or not.) Information within the structure can be accessed only through coded language that unlocks the coded system. The "linguistic" codes might be recognizable words, symbols, numbers, or combinations of all three. They may take the form of computer languages for programming, passwords for accessing, URLs for locating, or hypertext for linking. In all instances, unless the correct language or combination of linguistic elements is used, access is denied.

Once one has navigated to a bulletin board, however, does the metaphor of linguistic determination hold up? Because they are working within the linguistic structure of the internet itself, are they not still caught in the tensions between the langue and parole of technological determinism? Since television programs and their corresponding web sites can be understood as expressions of corporate strategy and allocational practices, it would be easy to fall into the political economy trap of Marxist determination. Concepts such as articulation and hegemony allow us to step outside of that trap by recognizing that meaning making, even when cued, is a complex process, and that articulations among corporate strategy, actual corporate operational practices, and cultural consumption also work to construct meaning. Returning to De Certeau, the *Soul Stories* participants tactically engaged in everyday practices of conversation, as negotiating agents that freely moved from idea to idea, regardless of any deterministic intentions. The monolithically deterministic models cannot account for the junctures where discursive struggles and contestations occur. Bulletin board regulars even have their own shorthand language. The *Soul Stories* participants both engage this shorthand language at the same time that they expand their social networking to include other sites outside of those maintained by Harpo Inc.

Inquiries into power relations on the internet also articulate with discourses circulating around public and private spaces, including the collapse of any distinctions between the two. Public events can be brought into the home, observed, and responded to globally. Private events can be digitally produced and distributed to the public. Scholars can engage in ethnographic espionage— observing without being observed. (My own microhistorical project positioned me as an outsider, in tension with my intentions, questioning how the language of the academy has formed my own subject position.)

As "first author" of her message boards, Winfrey is the controlling authority. It is Winfrey's invitation that participants respond to—an invitation that corresponds to a book, an author, a subject, and a message of her own selection. As primary authority, therefore, Winfrey imposes the institutional limits of strategy. The participants are guided to an idea of power as selected, authorized, and approved by Winfrey. First and foremost, the Winfrey message is reflected in the message board. We understand that the participants do not have agency within the production, exhibition, or distribution of the boards. But they do have limited agency in the production, exhibition, and distribution of their posts. And we could argue that the participants have sought out a site that emphasizes spiritual growth and therefore they may not fit the profile of a causal agent. Their interests and intentions perhaps are other-directed.

Even with these limitations, however, the board provides a unique access to community practices as participants strive to construct their own community and conversation within certain proscriptions. Claudiag writes, "It's so nice to start the day reading your messages. It's great to feel that special conection that is deeper than most friendships I have with some people in my surrounding." Theledge31 writes that the community they have formed, "us," works differently than the outside world. Joyefull writes, "Isn't it wonderful to know there is a place that positive energy is so abundant that you can just bathe in the Love and Light several times a day! I have learned so much from the collective Light and the shared Love and support here on these Message Boards." And they look out for each other. From Assenav: "I just realized I've missed Sageman late . . . * miss u, come back soon!" As a community they welcome newcomers. PamelaSWOregon welcomes BattyK, "you've plopped yourself down in a wonderful group of souls many of whom will be happy to help you. . . . we are becoming known to each other on deeper levels and to ourselves on inner levels as well . . * We share joy, laughter, annectodes, prays for the spots on the planet that we feel need group prayer . . * and we reach out to newcomers to help however we can . . *"

Soulgiver and BeingButterfly see this message board as a kind of soul circle. BeingButterfly writes, "We are like a . . . * soul gathering . . . * we affirm and encourage soulful journeys, we even have parties!" Cdnartist says, "We are walking Sarah's Circle together."[3] They even discuss all getting together face-to-face, meeting somewhere as a group. Since they are an international group, this may have turned out to be too great of a logistical challenge; that discussion was not pursued completely—at least not here on this message board.

There are misunderstandings and potential misunderstandings, but they work within the constraints of the medium. Cdnartist feels that a reference to BeingButterfly's menopause may have insulted her. She writes, "Something I still struggle with is the lack of audio and therefore intonation on these boards. I find myself struggling with this now as I read your message and I am wondering if perhaps in my feeble attempt to make a light-hearted remark, it did not read that way." Assenav responds, "When we speak with our voice, a message is a message due to our tone of voice, but weritten down it is so easily misenterpreted . . . *which is why we take much more time reflecting on what we want to say . . . with one another. . . . When we post a message . . . we are bound to sometimes misread the itnention of the other. . . . However, this is such a comforting and loving place . . . * Let us all smile in retrospect . . . * mistakes are easily made and easily rectified among friends . . . * Group huddle and hug . . . * " BeingButterfly answers, "I need a group hug . . . *(oooooooooo). Cdnartist, I think it was my response that was misinterpreted, but now I don't know what the ____ we're trying to say!!! I just know that I feel very comfortable here and only occasionally get my nose bent out of place."

Without the internet, this community would not exist. The women live in different countries, different continents, yet they can collapse space into friendship. When Assenav joins this group, she writes, "I love it when positive comes out of our technological abilities . . . * distance (in a physical sense) is no more thanks to internet and e-mail. I love it, I love it, I love you!! Needless to say that I'm always here for you too, if you need me . . * just thought I'd mention it anyway . . * THANKS!"

Into the Margins

Francine Prose argues in a February 13, 2000, *New York Times* article, that women's websites are "a symptom of the cultural separatism currently generating a profusion of products and services created specifically for women." She further argues that "In theory, 'women's culture' sounds like a good idea but the apparently subversive subtext . . . suggests that women, tired of being denied power in a man's world, have decided to take their toys and play elsewhere." In the case of *Soul Stories,* a seemingly considerable male intrusion drove many of the women elsewhere, and the board was retired shortly afterwards. This would suggest that the need to "play elsewhere" is compelling.

A little past midnight on November 24, 2000, an entry from someone identified as PixelBaby violated the board's protocols with obscene pictures and messages. As it happens, I was online when it occurred. I both saw and printed the material before the board was sanitized. My guess is that the violator was male because of the content of the photographs (one photo of a naked male spreading his anus toward the camera, and one photo of a lounging naked male with an anatomically impossibly large erect penis), but I have to acknowledge that anyone could post these photos. Within two hours, all traces of the incident were erased from the board. There was one new message from PamelaS-WOregon: "Anyone looking for Sunday's prayer chain . . * go to the Coming Home section of the weekly boards." Some of the women did not return to the *Soul Stories* board, but enough of them did, and new women joined them, but the board was retired soon after.

This hacking incident replicates the experience of many women who, seeking safe communion, are driven to the margins. This is one of the reasons that sites such as Oprah's Message Boards are regulated so strictly. Had I not been online at the precise moment I was, I probably would never have known this incident occurred. The participants rely on Harpo Inc. to create and maintain this site for the safety and comfort of its participants. It would appear that a certain amount of agency is willingly surrendered for security reasons. But where did the core group of 15 participants go? Did their community continue?

During this same period of time, the National Organization of Women's website was experiencing a hostile male intrusion precipitating a heated, sometimes bitter discussion on the NOW bulletin boards. A man, David Byron, who had been banned from NOW and who was previously banned from the *Ms.* boards, continued to dominate one discussion. In an April 2001 threaded discussion on the NOW Issues board, NOW member Ripley writes: "David Byron blew onto the *Ms. Magazine* boards about 13 months ago. Before him we had a nice quiet place that was mostly free of antifeminists. He was the reason *Ms.* had to start moderating so much. Well, him and a bunch of pro-gun morons (including one named Libertarian, possibly the same idiot). He was the first person to be banned off *Ms.* He was on there a few weeks. He hasn't changed." Other participants on the NOW boards, identifying themselves as men, argued from such entrenched and extreme religious and pro-life positions that it is difficult to separate the patriarchal from the maniacal, making the work of building political coalition on the NOW boards difficult if not impossible. Ripley continued:

I don't think he's [Byron] any different from any other antifeminist on these boards. He's just the most prolific. They should all be banned. There are plenty of places for womyn [sic] haters to spew their vileness. This is a feminist place. A wise person once related to me: I'm tired of talking about WHY feminism, I want to focus on HOW feminism. That is what I want. I want to focus on real feminist discussion that will accomplish something. Telling assholes off only serves to distract us from doing anything worthwhile.

The anti-feminist voices were the loudest on the NOW bulletin boards, shouting down both the reactionary anger and the calm reason of the participants identifying themselves as feminists. As I read the threads, I noted complaints that NOW's web administrators do not monitor the sites well, that the abusive and hostile threats should have been removed, that the abusers should be banned, and the web site should be made private—for members only—following the *Ms.* lead.

Both the National Organization for Women and Oprah Winfrey summon charged emotions from their detractors, but the difference in the tone of the conversations *appears* to be related to administrative responses to hostility. That NOW does not police its boards from these barbs might speak to a commitment to open discourse, but open discourse is a messy business. Since all references to any disruption are removed as though the event never happened, the Oprah.com boards signal safe harbor to their readers, most of whom are not exposed to the disruptions. We could argue that the Oprah.com boards respond to one of the consequences of open discourse by foreclosing this discourse in order to eliminate hostile attacks.

Both NOW and Oprah.com speak in some way to larger social problems. The silencing of the hostile and abusive dissent on the Oprah boards by the administrators, and the uncensored corollary of the loud and sometimes menacing voices of dissent on the NOW boards, are dual responses to a seeming misogynistic impulse that seeks to humiliate and control women.

Internet bulletin boards can serve as a form of communal diary. They give us access to hundreds and thousands of intimate conversations that we would not get from any other source. The *Soul Stories* Message Board specifically reveals dozens of women sharing intimate stories of fear, loss, love, spirituality, frustration, and questioning. As a form of microhistory, they offer unprecedented access into the everyday lives of women. Because the boards are monitored, they offer Winfrey's fans a relatively safe common site where they can share their common interests, and they provide them a jumping off place where they can engage in more intimate conversations. For these women, it was the opportunity to share the narratives of their lives with others that was the impetus for their community-building. Moreover, the narrative trajectory reflects the Winfrey message of self-empowerment—that we can overcome difficulties through spiritual transcendence.

While Harpo regulators proscribe the conversation from moving too far away from the board's designated purpose, the emergence of a fluid conversation forming into its own community of participants suggests an element of negotiation. The message boards offer an opportunity to observe whether Winfrey's readers/fans question Winfrey's authorial function, to understand the possibilities the boards might serve as an interruption of dominant ideologies. Specifically, the *Soul Stories* Message Board exemplifies the possibility for subversive ways that women can find voice in the media. While well-monitored and sanitized, the conversation that emerges among its participants is just under the radar of widespread scrutiny. In this way it presents a challenge to the underlying assumptions about gender and the media, and whose voice gets past the cultural gatekeepers. On the other hand, it is well-monitored by Harpo regulators; therefore the participants use the site primarily as it is intended, and they move outside the site for more privacy. In this way the board serves as both a communal forum and a jumping-off place for more intimate discussions.

I agree with Shawn P. Wilbur that we need to adopt a position of critical inquiry when we evaluate these boards as authentic communities. I also think, however, that perhaps we need to find new paradigms for thinking about these spaces, that perhaps the old models simply do not fit. What might the new questions be? How do we make sense of these boards?

Culture is complex and the internet makes it only more so. The challenge of cultural studies is to find models and ways of thinking about the emerging alliance between television programs and their corresponding web sites, as sites for multivalent cultural expressions. The cultural studies project is, of necessity, moving to negotiate and navigate a pre-digital consciousness in a rapidly changing digital culture, to investigate how these cultural practices circulating around the internet represent the "real" lived experiences of people.

While television studies was slower to find legitimacy in the scholarly investigations into popular culture than was film studies, new media technologies—perhaps because they originated as a scientific and medical tool—have raised the cultural capital necessary for scholarly inquiry in a brief amount of time. With the marriage of the internet and commerce, however, and the growth of female internet participation as a result of television's construction of corresponding web sites and specific commercial targeting, the internet as the site for social formations has moved into a new era.

What models do we use to address these spaces? How do we comprehend the transcendent nature of the *Soul Stories* board? How do the message boards reflect women's experiences on and off the boards, both the manners in which they are represented, and the manners in which they are driven further into the margins? With both elements of community and market present, how do we read these message boards as branded community? And finally, how do we interrogate relations of power and the manners in which empowerment is enacted in the everyday lives of women? The *Soul Stories* Message Board raises vexing questions for how we can engage in a cultural critique of this vast and fluid medium.

Notes

1. The postings in this message board contain many spelling, grammatical, and proofreading errors. I have chosen not to include the standard [sic] following these errors, and I have also chosen not to correct them. I want to represent the women's comments as close as possible to the way that they were written. However, for those entries that I have quoted from in part, I use standard ellipses when indicated. Since many of the original messages contain ellipsis points for emphasis or to serve other punctuation needs, I have tried to indicate with a "*" when the ellipses belong to the author.

2. Shattuc differs from them, however, in her focus on the constitution of the audience "as a result of industrial needs, psychological theory, and the conservative agenda in the 1980s and 1990s." She asks for whom the real women speak: "themselves or a bourgeois notion of the underclass as victims or an uncontrolled mass" (Shattuc 1997, 9). In this way Shattuc agrees with Ien Ang's assessment that a quantifiable audience exists solely in a discursive form, not as an entity that can be measured.

3. This is a reference to Joan Borysenko's *A Woman's Journey to God,* about women looking within to discover the light that has been there all along.

Works Cited

De Certeau, Michel. 1988. *The Practice of Everyday Life.* Translated by Steven Rendall. Berkeley : University of California Press.

DeLoach, Anita. 1996. "Grrrls Exude Attitude." *Computer-Mediated Communication Magazine.* http://www.december.com/cmc/mag/1996/mar/deloach.html (accessed April 25, 2001).

Gary Zukav Home Page. 2000. "About Gary Zukav." http://www.zukav.com/index.htm, (accessed November 19).

Gary Zukav Home Page. 2000. "Welcome." http://www.zukav.com/frames/introducton.htm, (accessed November 19).

Goatse. 2000. "Woah." http://www.goatse.cx/giver.html (accessed November 26).

Geocities. 2000. "Your Title Here." http://www.geocities.com/fiwer/ (accessed November 26).

Jenkins, Henry. 1991. *Textual Poachers: Television Fans and Participatory Culture.* New York: Routledge.

Johnson, Richard. 1986/87. "What is Cultural Studies Anyway?" *Social Text.* 16 (Winter): 38–80.

Joyrich, Lynn. 1996. "Networking: Interlacing Feminism, Postmodernism, and Television Studies." In *Re-Viewing Reception: Television, Gender, and Postmodern Culture,* 166–77. Bloomington: Indiana UP.

National Organization for Women. 2001. "Issues." http://63.111.42.146/NOW_Village/default.asp. (15 April).

Oprah's Message Boards. 2000. "Gary Zukav and *Soul Stories.*" http://boards.oprah.com/cgi-bin/winfrey/webx?WEBX (accessed November 28).

Oxygen. 2000. "Guides and Teachers." http://oprah.com/rys/gary/rys_gary_main.html (accessed November 19).

Prose, Francine. 2000. "A Wasteland of One's Own." *New York Times,* February 13.

Radway, Janice A. 1991. *Reading the Romance: Women, Patriarchy, and Popular Literature.* Chapel Hill: University of North Carolina Press.

Shattuc, Jane M. 1997. *The Talking Cure: TV Talk Shows and Women.* New York, Routledge.

Squire, Corinne. [1994] 1997. "Empowering Women? *The Oprah Winfrey Show.*" In *Feminist Television Criticism: A Reader*, edited by Charlotte Brunsdon, et. al., 98–113. Oxford: Clarendon Press, 1997.

Striphas, Ted. 2003. "A Dialectic With the Everyday: Communication and Cultural Politics on Oprah Winfrey's Book Club." *Critical Studies in Mass Communication* 287: 295–317, http://www.epnet.com (accessed August 20, 2005).

Wakeford, Nina. 2000. "Networking Women and Grrrls with Information? Communication Technology: Surfing Tales of the World Wide Web." In *The Cybercultures Reader*, edited by David Bell and Barbara M. Kennedy, 350–59. London: Routledge.

Wilbur, Shawn P. 2000. "An Archaeology of Cyberspaces: Virtuality, Community, Identity." In *The Cybercultures Reader*, edited by David Bell and Barbara M. Kennedy, 45–55. London: Routledge.

CHAPTER FIVE

Oprah para Mujeres Chicanas

A Survey of the Impact of Oprah's Message on Chicanas

ADRIANA KATZEW AND LILIA DE KATZEW

Oprah's success in a predominantly man's world and in a predominantly white U.S. environment has been attributed to her ability to reach a diverse segment of the U.S. society and the global community at large. Sociologists such as Katrina Bell McDonald further argue that virtually everyone in the United States—black, white, Latino/a, or Asian—embraces Oprah's persona and message (2007, 1). Oprah's supposed ability to reach women of all ethnicities relies on the assumption that women's suffering and women's issues are universal. Indeed Oprah claims in her television show that "*I'm every woman*" (the advertising theme song played in earlier segments of Oprah's TV show). But has her message indeed reached and transformed the lives of Chicana[1] women whose demographic importance is enormous in the United States?

This chapter is a preliminary study of the impact of Oprah Winfrey's message on a selected group of Chicanas in California's Central Valley comprised of college students (ranging in age from nineteen to fifty-two years old) and professionals. Given the different levels of acculturation and assimilation among these women, we were interested in finding out if, and if so how, the power of Oprah's message in the media, specifically television, has transformed their attitudes, behavior, and identity construct. We were also interested in exploring whether these women thought that Oprah's message addresses issues and situations faced specifically by Chicana women.

Selection of Participants

For this preliminary study, we designed a survey with questions that would allow us better to understand the impact of Oprah's TV show and her message on our participants. We purposefully selected twenty-two Chicanas, all of whom are either students at California State University, Stanislaus (CSU, Stanislaus), or professional women who graduated from this institution or who work there.[2] We selected these women for several reasons. First, they are all either pursuing higher education or have at least a bachelor's degree, and they all have had exposure to courses in ethnic studies. We deliberately selected Mexican American women with higher education because we thought that, through their exposure to specific courses in ethnic studies, as well as their life experiences, they would have the tools to reflect critically on Oprah's core message in her TV show—the empowerment of women—and to reflect on the assumption that Oprah's TV show crosses ethnic lines and applies to issues affecting Chicana women.

We also selected these women because of their different generational status in the United States since we wanted to investigate if that made a difference in their "reading" of Oprah's TV show and her message. The first group consists mostly of college students (ages nineteen to forty-two) and some of the professionals. They are the first generation who were either born in the United States of Mexican-born parents (who came as adults to the United States) or were born in Mexico and came to the United States at a young age and/or have been educated in the U.S. educational system. Their primary language is English, and they have been largely socialized by the mass media. The second group consists of Chicana professionals in their mid-to-late-fifties who lived through, participated in, and are the generational product of the Chicano/a civil rights movement of the 1960s and 70s. They were all born in the United States, and some of them can trace their roots in the United States back several generations. They too are literate in U.S. mainstream media. The third group consists of a fifty-two-year-old Mexican immigrant woman–now a student at CSU, Stanislaus–who came to the United States as an adult, who was not socialized in the U.S. educational system, and for whom English is not her first language. This woman has wide access to the U.S. mass media as well.[3]

The majority of the women who participated in this preliminary study were born in the United States.[4] All but one of them were socialized in the U.S. educational system,[5] and all of them are the first generation in their families to go to college (some of them are actually the first members in their family to go to college). All the participants are bilingual in English and Spanish.

The retention of Spanish for these participants might be directly associated with the fact that all of them have at least one parent who was born in Mexico (and for most of them, both parents were born in Mexico).[6] The immigrant woman who came to the United States as an adult presents an interesting and contrasting language dynamic situation in that she has systematically engaged in the acquisition of English and of higher education, which might not be the case for other Mexican immigrant women who arrive in the United States as adults and who do not attain English proficiency.

To contextualize the Chicanas selected for this research, it is important to provide a socioeconomic, educational, and cultural profile of Mexican Americans in California's Central Valley, where CSU, Stanislaus, is located and where these women reside.

Chicanas/os in the United States and California's Central Valley

The Chicanas who participated in this study reside in California's Central Valley, mostly in the counties of Stanislaus, Merced, and San Joaquin. A sociodemographic portrait of the Valley shows that the agricultural industry is still the economic bedrock, accounting for approximately 20 percent of the jobs (*San Francisco Chronicle* 2005), and it is intimately linked with an assortment of manufacturing jobs dominated by food processing, including dairy products, wine, poultry, fruit, tomatoes, and nuts (U.S. Census Bureau 2005b). The Valley's agricultural industry has historically invited a large force of cheap labor—usually from Mexico—that has dramatically shifted the ethnic balance in the region over time. Consequently, the ever-increasing Mexican and Chicana/o presence in the Valley has also brought intense fears of a Valley split in two with its residents sharply divided by economics, culture, language, and educational attainment, among other factors.[7]

The Valley's changing demographics mirrors, in fact, that of the state, which also reflects a dramatic population shift in terms of race and ethnicity. Latinos are now the majority in Merced County (51.5 percent), and their numbers are rapidly increasing in Stanislaus and San Joaquin counties, where they comprise, respectively, 37.8 percent and 34.8 percent of the total population.[8] Approximately 40.1 percent of Merced County residents speak Spanish at home; in the counties of Stanislaus and San Joaquin, the percentages of residents who speak Spanish at home are 29.3 percent and 23.4 percent respectively (U.S. Census Bureau 2005a). Language, then, is not only a cultural indicator that speaks about identity and group affiliation but, in this case, also reflects the extraordinary surge of Mexican immigration during the past decade. Consequently, the language variable not only is important to gauge the levels of acculturation but is also the main factor that allows the participants to understand Oprah's message. In this preliminary study, our aim was to understand how these women "read" Oprah and the message of her TV show and how that may be mediated by age, generational status in the United States, predominant language, different levels of assimilation and/or acculturation, and socialization into U.S. mass media.

Findings

Since our selection of participants was targeted, we do not claim that we can generalize from our preliminary findings to the entire Chicana population; we can only offer glimpses into the understanding that a group of educated Chicanas have in an area of California, the Central Valley, which has a large percentage of Mexican Americans and Mexican immigrant population owing to a significant agricultural industry in the area. These glimpses will be useful in designing a larger study with a larger sample size that would encompass a more diverse segment of the Chicana population, including Chicanas who have not attended institutions of higher education, recent Mexican immigrant women, Chicanas of low, middle, and high socioeconomic status (SES), and Chicanas in different geographical regions of the country and with differing access to Spanish-language programs on television. In doing so, we will learn whether the findings from this study hold in a more comprehensive, larger-scale study or are further complicated.

Everyone Knows Oprah

Although only some of the participants watch *The Oprah Winfrey Show* regularly, all of them know who Oprah is and also know in general terms what the message of her TV show is, regardless of their different levels of acculturation and assimilation, their generational status in the United States, their media preferences in terms of television shows and/or TV stations, and their language skills. They know that she is a black woman and a television talk show hostess who is very wealthy, who helps people, and who fights for what she believes—specifically the empowerment of women. The inescapable conclusion, therefore, is that the power of the mainstream media is enormous. One of the reasons seems to be, at least for these participants, the presence of a television in their homes regardless of their socioeconomic status (SES) and the fact that they are all television viewers who watch an average of fifteen hours per week. The mere act of watching television (whether mainstream English-language stations or Spanish-language stations[9]) is an indicator of the levels of acculturation[10] experienced by Mexican immigrant women and by Chicanas. Therefore, the fact that all of the participants have heard of Oprah only reconfirms that watching U.S. media provides a formidable exposure—specifically for ethnic groups—to U.S. mainstream culture as reflected by TV. Consequently, the levels of acculturation increase, whether it be to a lesser or higher degree, and "cultural learning and behavioral adaptation takes place" (Valencia 2005, 241).[11] In order to be able to follow and to accept—or not—Oprah's message, however, the viewers must grasp the premise of her message, that is, they must be sufficiently literate in English to understand what is at play in *The Oprah Winfrey Show*. In this study, all the participants are English literate and bilingual, and their responses reflected their age interests, their generational status in the United States, and their socialization into the U.S. mass media.

Oprah's Limited Impact

One of the key questions we wanted to explore in this preliminary study was whether Oprah has in any way transformed or influenced the lives or views of our participants.[12] Overall, most of our participants felt that she had not transformed their lives and/or views; however, age and acculturation seemed to be linked in this preliminary study to those who did or did not feel that Oprah's message has influenced their lives and/or views. All of the youngest participants in the study—nineteen-year-old first-year college students—stated that Oprah has not transformed or influenced their lives. Their comments and answers to this question may reveal the fact that they are not tuning into Oprah's media scenario of electronic confessional about how to empower women and the scripted steps to do so. Most of them seem to be spending more time with friends, school, and family.[13] Furthermore, the fact that all of these respondents still live at home with parents who are Mexican immigrants and speak mainly Spanish might explain their media experience, which is watching the Spanish-language television stations—mostly soap operas—with family members in what is traditionally a family activity among Mexicans and Mexican Americans.

We found, however, that the students who were older differed from their younger counterparts. More of these older students watch Oprah's TV show regularly, and more of them noted that Oprah's message reaches them and has an influence in their lives.[14] While a majority of the students in their twenties do not feel that Oprah has transformed their lives and/or views, some do, as do a majority of even older students—students in their mid-thirties through early fifties.[15] Following is a discussion of some of the reasons offered by those students who feel that Oprah has changed their lives and/or views.

Some of the students point to the fact that Oprah encourages women to empower themselves. For example, one student (a single woman who owns her home and defines herself in the middle-high SES) stated, "I love the fact that Oprah is helping her community. She models good behavior and is funny to watch. She has a desire to help others, but [I] specially [like] her ability to speak to women to empower themselves." Along similar lines, another participant explains why she feels that Oprah's message has changed her life: "She . . . motivates me, as a woman, to do the best I can." Another student believes that Oprah's message that "women can achieve great things, even when they are oppressed" has also transformed her life and views. One student finds Oprah to be "an inspiration to me and to all women" based on the fact that "Oprah was abused as a child; however, she didn't let that experience destroy her spirit." She adds that "Oprah has encouraged me through her shows to get educated." For another of our student participants, Oprah has enforced her points of view. Media scholar Sherryl Wilson points out that, indeed, Oprah's television program "presents a selfhood that emerges from relating stories of experiencing/overcoming problems of varying degrees." Oprah's message is often hinged in women's ability to recognize that transcending problems takes endurance and leads to self-realization (2003, 3).

Some of the participants in their twenties acknowledge Oprah's message of empowerment, specifically referencing her struggles with weight and body image. It is interesting that these Chicana students identify Oprah as a successful African American woman who continuously fights her weight in order to fit in with the conventional ideal body image so predicated for celebrities in the U.S. media. Wilson readily points to this contradictory dynamic in Oprah that ultimately endears her to her female audience. She argues that as an African American woman "whose public biography of abuse, rejection and self-loathing—articulated through her perception of her (large) body—Oprah is the antithesis of that which is considered desirable in the official discourse" (192); yet, at the same time, "Oprah-as-celebrity epitomizes success, wealth, and power and stands as a testimony to the possibility of renewal, regeneration and self realization" (192–93).

For another student, the fifty-two-year-old immigrant woman who came to the United States as an adult and is now a student at the university, Oprah provided help and inspiration in her process of acculturation to U.S. society.

"When I came to this country," she recalls, "I started watching TV and I kept changing channels. I thought that [Oprah] was very clear in her speaking and I just like her because her words are very powerful and strong and makes us think and learn." Furthermore, Oprah's "shows have helped me to speak the language; she inspired me to continue with my education." This perspective gives us an insight as to an immigrant's use of the English-language media as a teaching guide, and it would be useful in a subsequent study to find out if other immigrant women have used it similarly (as a teaching tool) or whether they are more likely to watch Spanish-speaking television stations.

Yet, for our participants who are loyal followers of Oprah, the issue of women's empowerment is central to their own individual journey in which they try to overcome social and familial pressures that tend to value traditional roles that could confine them as individuals and as women. In Oprah's show they find guidelines and quick recipes for healing, for self-realization, and ultimately for redemption. They also find a site or stage where they can hear the testimonies, the public confessions of other women's experiences, where "the suffering of women is universal, unabated, and endured only through solidarity with other women" (Lofton 2006, 613), and where Oprah has become a guiding light "at the heart of the most pressing moral questions of our lives" (Illouz 2003, 15) and the "embodiment of the latter-day American Dream" (Abdt and Mustazza 1997, 64). In other words, they have found what English scholar Jeffrey Louis Decker calls *Saint Oprah* or a "post-modern priestess—an icon of church-free spirituality" (Taylor 2002, 38).

The growing level of acculturation may be a strong factor that allows a greater number of older Chicana students to follow Oprah's message and feel it influences their lives. With no language barrier and with a wider access to the mainstream media (half of them watch English-language stations only, while the others watch both Spanish- and English-language channels), Oprah's message has resonated with them in terms of witnessing and identifying themselves in a public "therapeutic discussion" about women's relationships, positions, contributions, and struggles in general. Consequently, empowerment for these Chicanas is directly related to a sense of individualism and empowerment as women. They have bought into what media scholar Janice Peck calls a "therapeutic 'mode of thinking about self and society'" (Peck 1994, 92, 94) that is prevalent in contemporary U.S. culture. This therapeutic mode of thinking is organized under the ideology that "'freedom' is connected (articulated) with individualism and the free market" (Hall 1981, 31)—that is, that in this capitalistic society, all individuals should have "equal access to the means to pursue their private ends." What resonates in Oprah's message is this therapeutic discourse in which problems can be solved through communication and through the recognition that individual feelings are sometimes more important than experience. This discourse serves to "privilege individual experience as the primary source of truth; and to encourage 'taking responsibility' for one's own feelings and behavior based on the belief that we are powerless to change anything beyond our own lives" (Peck 1994, 94).

As to the professional Chicana women who participated in the preliminary study, most did not feel that Oprah has in any way transformed or influenced their lives or views. This is the case for both the young professionals in their mid-twenties to mid-thirties working as public school teachers or as administrators at CSU, Stanislaus, as well as the administrators at this university who are in their fifties, who lived through and participated in the Chicano/a civil rights movement of the 1960s and now dedicate their professional lives to serve, counsel, recruit, and encourage Chicana and Chicano students to remain in the educational pipeline and to pursue higher education.[16] Of the few professional Chicana participants who did feel that Oprah has transformed their views or lives, one pointed to Oprah's shows that deal with medical issues because "[t]hey provide information on topics that are not usually discussed openly such as menopause or breast cancer." On the other hand, those who do not feel that Oprah has changed their lives or views, express varied reasons. A young Chicana counselor, for example, stated that "I can see how [Oprah] can make an impact on others, especially women and African American women in particular. I don't feel as though she transformed or influenced my life, only because I looked up to some strong women in my life: my mother, Dolores Huerta, Gloria Sandoval, and others." A participant who grew up in the 1960s says that "except for [Oprah's] generosity to victims, I do not really relate to her."

Why do some Chicanas who have been in the United States for a significant period of time or have been born and raised in the United States acculturate to and embrace the country's all-too enveloping individualist mantra, which Oprah's show espouses, as is the case for so many of the participants in this study who are students in their mid-thirties through early fifties? And why have other Chicanas, as is the case for the majority of the professionals in this study who are in their mid-to-late-fifties, chosen to reject Oprah's individualist message? This is a question that needs further research, but at this point we can theorize that the level of exogamy, media-watching patterns (watching only English-language stations versus watching both Spanish- and English-language stations), and connection or rejection of Mexican values and traditions are all factors that may influence the type of reception that a media personality such as Oprah will receive.

Failing to Address Issues Relevant to Chicanas

Another main question we wanted to investigate in this preliminary study was whether our participants thought that Oprah's message addresses Chicanas' issues, problems, lives, and/or cultural situations[17] that impact their identity construct. Overall, most of our participants did not think that Oprah's message addresses issues affecting Chicana women. Interestingly, only half of the youngest students who participated in this study (nineteen-year-old college students) responded as such, while the other half stated that they did not know enough to give an opinion.

Most surprising, however, was the fact that all of the participants in the group with the highest number of people who felt that Oprah had influenced their lives or views (college students thirty-six to fifty-two years old) expressed the view that Oprah has not addressed Chicanas' issues, problems, culture, or life situations through her message or television show. One of these students, while a devoted Oprah fan, stated that "[s]he really has not addressed issues solely concerning Chicanas," while another fan asserted that "hardly any Chicanas come on her show," adding that Oprah "doesn't talk about Chicanas/os' problems in education." This paradox raises an important issue: that Chicana women may think of themselves as having not one identity but multiple, intersecting identities. That is, on the one hand, these women may see themselves simply as women at some point, which would help explain why they identify with the concept of the universal woman that Oprah promotes; at the same time, however, their opinion that Oprah does not address issues affecting Chicanas seems to point to the fact that they see their role as women within their ethnic group as different or more complex than the role of "woman" of which Oprah speaks, one whereby ethnicity and gender intersects and creates a multifaceted identity or set of identities. It would be important to see, however, if this finding holds in a larger-scale study.

It is also important to note that one of the reasons that the Chicana women who participated in this study did not think that Oprah's message addresses issues of concern to Chicana women might have to do with the individualist ideology that Oprah espouses, which stands in contrast to the Chicana/o culture. The Chicana/o culture is still "more oriented toward the group and seek[ing] to enhance its welfare." Sociologist Alfredo Mirande argues that Anglos "are more individualistic, so that even the family itself idealizes the developments and accomplishments of the individual." Chicanas/os, however, generally seem to "derive more emotional gratification from the family than the Anglos," and individuals frequently place the needs and welfare of the family above their own. One of the most important features of the Chicano culture is, therefore, the family, and its members are very much vested in its survival and integrity. In fact, "achievement and success are measured according to the contributions made to the family" (Mirande and Enriquez 1981, 107). Further- more, a public therapeutic discourse among strangers, which is the formula in Oprah's show, is not a way of solving problems in the Chicana/o culture, where familialism is still strong enough to "provide help and comfort to one another" (108). Furthermore, even though the Chicano family is "ostensibly patriarchal, it is in fact mother centered" (Baca Zinn 1975b, 26), and even if this pattern might appear contradictory, we find it is not, since "both sexes have responsibility in their own spheres" (27) and they each exercise power and authority within their respective spheres (Mirande and Enriquez 1981, 117). Consequently, the integrity of the group heavily depends on the integrity of the family, and as such traditional roles also evolve, specifically in shared-decision making. But perhaps the change in traditional roles is not coming fast enough for Chicanas whose acculturation process is rapidly expanding and is subject to their individual experiences in the United States. The issues discussed here about the Mexican and Mexican American family are of great importance to Chicanas, yet have not been addressed on *The Oprah Winfrey Show*.

Some of our participants also noted that Oprah tends to cater to white and/or African American audiences. One young professional, for instance, expressed that "[Oprah] appears to have forgotten her African American roots. She's very whitewashed," while another participant remarked that "[s]he is pro-black and doesn't relate to other ethnicities with the same level of interest." Even a participant who is an avid fan of *The Oprah Winfrey Show* observed that "[Oprah] recently addressed the Imus issue and brought together leaders and rappers.[18] She is aware of the black issues, but she is ignorant of issues that deal with other ethnicities. In a recent episode she discussed the issue of eye creases in Asian Americans." This observation is in line with Kathryn Lofton's research. Kathryn Lofton points to Oprah's ignorance of other ethnic distinctions and the social implications, evidenced, for example, in the October 5, 2001, episode of *The Oprah Winfrey Show* titled "Islam 101," which included an interview with an Islamic Studies professor, an interview with Queen Rania of Jordan, and a profile of Noreen, a *Chicago Tribune* reporter who is a Muslim woman. In this profile, Oprah classified Noreen as a modern Islamic woman because, in Oprah's words, she "incorporates Islamic traditions into her modern life" (quoted in Lofton 2006, 615). After Noreen's profile was shown, Oprah opened the conversation to the audience, which included several Muslim women. The discussion emphasized the "universality of women's issues regardless of religious affiliation," especially considering the threats that Muslim-American communities were facing after the September 11 attack. At the end of her show, Oprah enthusiastically thanked several times the "modern Muslim women!" In her analysis of this episode, Lofton claims that, for Oprah, "[t]hese women were not ordinary Muslims, they were *modern* Muslims, Muslims who worked and raised children and bought Victoria's Secret lingerie. Religious yet accessible, faithful yet earthly, moral yet hip: Modern Muslim women!" Lofton argues that, for Oprah, a modern Muslim woman is a "religious believer who does not allow religion to interfere with her love of country or consumption." For Oprah, "'Muslims are just like any other American,' except with different accessories. Religious difference in Oprah's America is a fashion choice rather than a theological commitment, a translatable cultural context rather than an exclusivist world-view" (616).

What we see, then, is not only the fact that, according to our participants, Oprah does not address issues particularly relevant to Chicanas but that she may not be addressing issues relevant to groups outside of white and African American audiences. A larger-scale study, however, would help us explore whether this finding holds.

Oprah as a Role Model to Some, Not to Others

To understand better the impact that Oprah has on our participants, we also asked them if they thought that she is an inspirational role model to U.S. women.[19] Overall, the majority of our participants felt that she is a role model to U.S. women, but many of them specified white and African American women. The majority of our participants, however, did not think that Oprah is a role model to Chicanas.

Some participants who thought that Oprah is an inspirational role model to U.S. women indicated that this is so because "she provides women with a forum to discuss issues which pertain to our everyday lives." Another participant pointed to the fact that "[m]any women relate to her because of her story, humbleness, and struggle." Interestingly, all of our participants who lived through and played a part in the Chicano/a movement of the 1960s stated that she is an inspirational role model to U.S. women because of what she represents as a woman. As one of them put it, "[Oprah] makes choices and sticks by them. She is independent and tells us that we do not need a man to be successful or happy . . . she lets us know that we can have dreams too." This comment falls within the historical experiences of women in the Chicano/a civil rights movement who witnessed the surge of Chicana feminism, which developed when Chicanas fighting in the *Movimiento* to end the oppression of Chicanos in terms of discrimination, education, poverty, and racism faced an internal oppression when they were expected to assume subordinated roles to their male counterparts. Not only did Chicanas begin to question their role in the *Movimiento*, but they also demanded an equal voice (Mirande and Enriquez 1981, 235; Blea 1995, 86–89). Not surprisingly, these Chicana participants view independence in women as a vital factor in their lives and they find in Oprah a mainstream media mouthpiece for these concerns. They also see Oprah's show as a forum in which they can experience the use of "the female voice to deconstruct the hierarchies that typically order public discourse" (Nudelman 1997, 307) and where "feminism is women talking" (Kaminer 1992, 31).

Other participants who agreed that she is a role model to U.S. women specified that she is a role model particularly to African American and white women. Media studies scholar Janice Peck confirms these students' perceptions by noting Winfrey's immense popularity among white women, yet her promotion of African American artists and educational achievement. One of our participants specified that Oprah is a role model "perhaps to middle/upper-class white women. She presents topics and invites guests that are relevant to affluent white women."

In general, our participants who selected their mothers as their role models see that, although not educated, their mothers are empowered women who have shown, time after time when faced with adversity, their indomitable spirit, activism, and strength of character. These mothers have placed the welfare of their family, in many instances, above their own individual interests. Interestingly, it is this kind of attitude that frequently becomes the centerpiece of discussion in *The Oprah Winfrey Show*, and it is redirected to follow a more individualistic position when Oprah suggests, in Lofton's study, that women "spend too much time on others, not enough on themselves," asking whether they are "like so many women I've talked to over the years who have suspended their deepest desires in order to accommodate everything and everyone else" (Lofton 2006, 610). There is a cultural gap that comes across in Oprah's message when her measure of happiness and self-fulfillment for women does not take into account the specific ethnic and cultural life-worlds of diverse women—specifically that of Chicanas who are determined to balance the welfare of their families without losing their particular dreams, desires, and educational and professional opportunities. In the Chicana/o world, issues of education, poverty, language, segregation, violence, and powerlessness are still prevalent. The survival and integrity of the Chicano family, therefore, is still regarded as a way of reaching socioeconomic advancement and of educational success.

Conclusion

The power of the mainstream media has obviously reached all the women who participated in this study since they were familiar with Oprah and her talk show. This TV program has provided an electronic space where "confessions of empathy from a largely female audience of 'sisters'" take place and where Oprah "speaks to other women who had themselves experienced victimization and powerlessness" (Timberg 2002, 139).

Through their answers, most of the participants in this preliminary study seem to be more acculturated in their beliefs that a public discourse about empowerment of all women in general, and of Chicanas in particular, must take place within a culture (theirs) that is still rich in familialism and traditional roles and where the expectation of women "is one of almost total devotion to the family" (Murillo 1971, 155). In fact, "despite the persistence of social roles which severely circumscribe the behavior of the female there is evidence that these roles are undergoing changes and modifications" (Mirande 2002, 158). Sociologist Alfredo Mirande argues that many Chicanas, especially the younger generation in urban areas, are challenging their traditional roles, and the better educated Chicanas are "seeking greater equality not only at the society at large, but also within the Chicano community" (ibid.). It is not surprising, then, that Oprah's message in the media has reached and made more of an impact within the thirty-to-forty-year-old student group of participants in this study who have families of their own and are experiencing a multiplicity of gender roles within their internal and external life spaces as women, mothers, wives, daughters, students, friends, sisters, and citizens.

However, if Oprah's basic premise in her message is about how women can be empowered in their everyday life choices by listening to other women's voices, by witnessing and validating guests' personal stories, and by actively taking steps for self-improvement (provided by Oprah), then her message has not reached, overall, the participant population in this study that consists of different generational levels of college-educated Chicanas in California's Central Valley. The vast majority of these participants do not believe that Oprah's message addresses issues, problems, and cultural or life situations that are particular to the Chicana experience.

Undoubtedly, Oprah is not only "a living legacy of black woman power" (McDonald 2007, 161) but also a role model to the vast white middle-class U.S. female audience to whom she caters. If Oprah's strength rests on the belief that she has connected all women through their suffering, which is universal and is "unabated and endured only through solidarity with other women" (Lofton 2006, 613), then she has been unsuccessful with the majority of women in this preliminary study. Most of the participants in this study, although sympathetic to women's suffering in general, are aware that Chicanas' experiences are different from white middle-class values, particularly as these values relate to a highlighted sense of individuality, "personal accountability, and virtuous uplift" (Decker 1997, 170). It is not surprising, then, that most of the Chicanas in this study cannot fully relate to the white middle-class U.S. female experience that usually predominates the critical discourse of *The Oprah Winfrey Show*. Chicanas/os on the whole are not yet significantly augmenting the ranks of the U.S. middle class since they are mostly the working poor. Sociologist Irene Blea argues that the working-class Chicana is disproportionately represented in overcrowded, rundown housing and has experienced discrimination and racism. For many working-class Chicanas, the main objective is marriage, an institution that conjures promises of independence and a better life. Although educational aspirations appear to be increasing, especially in terms of higher education, the socioeconomic structure and family pressures can push Chicanas to join the ranks of those with early jobs and work responsibilities. "While middle-income youth are engaging in sports, hobbies, homework, and dating, Chicano working-class youth are working and/or married" (Blea 1995, 88).

The participants in this study, who are college-educated or attending college and who could perhaps be more susceptible or ready to embrace Oprah's message, do not, overall, appear to have done so. These Chicanas believe that fully embracing Oprah's message of the universality of women's problems would be done at the expense of ignoring the idiosyncratic problems affecting Chicanas. The participants' sociohistorical memory of the Mexican American and Chicana experience has not only affected their sense (and choice) of identity but has also contributed to their awareness of the specific issues and quandaries facing Chicanas and their communities. Their identity construct does not appear in a vacuum. It is still linked with what Gloria Anzaldúa—the great Chicana poet, writer, and philosopher—called the ways that Chicanas "internalize identification, especially in the forms of images and emotions" (Anzaldua 1999, 83) and have a consciousness of the issues that are putting Chicano communities at risk. Therefore, these participants' sense of identity also reveals their generational levels of acculturation and assimilation; and even if some are experiencing greater assimilation levels, they still seem to retain a sense of group loyalty when they mostly define themselves as Chicanas, Mexicans, or Mexican American women, and reject for themselves the generic labels of "Hispanic" or "Latina."

The National Research Council has recently reported that with the process of acculturation, Latino family size tends to shrink.[20] Acculturation increases the longer the immigrant stays in the United States, and assimilation trends are more evident when Mexican Americans and Latinos are socialized in the U.S. educational system, are more exposed to U.S. culture, and practice exogamy. At first many of the children of immigrants will be bilingual, but successive U.S.-born generations will speak only English (National Research Council 2006). If that is the scenario awaiting Chicanas/os, Oprah's message will, most probably, have a greater resonance with more assimilated generations of monolingual Chicanas; however, this prediction should also take into account the uniqueness of the Mexican immigrant experience, which is embedded in geography: Mexico shares its northern border with the United States. As Mexican essayist, poet, philosopher, writer, and Nobel Prize winner Octavio Paz frequently pointed out in conversation with the authors, "geography is the mother of history." In this case, and as long as the U.S. demand for Mexican labor persists, Mexican immigrants will readily supply it while their economic needs are not being met in their own country. These Mexican immigrants easily cross the border and make their home in the Mexican American barrios throughout the United States. They bring with them the Spanish language and Mexican traditions and culture, which they reinforce not only with their social integration into the already established Mexican American communities but also through their very frequent intermarriage patterns with more acculturated Mexicans Americans. This specific sociohistorical pattern of cross-generational intermarriage between Mexican immigrants and Mexican Americans has affected the acculturation and assimilation process of the whole group and is one of the reasons for the extraordinary success of the Spanish-language television stations throughout the United States.

The inevitable influence of popular television media on the social patterns of behavior of ethnic groups in the United States shifts their process of acculturation, assimilation, and identity construct. Chicanas/os are exposed, by means of the electronic media, to the values and priorities of the mainstream population and are co-opted as consumers since they are not in control of producing or mirroring their own sociocultural experiences in the media, as evidenced by the minimal presence of Chicana/o actors, characters, and/or show hosts in mainstream television. An interesting question that arises is how would a Mexican American TV talk show host similar in style to Oprah accelerate (or not) the acculturation and assimilation process of Mexican immigrant women? Would these immigrant women buy into a message of liberation through a spiritual brand of individualism, and if so, how would that message change their lives and that of their families and communities? Would they actively encourage their daughters and granddaughters "to find truths for [their] revolution" (Lofton 2006, 599) and "to look at their lives differently" (Granatstein 2000, 74)? Would this new surge of individualism change the internal and external social mechanisms of the Chicano family?[21] Could a Mexican American Oprah-style TV talk show host become a sort of a benevolent fairy godmother who could effectively be the "[peddler] of dreams and goods" (Lofton 2006, 600) by providing her "instruction manual for viewer consumption and her inner revolution" (605), and if so, how would she change (or not) the economic and cultural marketplace for Chicanas/os and Latinas/os? Furthermore, how would Mexican immigrant women balance their new brand of individualism while facing socioeconomic and labor struggles, family responsibilities, lack of education (most of them come to the United States with barely any elementary education), and lack of English fluency? Would Mexican immigrant women, Mexican American women, and Chicanas—who are still facing extraordinary socioeconomic hardships and who are still at the bottom of the Latino ladder in terms of educational attainment—survive without substantial family, group, or community support?

In this focused study of a targeted population of educated Chicanas of California's Central Valley, the common thread among the professional Chicanas and the college Chicana students is that they believe in the power of women in general and of Chicanas in particular. They also believe that the core of Chicanas' power lies in their ability and determination to pursue their individual dreams without rejecting their family, their culture, and their identity as Chicana, Mexican, or Mexican American women, even if they do not see their experiences reflected in the mainstream media and in Oprah's message. Further research will allow us to see if these findings hold true for Chicanas and Mexican immigrant women of different socioeconomic status and educational levels, with different access to mainstream English-language media and to Spanish-language stations, with different levels of English and Spanish language skills, and from different geographic regions of the United States.

Appendix

Mexican Americans comprise today the largest percentage (66.9 percent) of the total U.S. Latino population, presently recognized as the largest ethnic minority population in this country (14.77 percent), surpassing African Americans (U.S. Census 2004). They are the country's fastest growing group and, not surprisingly, the most powerful emerging demographic force. In the state of California—ranked as the world's fifth largest economy, and where this study took place—the ethnic shift in population from July 1, 2000, to July 1, 2006, has been dramatic: the white and African American populations have shrunk, while the Asian and Latino[22] populations have increased, with Latinos showing the most significant growth.[23] For California's nearly 36.5 million residents, there is no specific racial/ethnic group that constitutes the majority. While whites are now the largest segment of the population (43 percent in 2006), Latinos (36 percent of the population in 2006) are predicted to outnumber whites around the year 2012. Furthermore, California has more Latinos than any other state (13.1 million).[24]

Notes

1. We use the terms "Chicana" interchangeably with Mexican American. For more detailed information about the specific usage of the term Chicano/a please refer to Isabel Blea and Alfredo Mirande (1995). Also, Arturo I. Rosales (1997) and Rodolfo Acuña (2003) add extraordinary critical insights and discussions about the geohistorical and sociocultural origins of the label and of the identity construction of the term *Chicana/o*.

2. Fifteen of the participants are students, five are administrators/staff at CSU, Stanislaus, and two are K-12 teachers who are graduates of CSU, Stanislaus—a public institution of higher education nestled in the agricultural fields of California's Central Valley designated a "Hispanic Serving Institution" (HSI). Out of its current 8,200 students, 26.5 percent are Latinos, the vast majority of which are Mexican Americans. In terms of gender distribution, approximately 66.7 percent of the total student population is female.

3. This immigrant woman is a student and throughout this article is included in the student group where the age bracket is recorded as 36–52.

4. Fourteen out of twenty-two of the women were born in the United States.

5. The fifty-two-year-old student participant was not socialized in the U.S. educational system.

6. For the fifteen students who participated, both of their parents were born in Mexico. For the seven participants who are professionals, some of them had one parent born in the United States. In some of those cases, not only were their parents born in the United States but also some of their grandparents and great-grandparents.

7. Valley residents are, overall, less educated than the national average, and the educational gap keeps widening. Adults are more likely to drop out of school before the ninth grade, and in San Joaquin County less than 17.3 percent of adults have bachelor's degrees compared to 14.6 percent in Stanislaus County and 13.5 percent in Merced County (Sbranti 2007, A1; U.S. Census Bureau 2005a).

8. Fertility rates are higher in the Valley than the national or state average. Families in Merced County have an average of 3.8 members compared with 3.18 nationwide and 3.53 in California. The same is true for Stanislaus County with 3.64 members per family and 3.69 for San Joaquin County. The Central Valley is also "home to one of the highest teen pregnancy rates in California" (Garcia and Jasek-Rysdahl 2007, 1). Not surprisingly, the population in these counties is younger than the U.S. average of 36.4 age in years. Merced County's median age in years is 28.9; in Stanislaus County it is 31.7 and in San Joaquin County it is 28.9 (U.S. Census Bureau 2005a).

9. U.S. Spanish language stations offer not only comprehensive regional, state, national, and international news, but also other programs that discuss or deal with socioeconomic, cultural, political, legal, and educational issues, policies and/or events.

10. Acculturation is understood as the "process by which one group (generally a minority or immigrant group) learns the culture of another group (generally the dominant group)" (Healey 2006,

533). This process involves "changes in cognition, language, and interpersonal interactions and has been shown to be a key construct for understanding behavior across a number of psychological, social, economic, and political contexts" (Valencia 2005, 241).

11. The levels of acculturation and assimilation also influence and dictate how Chicanas define and view themselves in terms of their identity as U.S. citizens or residents of Mexican descent.

12. In our survey, we asked the following question: "Has Oprah Winfrey in any way transformed or influenced your life/views?" followed up by questions that asked "If so, how, and why?" and "If not, why not?"

13. Three of the four nineteen-year-old students do not work and are full-time students, reflecting, most likely, their family's increasing upper economic mobility.

14. Two of the four students in the 36–42 age group stated that they feel Oprah has transformed their lives/views.

15. There were five participants in this age group with four ranging in age between thirty-six and forty-two years old. The other participant was the fifty-two-year-old woman who migrated to the United States as an adult. Three of the five participants in this group felt that Oprah has transformed their lives and/or views.

16. Seven of our participants are professionals.

17. In our survey, we asked the following question: "Do you think Oprah's message addresses Chicanas' issues/problems/life/cultural situation?" followed up by questions that asked "If yes, how?" and "If not, why not?"

18. The Imus issue refers to the media incident that took place in the April 4, 2007, edition of MSNBC's *Imus in the Morning*. The host of the show, Don Imus, referred to the Rutgers University women's basketball team, which is comprised of eight African-American and two white players, as "nappy-headed hos." His comment stirred much discussion and criticism throughout the mass media.

19. In the survey we asked: "Do you think she's an inspirational role model to U.S. women?" followed up by the questions "If yes, how?" and "If not, why not?"

20. Immigrant Mexican women, for instance, have 2.7 children on the average, while second-generation Mexican American women have 2.1 children.

21. The Chicano or Mexican American family has been historically judged as dysfunctional by mainstream social scientists who believe that the sense of collectivity/group that characterizes the family structure is an impediment to the success of its members in the U.S. society since it stifles the individual needs in favor of the welfare and interests of the family (Humphrey 1944; Jones 1948; Penalosa 1968; Madsern 1973; Carroll 1980; Heller 1966; Rudoff 1971; Sowell 1981).

22. The term "Latino" refers to people not only of Mexican descent but also who are (or are descendants) from other Spanish-speaking countries in the Americas.

23. The white population shrank from 46 percent in 2000 to 43 percent in 2006; the black population showed a decrease from 7 percent in 2000 to 6 percent in 2006. Conversely, the Asian population increased during the same time period from 11 to 12 percent, and Latinos showed the most significant growth from 33 to 36 percent.

24. New Mexico, however, has the largest percentage of Latinos (44 percent) of any state (US Census Bureau 2006).

Works Cited

Abt, Vicki, and Leonard Mustazza. 1997. *Coming After Oprah: Cultural Fallout in the Age of the TV Talk Show*. Bowling Green, Ohio: Bowling Green University Popular Press.

Acuña, Rodolfo. 2003. *Occupied America. A History of Chicanos*. New York: Pearson Longman.

Anzaldúa, Gloria. 1999. *Borderlands. La Frontera*. San Francisco: Aunt Lute Books Publisher.

Baca Zinn, M. 1975. Chicanas: Power and Control in the Domestic Sphere. *De Colores* 2 (3): 19–31.

Blea, Irene Isabel. 1995. *Researching Chicano Communities*. Westport, Conn.: Praeger.

Carroll, Joseph C. 1980. "A Cultural Consistency Theory of Family Violence in Mexican American and Jewish Ethnic Groups." *The Social Causes of Husband-Wife Violence*. Ed. Murray A Strauss and Gerald T. Hotaling. Minneapolis: University of Minnesota Press, 1980.

Decker, Jeffrey Louis. 1997. *Made in America. Self-Styled Success from Horatio Alger to Oprah Winfrey*. Minneapolis: University of Minnesota Press.

———. 2006. "Saint Oprah." *MFS Modern Fiction Studies* 52.1 (Spring): 169–78.

Garcia, J., and K. Jasek-Rysdhal. 2007. "Community Inquiry: Community Problem Solving To Improve Public Policy." Unpublished manuscript by The Center of Public Policy Studies, California State University Stanislaus.

Granatstein, L. 2000. "Spiritual Awakening." *Mediaweek* 3 (April): 74–75

Hall, Stuart. 1981. "The Whites of their Eyes: Racist Ideologies and the Media." In *Silver Linings*, ed. Bridges, G and R. Bruoit, 28–52. London: Lawrence and Wishart.

Hayes-Bautista, David E. 2004. *La Nueva California: Latinos in the Golden State*. Berkeley: University of California Press.

Healey, Joseph F. 2006 *Race, Ethnicity, Gender, and Class. The Sociology of Group Conflict and Change*. Thousand Oaks, Calif.: Pine Forge Press.

Heller, Celia. 1966. *Mexican American Youth: Forgotten Youth at the Crossroads*. New York: Random House.

Hikel, Sabine. 2004. "Oprah Winfrey and the Glamour of Misery: An Essay on Popular Culture." *The Journal of American Culture* 27 (4): 453–54. December.

Humprey, Norman Daymond. 1944 "The Changing Structure of the Detroit Mexican Family: An Index of Acculturation." *American Sociological Review* 9 (December): 622–26.

Illouz, E. 2003. *Oprah Winfrey and the Glamour of Misery. An Essay on Popular Culture*. New York: Columbia University Press.

Jones, Robert C. 1948. "Ethnic Family Patterns: The Mexican Family in the United States." *American Journal of Sociology* 53 (May): 450–52.

Kaminer, W. 1992. *I'm Dysfunctional, You're Dysfunctional: The Recovery Movement And Other Self-Help Fashions*. Reading, Mass.: Addison-Wesley.

Lofton, Kathryn. 2006. "Practicing Oprah, or, the Prescriptive Compulsion of a Spiritual Capitalism." *The Journal of Popular Culture* 39.4: 599–621.

Madsen, William. 1964. *The Mexican Americans of South Texas*. N.Y.: Holt, Rinehart and Winston, Inc.

McDonald, Katrina Bell. 2007. *Embracing Sisterhood. Class Identity, and Contemporary Black Women*. Lanham. Md.: Rowman & Littlefield Publishers.

Mirandé, Alfredo. 2002. *The Chicano Experience. An Alternative Perspective*. Notre Dame: University of Notre Dame Press.

Mirandé, Alfredo, and Evangelina Enríquez. 1981. *La Chicana. The Mexican American Woman*. Chicago: The University of Chicago Press.

Murillo, N. 1971. The Mexican American Family. In *Chicanos Social and Psychological Perspectives*. ed. Wagner, N. N. and M. J. Haug, 97–108. St. Louis: Mosby.

National Research Council. 2006. *Multiple Origins. Uncertain Destinies: Hispanics and the American Future*. 2006 Report. Washington, D.C.

Nudelman, Fanny. 1997. "Beyond the Talking Cure: Listening to Female Testimony on The Oprah Show." *Inventing the Psychological. Toward a Cultural History of Emotional Life in America*. Ed. Joel Pfister and Nancy Schnog. New Haven, Conn.: Yale University Press.

Peck, Janice. 1994. "Talk about Racism: Framing a Popular Discourse of Race on Oprah Winfrey." *Cultural Critique* 27 (Spring): 89–126.

Peñalosa, Fernando. 1968. "Mexican Family Roles." *Journal of Marriage and the Family*. 30 (November): 680–89.

Rosales, Arturo F. 1997. *Chicano! The History of the Mexican American Civil Rights Movement*. Houston: University of Houston. Arte Publico Press.

Rudoff, Alvin. 1971. "The Incarcerated Mexican American Delinquent." *Journal of Criminal Law, Criminology, and Police Science* 62 (June): 224–38.

San Francisco Chronicle. 2005. *A Great Valley's Divide*. Editorial (January 24).

Sbranti, J. N. 2007. *Valley Growth Spurt*. The Modesto Bee (March 22): A1+.

Schaefer, Richard T. 2006. *Racial and Ethnic Groups*. Upper Saddle River, N.J.: Pearson/Prentice Hall.

Sowell, Thomas. 1981. *Ethnic America. A History*. New York: Basic Books.

Taylor, L.T. 2002. The Church of O. *Christianity Today*. 1 (April): 38.

Timberg, Bernard. 2002. *Television. A History of the TV Talk Show*. Austin: University of Texas Press.

U.S. Census Bureau. 2003. *The Hispanic Population in the United States*. June.

———. 2004. U.S. Department of Commerce. *Population Report*. Population Division.

———. 2005a. *American Community Survey*. American Community Survey Office.

———. 2005b. U.S. Department of Commerce. *Population Report*. Population Division.

———. 2006. *Population Report*. Population Division.

Valencia, Richard, ed. 2005. *Chicano School Failure and Success*. New York: Routledge/Falmer.

Wilson, Sherryl. 2003. *Oprah, Celebrity and Formations of Self*. New York: Palgrave Macmillan.

CHAPTER SIX

Confessions from At-Risk Teens

Abstinence, the Social Construction of Promiscuity, and
The Oprah Winfrey Show

KATHERINE GREGORY

"Abstain from sex to attain your goals," reads a billboard along a highway in central Illinois. Associating abstinence and economic/educational potential for young females is unavoidable when addressing teen sexuality in the United States. From public service announcements advocated by public health departments to emotional confessions disclosed on *The Oprah Winfrey Show*, the media climate suggests multiple strategies for instructing teens to abstain from sex rather than face the consequences of their sexuality. Sound bites, like those heard on *The Oprah Winfrey Show*, warn teens—disarmed without the knowledge of safe sex practices—of a recipe for failure awaiting those who succumb to their carnal, hetero-normative impulses before an arbitrarily prescribed time in adulthood. In this chapter, I will explore the regime of abstinence and what messages are circulating about teen sexuality, social agency, and stigma on *The Oprah Winfrey Show*.

In this instance the term "regime" is intended as an ideologically driven policy excluding all other methods of reproductive control and is used to suggest an entire social prescription that a teen must conform to in order to be perceived as "normal." Furthermore, I challenge the media construction of promiscuity and social capital attached to "purity" and argue for a media-based discourse that breaks from the dominant messages and informs teens how to "manage" their sexuality in constructive ways without pathologizing their actions or replicating traditional constructs around femininity.

The locus of cultural meaning in our society, says Foucault, is inextricably linked to a system of codes, representations, and vernacular known as discourse (Foucault 1971, 90). What emerges from this discourse is a hierarchy of meaning, or an "order of truth," that is shaped by the interests of various institutions, including the media, to dictate what is of importance to society. Therefore, discourse becomes the converging intersection of where knowledge and power meet (O'Farrell 2005, 81). The purpose of this chapter is to map out what mediated messages about appropriate sexual conduct for female teen heterosexuals are constructed on *The Oprah Winfrey Show* and how might those messages shape public discourse. In the last few years, *The Oprah Winfrey Show* has made the "secret" daily practices of teens in the United States the focus of many episodes. Unfortunately, a paradigmatic shift from conservative institutional agendas around teen sexuality issues is not evident. In fact, to frame the seriousness of teen sexuality as a nonconsensual act and a social problem, the most extreme cases and behavioral problems are presented and/or linked to set the stage for disciplining the body of the teen. Once this message is disseminated to viewers, it's intended to be internalized by teens and reinforced by their parental control to ensure policing of budding teen sexuality. Meanwhile, new ancillary media platforms, such as *O, The Oprah Magazine*, and the Oprah website, complement these overarching messages while at the same time encouraging simulation of teen desirability through promotional products and consumption of commodities—cosmetic teen makeovers, fashion shows and accessories, diets, and other marketed driven products—to indirectly accelerate the development of teen sexuality through acts of display and physical discipline. Teen heterosexuality is rarely, if ever, constructed as part of a healthy process toward sexual development outside of commodity culture and heteronormative practices. Rather, greater material rewards await those who practice abstinence, Oprah promises, clearly contradicting the consumer habits advertised for her multiple media outlets.

The Moral Authority of Oprah

Shattuc (1997) and others (Acosta-Alzura 2003) identify "structural" features that make up the talk show format. Key features of a talk show include a focus on "issues-oriented" content, "audience participation," appeal to "female viewers," and, maybe most significant for this project, a host or hostess who holds some "moral authority" and "educated knowledge" when engaging topics or judging guests (Acosta-Azura 2003, 138). Why is the genre of the talk show, and *The Oprah Winfrey Show* in particular, so effective at shaping the cultural mindset of millions of Americans? If "image controls emotion and emotion controls politics" (Dinerman, 1999), it is possible to imagine the emotional grip the host holds on viewers and how messages communicated on the show serve as a vehicle through which to convey "soft" hegemonic cultural powers, whether they are in the interest of corporate sponsors, Oprah Winfrey, or the reproduction of dominant societal values and norms (293, 299).

Of all the American talk shows, *The Oprah Winfrey Show* is considered to be at the "high end" of such a format because, among other things, the hostess produces a strong synergy with her audience. In the case of Oprah, her charismatic delivery and spiritual overtones give her a platform through which to communicate effectively. Her focus on makeovers, personal transformations, and spiritual adages, makes for the possibility of personal reinvention. Winfrey's own personal narrative weaves with the story lines and personal struggles often presented during each episode. As regards how teens are represented, the talk show format "revolves around the performance of talk" (Tolson 2001), which includes extreme, graphic, and emotionally charged language, along with the psychological authority of a mental health professional to capture the credibility of any given audience. These combined features help to validate the framework used to present the topic. Rarely is a dissenting view presented on the panel when discussing serious social issues. Hence, this method for shaping audience perception, and in some cases evoking a moral panic,[1] requires packaging social problems in broad sound bites through "shocking" discoveries that often put middle-class problems at the center of attention.

In the mid-1990s, Oprah Winfrey made numerous declarations that she was tired of the old sensational format that delved into family systems and carnivalesque storylines (Lofton 2006, 603). Her talk show format began to center on "individually oriented" features placing greater focus on individual spiritual growth and responsibility. Through the prism of spirituality there were multiple programs devoted to the commodification of personal growth and awareness in association with practices of capitalism (599). Oprah employed spiritual principles to further blur what has been described as the "peddl[ing] [of] dreams and goods." In one episode analyzed by Lofton, the topic incorporates the actualization of the lost dreams of four women who are crowned "princess for a day." Each woman's narrative depicts a lack of material stability or heavy emotional obligations, but after being selected as the subject for the episode, each is "reified" and "sanctified" with a dose of Oprah's material giveaways (600). Anyone who does not conform to her strict moral expectations, in contrast, has no place in this world. They are relegated to stigmatized episodes in which confession is expected and atonement doled out. The teens who transgress do not get awarded with a new wardrobe or appliances or an audition on a reality show.

Sexualized problems fit into a new format that emerged in the last few years. The format style went through another transformation as *The Oprah Winfrey Show* programming shifted toward "Change Your Life TV" (603). Implicit in the programming format was the overarching message that one could transform one's life by "behave[ing] your way to success" (605). How do the tenets of Oprah's "spiritual change through material means" (606) overlap with teen sexuality? In effect, the layered message of teen sexuality inhibits the pathway to success. Even without the threat of an unwanted pregnancy or an STD, teens that focus on their sexual relationships and emotional needs over education and professional development miss out on material opportunities and gratification. Focus on education at the expense of sexual interests is a ticket to professional and financial opportunity. In fact, "self-improvement" drives content production throughout all of the Oprah multimedia outlets (607). On the Oprah website, the act of journaling is recommended as a daily practice. This includes devoting an entire journal to reflecting on past actions as a way to transform one's life (611). Therefore, any behavior labeled as transgressive becomes a negative factor in the framing of the lives of young females and requires a variety of regulatory methods to maintain control.

In the case of the raced and classed female teen, her body becomes "central to the deployment of internalized disciplinary mechanisms and desires" (Barry, 1985). In his "repressive hypothesis" Foucault determined that over the past three hundred years regulatory forces construed a series of sexual "prohibitions" were to restrict individual pleasures through the body. As a result, sexual relations were then "relegated to the domestic sphere and only heterosexual procreative relations were sanctified" (Barry 1985, 94–97).

These different institutional powers—whether religious, medical, scientific, or state—regulate populations and reproduction through the production of controlling knowledge. It is fair to contend that the problematization of teen sexuality predates *The Oprah Winfrey Show*, dating back to early Kinsey reports that suggested that many young women partook in premarital sexual intercourse or other "risky" sexual behavior in the 1950s (Kinsey quoted by Atwood 2006, 451). This same fear-based rhetoric is used today under the guise of scientific knowledge as reports emerge about the age at which a person becomes sexually active has dropped over the past fifty years. Charting of this development as evidence of a social problem, however, does not always take into account that women are delaying marriage or that marital delays are the direct result of greater numbers of women gaining access to higher education. Race and ethnicity also account for differentials in teen sexual activity. African American and Latina teens are more likely than white females to have engaged in sex before age eighteen (450). The depiction of teen sexual recklessness, however, cuts across ethnicity and social class. In more recent constructs, a group mindset is presented as a reflection of teens' complete disregard for what health risks are at stake when engaging in unprotected sexual behavior (452–53). Furthermore, mainstream media's negative focus on teen sexual behavior draws attention to teens' inability to take responsibility for their sexual actions, particularly when it comes to what teens qualify as sex. Findings for these studies often highlight how teens do not consider oral sex or other high-risk sexual behavior as a form of sex and in many cases do not consider health risks of this type of behavior. What is often not communicated in these sweeping assumptions about teen sexuality is that fewer and fewer of them are armed with any knowledge about contraception because of the enforcement of community-based abstinence-only education.[2]

Rims and Rainbows: Exposing Teen Sexual Practices

The talk show format has long been documented as a site of the confessional spectacle in cultural and media studies. This mode of communication reenacts other historical dyads found between confessant and clergy member or confessant and psychoanalyst. This act of expunging oneself through disclosure of one's deepest secrets gives tremendous power to the interpreter, resulting in a gross power differential (Foucault 1990). During an episode about "at risk teens," weepy female teens of all races, ethnicities, and classes purge themselves of "shameful" indiscretions in search of ways to repair their embattled self-esteem as Oprah listens on in the role of moral authority. Her responses are replete with chunks of advice digestible for any global audience. Oprah's larger goal in addressing teens at risk is to encourage education in susceptible teens, but this narrative also triggers Oprah's early televised admissions that her sexual development was marked by repeated sexual assaults and an early pregnancy, with the infant dying several weeks after birth. This early tragedy in her iconic life functions as personal testimony and serves as an example of how young women stigmatized by their sexuality may reinvent themselves, presuming there is no "evidence"—in the form of teen pregnancy or a child—of a sexual past. There seems to be, however, a disconnect between how Oprah has treated her triumphs over personal powerlessness and the lack of sexual choices many young women have when faced with sexual predators and violence in all facets of their everyday lives. Furthermore, this method of moral instruction does not erase the tension between normalized messages about abstinence and teen sexual activity in the United States, particularly given the extraordinary meaning and power placed on the lived and imaginary sexual lives of teens. In recent years, Oprah has distanced herself from her own narrative setbacks of bad breakups and low self-esteem but remains committed to related topics because of its impact on young girls' education. The question, however, remains whether or not her moral utterances and framing of teen sexual activity effectively counter hypersexualized representations of teens in the media. After all, Oprah's audience is not composed of teens, per se, but of their stay-at-home mothers, who are being informed of purported oral and anal sexual practices taken up by their teens.

This knowledge production operates as a way to facilitate adult control over "unmanageable" children and to maintain Oprah's high ratings, the consequences of which may vary or be difficult to measure because *The Oprah Winfrey Show* must compete with teen magazines that have their finger on the zeitgeist of teen culture. For example, *Teen Vogue* has more than 4.5 million readers with a circulation of 1.29 million. Their average reader is 16.3 years of age (Teenvogue.com). These figures underscore the importance of a content analysis of such magazines and the messages they promote about teen sexuality. In effect, these messages encourage a double life, leading to a covert world of teen girls, often uncovered by Oprah, but out of the watchful view of adults nonetheless. There is reason to believe abstinence campaigns have resulted in lower teen pregnancy rates, which have dropped from 61.1 births per 1000 people age 15 to 19 in 1991 to 47.7 births in 2000 (The Alan Guttmacher Institute 2006–7). But the campaigns may also be resulting in specific health issues that have become more prevalent in U.S. teens, across race, ethnicity, and class; in particular, mixed messages about teen competition and need for attention may be linked to increased eating disorders and relational aggression in girls (www.opheliaproject.org), which includes communication tactics such as alliance building, gossip spreading, and other exclusionary behavior intended to alienate a social clique's target.

A thorough content analysis of *The Oprah Winfrey Show* will afford readers an understanding of how cultural norms about teen sexuality are constructed and deployed by both parents and the media. These messages are contradictory at best, even on *The Oprah Winfrey Show*. There are alternative methods for communicating sexuality to female teens that are open and honest (see Girls, Inc., YWCA, Planned Parenthood, AIDS Fonds, and so forth); however, the moral imperative of *The Oprah Winfrey Show* cannot afford to deviate from its ideological underpinnings, given the uncompromising agenda of the abstinence-only movement (Else-Quest, Hyde, and DeLemater 2005), cultural climate, market share, and a programming schedule that reaches U.S. households in the afternoon during prime family viewing.

The most compelling *Oprah* episode on teen sexuality occurred in late 2003, arousing in its audience what could be described as a "moral panic" regarding changing sexual mores of youth in America. In many ways, the impetus for the program "Is your child leading a double life?" (October 2003/April 18, 2004) coincided with the release of the film *Thirteen* (2003). The revelatory aspects of the film's sexually explicit content to many middle-class parents about young white teens were as much of a cultural eye opener as the multicultural film *Kids* (1995) was a decade earlier. The program "Is your child leading a double life?" in effect, cross-platformed content featured in an upcoming article in *O, The Oprah Magazine,* that focused on the troubling secret sex lives of female teens. *O Magazine* writer Michelle Burford presented explicit details about teen sexual practices that she "de-coded" for her audience. Part of the justification for the explicit language was to make parents aware of how their children might be conducting a "secret life" without their knowledge through use of an evolving slang around sexual practices and misleading check-in calls by cell phone.

In the process of unpacking teen codes, the episode prompted many Howard Stern fans to write letters of complaint to the FCC for the episode's use of explicit language during daytime programming, when children could be watching. Notable sound bites that emerged from the episode and had a life of their own at various internet sites related to group sexual practices and sexual contact that did not fall within the parameters of strict heteronormative courtship. Burford told audiences "to hold on to their underwear" when she described "rainbow parties" during which female teens, wearing different shades of lipstick and anonymously moving between partners, would sit under a table while performing oral sex on multiple boys seated above. The object of the game, she reported, was to determine which girl could put a penis the deepest in her mouth. The lipstick marker therefore created both a rainbow effect on the boys' penises and determined who the winner of the game was. This antic as described on *The Oprah Winfrey Show* was supposed to be an example of a lack of parental awareness but, more important, framed teen sexuality as rooted in a form of recklessness whereby teens displayed a lack of agency, deriving little if any pleasure or relationship from the act. Moreover, it was emphasized that female teens were not protecting themselves with a condom because they did not consider oral sex as sex. This depiction of a casual group encounter was coupled with a depiction of "tossing the salad," in which a taboo oral-to-anal contact was performed. Slang, the author claimed, was one way teens could conceal such activities from their parents. Adult assumptions embedded in the finding signaled what is socially acceptable teen behavior: the author was surprised that teens were found to have a "lack of shame" associated with casual sex. Consequently, stigmatization associated with becoming sexually active at "too young" an age or having "too many" partners seemed inconsequential to them.

More recently, Oprah has invited entertainers and a resident psychologist to link other behavioral conduct to teen sexual activity. During a two-part episode (March 30, 2005/March 13, 2006) with Venus and Serena Williams, Jada Pinkett Smith, and Dr. Robin Smith, Oprah draws on the advice from her guests on dating and sex, claiming that her teen guests treat themselves like "trash cans." Oprah introduces her first guest as "[a teen who] already has had sex with eight boys." This admission is a threat to a monogamous relational model and marks the end of a rightful stage of innocence. When the guest is introduced, she is there to "admit" her transgression rather than discuss her actions. Embedded in the language of authority are assumptions about what are considered to be "normal" rules of heterosexual engagement. If such sexual transgressions have taken place outside of monogamy, only through a process of confessional discourse before an authoritative panel may the guest find her vindication. Ultimately the guest is told to put an end to such actions. In the process of pathologization, the psychologist describes her case as a means to fill her hunger. Teen sex is then framed as unhealthy, "painful," and something that can make a teen "sick." The female body is, again, described as a "trash can," nothing more then a passive vessel for "boys' sperm" and "boys' insecurity." Sperm in this case is signified as a profane, contaminating substance. These scare tactics fail to teach young women how to negotiate their sexual and emotional needs. Although not explicitly recommended, the "revolution" Oprah declares should happen can only lead to abstinence. Constructing the guest's behavior as nonconsensual and harmful also sits well with the ideological schema of the abstinence-only movement that propagates the notion that all premarital sex is damaging to a woman's emotional and physical health, following her well into adulthood (Else-Quest, Hyde, and DeLemater 2005).

In another episode, "Suburban Teens: The New Prostitutes" (September 25, 2003), teens who "come from good homes" in the suburbs are lured into prostitution with the promise of making "easy money" to fulfill their consumer practices. The video cutaway over the narration is a black-and-white shot of a single white female streetwalking on a desolate highway with motor vehicles passing. Oprah narrates the severity of the problem: male and female pimps target middle-class teens by approaching them in privatized "public" spaces such as the mall or a fast-food restaurant to work as prostitutes. Viewers are led to believe that no suburban space is deemed safe, as teens report having sold sex in their bedrooms in their family homes. During the program, a small group of multiethnic teens relay their ordeal, ready to divulge their actions and find atonement while seated across from Oprah, who is dressed in a sweeping black and white floor-length gown.

The dominant assumption circulating on this program is that only teens from "broken homes" or living in poverty are compelled to behave in such a way. This story is different in that it strikes at the heart of middle-class stability and social space, suggesting that prostitution, an urban vice, has now reached gated communities. The prostitutes are none other than members of those sheltered spaces that were set up to guarantee idyllic childhoods and a postponement of all things corruptive. The message suggests a menacing threat to the gated communities and reminds us that the myth that all things outside of the sanctified heteronormative paradigm take place elsewhere is false. Oprah's online site asks users if this could "happen to your daughter," stimulating a visceral experience of what their mothers must be experiencing. It would be interesting to know whether any long-standing social stigmatization will be attached to the teens who disclosed their brush with prostitution or whether the entire episode will be silently erased as a youthful indiscretion.

Episodes where links between sex and teens are not direct, such as the second part on the Venus and Serena Williams, Jada Pinkett Smith, and Dr. Robin Smith episode, "The secret lives of teen-age girls" (April 15, 2005), continue to blur issues around sexual conduct. In this case, drinking, cutting, and other behaviors are associated with inappropriate sex as part of a larger narrative about teens who are out of control. Most of the guests are middle class and college-bound; however, they are depicted as lacking self-esteem and therefore unable to set personal boundaries. Clearly, the problematization of mostly white middle-class teens is earmarked for special episodes that undermine the construction of middle-class life and popular assumptions about what type of person ends up losing control and acting out sexually.

Methods of controlling female teen sexuality are not limited to episodes that focus solely on their issues. For the episode "Women who use sex to find love" (February 23, 2006), the focus is on a self-described adult "sex addict" whom Oprah introduces by identifying the sensational number of sexual partners the women purports to have had. Oprah interjects between the guest's narrative, perhaps to disrupt the reflex of the audience to harshly judge her, by equating her own food addiction to that of any other addiction. But she distinguishes between her own and her guest's outlet when she openly admits that she could not transfer her addiction to such an activity because of the thought of seeing so many "strange penises." The cumulative thought of experiencing all of the guest's sexual encounters is the equivalent of gorging oneself on all the food that Winfrey has ever consumed during a single sitting. And while she purports to be without any judgment toward her female guest, she uses the woman's sexual behavior as a teaser for each segment. The woman is described to be without "desire" or agency, instead using sex wherever there is an opportunity. Even when the topic relates to sex between consenting adults, the woman's teenage behavior is framed as a signal of an emerging problem explicit in her narrative.

Although self-described as "not very promiscuous" as a teenager, thus meaning she was perhaps middle class and "not out of control" in her youth, the guest reveals subsequent exposure to pornography and the first of many "one-night stands" after experiencing a betrayal from her boyfriend while still in her teens. These marking events could be read as precursors to downwardly spiraling behavior but also as a forewarning to all viewing parents about how their teens' current sexual conduct might harm them in adulthood. To reinforce the construction of the guest as a woman "out of control" and a disgrace to her family rather than as a twenty-five-year-old consenting adult, not surprisingly, her mother is introduced in the next segment. At this stage of the episode, the interview segues to how moral values were communicated and provided stability for the guest until the time of her parents' divorce. This allows viewers vicariously to feel the shame a mother must endure knowing that her daughter has slept with ninety men. What is not established, though, is what constitutes as a sound, "normal" number of heterosexual partnerships one might have in adulthood. Social rules of compulsory heterosexuality around "appropriate" sexual activity are reinforced through a patriarchal concept of what is unacceptable conduct. Singling out a traumatizing event that took place before the subject had sexual agency has the potential to neutralize any stigmatizing implications of her actions as an adult.

The guest who is notoriously identified by her number of sexual partners is also framed within a mental health model. She is situated on the social margins, thereby limiting any lifestyle options put forward during this episode. The framing of this topic is not intended to sway beyond the existing "sexual hierarchies," nor is it intended to evoke "forms of resistance to sanctified heterosexual relations." In effect, the ideas put forth simply reproduce a "hegemonic familial structure" and "reproductive heterosexist roles" at the complete exclusion of any other forms of sexual identity or family structure (Ingraham 1996). Furthermore, these same principles of institutional heterosexuality give heterosexual women the repressive power to police each other's sexual relations, by punishing and labeling other women who do not conform to the rules of domesticity and monogamy. Meanwhile, this ideology perpetuates a double standard that continues to bestow heterosexual males with status based on their sexual prowess. Consequently, an arbitrary number assigned to the label "promiscuous" based on any sexual activity only reinforces a heteronormative, monogamous domestic imperative that the audience is eager to validate.

As stated earlier, whoever controls the discourse controls the meaning assigned to any act or anyone participating in it. A cross-platform of online information on parenting reinforces the messages made during any related television episode. All related online content from a specific program or related topics leads to methods a parent can deploy to gain control over a teen's life. This inevitably links parental loss of control to teen "dating" and other activities deemed not suitable for a minor. The online site for the program titled "Is your child leading a double life?" links to related programming content about media influence on teen values and how to manage budding teen sexuality, including "Teenagers and Dating: When's the right time?" The expert in this case is Dr. Mike Riera, a psychologist and author, who stresses that dating before high school should be discouraged. This gives a tremendous amount of control to parents to decide when their child is "ready" to date.

Pre-high-school dating in this context is largely described as innocuous "hand holding" or "talking on the phone"; however; parents are warned to pay attention to signs that might indicate that *more* is taking place. The psychologist recommends parents use a variety of conversational angles to spell out for their children why they are too young to date, namely stating that their stage of development does not allow them to know themselves well enough to date and that dating will await them in "a year or two." Meantime, parents are advised to express their understanding of their children's feelings. In a video link to "Is your child leading a double life?" Dr. Pinsky's recommendation to parents opens with the statement that it takes great effort for parents to know what their children are up to because teens go to great lengths to conceal their lives from adults. The cutaway video shows a wide shot of a group of male teens who disappear from view as they walk behind a large pine tree into what could be the neighbor's yard or off family property. Once out of sight of the parental gaze, the cutaway suggests, teens are apt to be exposed to sinister behavior. Dr. Pinsky advises parents to "be aware of the world children are being exposed to," implying it is a universe unknown to adults. The job of a parent includes playing the role of "policeman" and "truant officer." Both examples require parents to play the role of "monitor" of what teens watch on television and the internet and who their friends are rather than simply setting an example. This sequence cuts to an outdoor scene with teens around a bonfire. The association is that of underage drinking and sex. All of these forces point to outside influences affecting a teen's judgment rather than what is practiced and communicated inside the home. Therefore, menacing forces lurking outside the sanctity of the home, which is decidedly middle class, suburban, and white, are the teen's greatest threat.

The cause of such teen problems is embedded in the televised construction and analysis of their narratives. Psychotherapeutic jargon that was once used as "professional theory and practice" has now been transformed into "a culturally dominant ideology" (Bellah et al. quoted in Lamanna 1999, 189) used by host, guests, and experts alike to frame adolescent sexual relations. Rhetoric from the abstinence-only movement that under Title V of the Social Security Act gets state and federal money for promoting the psychological and physical health risks of premarital sex would lead the public to believe that "age and relationship status" makes teen sex ultimately dangerous (Else-Quest, Hyde, and DeLemater 2005). Who or what social forces will be made a scapegoat as the source of influence on this behavior? Many audience members and psychological experts on *The Oprah Winfrey Show* have singled out sexually explicit content found on TV and on the internet as possible reasons for sexual misinformation or, worse, encouraging young people to engage in sexual behavior. Parental negligence is, however, often ignored by these studies (Lamann 1999). Meanwhile, the degree to which a teen's behavior is deemed unhealthy or pathological is inextricably related to the number of her sexual encounters. Hence, an arbitrary number determines if a teen is labeled "promiscuous." All other forms of sexual experimentation—with the exception of traditional definitions of sex—are disqualified from this numeric calculation.

If we as social agents are the product of the social and historical forces in which we are immersed, those same forces are assumed to shape the direction of our collective consciousness about social reality (Namaste 1996). This impact shapes where "subjects can appear and in what capacity" (195), producing forms of social regulation and institutionalization as by-products of these controlling forces. It was Foucault who identified ways in which historical forces dictated the classifications of sexual identities during the Victorian era, hence inventing the label of "homosexual" as a way to control and regulate entire populations (Namaste 1996). This example of the social construction of the "homosexual" makes it possible to then consider how the construction of female teenager in the context of American life is a product of regulatory forces, social control and sexual discourse. Overall, teen sexuality is portrayed during one episode as "painful," destructive, and a practice that "can make you sick." How affective are these judgmental scare tactics in controlling teen behavior and shaping public opinion about what is best for teenagers? By assigning negative outcomes to the experience, teens are not being taught how to negotiate their desires because their needs are totally negated behind a veil of abstinence. Every expression of casual sexual experimentation is framed within a mental health model. By constructing teens as irresponsible and developmentally incapable of being a sexual agent in the media, acts of sexual experimentation are set at a great personal cost and irrevocably destructive. Even the program about "adult sex addicts" is contextualized in terms of teen sexual trauma. Rather than the guest being called "whore" and "slut," she is characterized as a passive dysfunctional vessel. The male sexual anatomy, meanwhile, is signified as foreign and corruptive.

Discourses about teen sexuality tell us more than what is considered to be a sex act. They inform us of what methods of control are being deployed to coerce teenagers into conforming to what is perceived as "normal" in our society. This is dictated by discourses that are mostly repressive and that govern who has the "right" to speak about teen sexuality. Those who are permitted to speak, says Foucault, have the power to naturalize what should be understood as a part of socialization and methods of control to coerce submission to our social norms (Atwood 2006, 465). This ideological agenda is not universal; for instance, in a culturally diverse place such as the Netherlands, state-sponsored sex education begins in middle school, where children learn how undesired pregnancy and the risks of STD transmission can be prevented (AIDS Fonds). This pragmatic approach is the result of statistics indicating that many children are experimenting with sex as early as the age of thirteen. Selling abstinence and guilt is useless if a society is to have an educated youth population that understands the consequences of their actions.

Notes

I gratefully acknowledge insightful comments from Trystan Cotten and Kimberly Springer.

1. "Panic" was used at some online sites to describe the sexual practices detailed during this episode.
2. "In 2002, only 62% of sexually experienced female teens had received instruction about contraception before they first had sex, compared to 72% in 1995" (The Alan Guttmacher Institute, 2007).

Works Cited

Acosta-Alzura, C. 2003. "Change Your Life! Confession and Conversion in Telemundo! Cambia Tu Vida," *Mass Communication & Society* 6, no. 2: 137–59.

AIDS Fonds. 2006. Interview with project manager. June. www.aidsfonds.nl.

The Alan Guttmacher Institute. 2006–7. http://www.guttmacher.org/pubs/state_pregnancy_trends .pdf (accessed August 14, 2006, and July 6, 2007).

Atwood, J. D. 2006. "Mommy's Little Angel, Daddy's Little Girl: Do You Know What Your Pre-Teens Are Doing?" *The American Journal of Family Therapy* 34, no. 5: 447–67.

Barry, K. 1985. *Female Sexual Slavery*. New York: New York University Press.

Bellah, R. N., et al. 1985. *Habits of the Heart: Individualism and Commitment in American Life*. Berkeley: University of California.

Brooker, P. 1999. *The Concise Glossary of Cultural Theory*. London: Hodder Arnold.

Else-Quest, N. M., J. Shibley Hyde, and J. D. DeLamater. 2005. "Context Counts: Long-Term Sequalae of Premarital Intercourse or Abstinence," *The Journal of Sex Research* 42, no. 2 (May): 102–12.

Epstein, D., and D.L. Steinberg. 2003. "Life in the Bleep-Cycle: Inventing Id-TV on the *Jerry Springer Show,*" *Discourse* 25, no. 3 (Fall): 90–114.

Foucault, M. 1971. *The Order of Things: An Archaeology of Human Sciences*. New York: Vintage.

———. 1990. *The History of Sexuality: An Introduction*. New York: Vintage.

Ingraham, Chrys. 1996. "'The Heterosexual Imaginary: Feminist Sociology and Theories of Gender,'" edited by Steven Seidman, *Queer Theory/Sociology*, Cambridge, Mass.: Blackwell.

"Is your child leading a double life?" *The Oprah Winfrey Show*, October 2003/April 18, 2004, Transcript.

Lamanna, M. A. 1999. "Living the Postmodern Dream: Adolescent Women's Discourse on Relationships, Sexuality, and Reproduction," *Journal of Family Issues* 20, no. 2, (March): 181–217.

Laramie, T. 2005. "Effects of Visual and Verbal Sexual Television Content and Perceived Realism on Attitudes and Beliefs," *The Journal of Sex Research* 42, no. 2, (May): 130–37.

Lofton, K. 2006. "Practicing Oprah; or, the prescriptive compulsion of a spiritual capitalism," *The Journal of Popular Culture* 39, no. 4: 599–621.

Media Kit. TeenVogue.com, checked on August 14, 2006.

Namaste, Ki. 1996. "The Politics of Inside/Out: Queer Theory, Poststructuralism, and a Sociological Approach to Sexuality," in *Queer Theory/Sociology*, ed. Steven Seidman. Cambridge: Blackwell.

O'Farrell. C. 2005. *Michel Foucault*. London: Sage.

The Ophelia Project. 2006. www.opheliaproject.org (accessed March 12).

"The Secret Lives of Teen-age Girls." 2005. *The Oprah Winfrey Show*, April 15, Transcript. Shattuc, J. 1997. *The Talking Cure: TV Talk Shows and Women*. New York: Routledge.

Smart, B. 1985. *Michel Foucault*. London: Routledge.

"Suburban Teens: The New Prostitutes." *The Oprah Winfrey Show* website. http://www.oprah.com/tows/pastshows/200309/tows_past_20030925.jhtml (accessed March 16, 2007).

"Teenagers and Dating: When's the right time?" 2007. *The Oprah Winfrey Show* website. http://www.oprah.com/relationships/relationships_content.jhtml?contentId=con_20030326_dating.xml&section=Family&subsection=Parenting (accessed March 12, 2007).

Tolson, A. 2001. "Introduction: The Talk Show Phenomenon." In *Television Talkshows: Discourse, Performance, Spectacle*, ed. A. Tolson. Mahwah, N.J.: Lawrence Erlbaum.

"Venus, Serena and Jada Pinkett Smith on Dating, Sex and Weight." 2005. *The Oprah Winfrey Show*, March 30, Transcript.

"Women Who Use Sex to Find Love." 2006. *The Oprah Winfrey Show*, February 23, Transcript.

CHAPTER SEVEN

Oprah Goes to Africa

Philanthropic Consumption and Political (Dis)Engagement

HEATHER LAINE TALLEY AND MONICA J. CASPER

> *"Celebrity itself is thus commodified; notoriety becomes a type of capital . . . The perceived ability to attract attention, regardless of what the attention is for, can be literally cashed in."*
> —JOSHUA GAMSON, 1994

In 2005, *Time Magazine* named as its Persons of the Year rock legend Bono of U2 fame and Microsoft founder Bill Gates and Melinda Gates, cofounders of the world's wealthiest charity. Bono was honored for his contributions to the One Campaign, while the Gates were honored for their global philanthropic work. The September 2006 issue of *In Style* carried a story about the "cause celeb" [sic] of the One Campaign, featuring "countless stars" dedicated to eliminating poverty and HIV/AIDS in Africa. The story featured well-groomed celebrities in black and white "One" t-shirts—which, according to a sidebar, can be purchased at Nordstrom for US$40. Consider the description: "The atmosphere at photo shoots held in Hollywood and Manhattan for Bono's AIDS and antipoverty campaign, One, was upbeat, but the serious cause behind the gatherings was never far from the participants' minds" (Sayers 2006, 562).

Also in 2006, noncelebrities Lia and Steve Purcell launched a web-based organization called Look to the Stars. On looktothestars.org, the couple wanted to publicize "the many wonderful things that celebrities are doing to help the world." The site profiles the philanthropic activities of more than four hundred celebrities including Bono, Bill (but not Melinda) Gates, and our subject of inquiry, Oprah Winfrey. Each profile includes biographical data, charities supported by the celebrity (with links), and glamorous publicity photographs. The site also contains a "news" section with stories about various fundraising and philanthropic activities in which featured celebrities are engaged.

What, exactly, is going on with these "do-gooder" celebrities? In this chapter, we address several interrelated issues: the cult(ure) of celebrity, its role in mediating philanthropy, political (dis)engagement, American consumption of/in Africa, and crucially, the ways that the figure of Oprah Winfrey enables us analytically to map the intersections of these. Oprah performs a vital role in American popular culture—linking the United States to Africa, African Americans to non-African Americans, women to men, people with HIV/AIDS to the sero-negative, capitalism to philanthropy, books to readers, a self-help population to "inspirational" resources, and most significantly for our purposes, consumers to merchandise and/or projects.

We draw specifically on the episode "Christmas Kindness" (2005), released as part of *The Oprah Winfrey Show: 20ᵗʰ Anniversary DVD Collection*, to interrogate Oprah's philanthropic activities in Africa.[1] We watch and analyze as Oprah chronicles her holiday adventure, working hard to convince viewers of the "joy" of giving to needy Africans. The superstar fosters her own celebrity status, while also charting a new kind of philanthropy at the intersection of consumption, celebrity, and self-improvement. Yet we suggest that while Oprah is "doing good," she is simultaneously displacing political engagement on the part of viewers/consumers with a weak and ultimately ineffective version of action. Oprah-style philanthropy may bring in dollars through appeals to emotion, but it precludes direct, sustained political engagement and thus ultimately lasting structural change.

Consuming Oprah, Consuming Africa

Oprah Winfrey is unlike any other celebrity in recent memory. As the introduction to this volume has shown, she rocketed to fame via daytime TV, but she is no mere talk show host. Oprah has created a hyper-successful media and merchandising empire that has penetrated every sector of the U.S. market and gone global. She has attached herself to so many consumer products and public figures—from candles to sheets, from John Travolta to Bill Clinton, from Tolstoy to Toni Morrison—that American consumption outside of Oprah's one-woman culture industry seems virtually impossible. *All* Americans consume Oprah whether they realize it or not.

Increasingly, this empire includes a range of charitable endeavors. While Oprah's Angel Network has funneled contributions into a variety of projects in the United States and elsewhere, clearly her major philanthropic cause is Africa, specifically South Africa, where HIV/AIDS is devastating bodies, families, and communities at astonishing rates and with devastating consequences (Karim and Karim 2005). Oprah's newest and most publicized venture is the opening of a selective school for South African girls, the Oprah Winfrey Leadership Academy for Girls in South Africa.

Why does Oprah care so much about this region? She has reported that "South Africans have more spirit and hope than any other people she has met. She's also crazy about the accent, loves the food . . . and says she has Zulu DNA" (Alexander 2005). In 2005, Oprah underwent genetic testing, hoping to show a biological (that is, "real") linkage to the country where she feels so "at home." The test initially revealed that Oprah could be Zulu, but controversy ensued. Historians were "baffled" by Oprah's claim, given that "there are few records of the Zulus having any connection to the African slave trade" (Munnion 2005). Not surprisingly, Henry Louis Gates's PBS special *Oprah's Roots: An African American Lives Special* demonstrates that not only is Oprah not Zulu, she is not even South African. Her family is descended from the Kpelle tribe of Liberia, located in West Africa (Gates 2007).

Oprah is not the only celebrity claiming to speak for Africa. Indeed, the entire continent has become a trend, an accessory, a destination, and a cause du jour for celebrities seeking good PR and a mission. Alex Williams writes in the *New York Times*, "That Madonna should suddenly be casting an ice-blue eye toward Africa should hardly be surprising. After all, she has always known how to spot a trend. And much as it may strain the limits of good taste to say it, Africa—rife with disease, famine, poverty, and civil war—is suddenly 'hot'" (Williams 2006, 9).

Michael Musto of the *Village Voice* "dismisses the current interest in Africa as merely the cause-of-the-moment among A-listers and charities." But, as Williams asks, "Where does all the good will leave Africa?" While celebrities have brought attention and glamour to African causes, what happens when the next new thing replaces Africa-the-trend? These pop culture critiques beg the question: Who will remain in Africa when the need for spin, PR, career advancement, and self-improvement fades? Can interest be sustained without a genuine (and/or genetic) connection to the land, people, and/or issues?

There is yet another disadvantage to the intense focus on Africa. Under colonialism, Africa was typically referred to as the "dark continent." This term, whose legacy continues in both obvious and subtle ways, relies upon and reproduces racism and imperialism. But it also makes reference to the sheer lack of exposure and knowledge of most Westerners to the world's second largest continent. Too many people in the West understand entirely too little about the diverse, complicated, culturally rich African continent with its multitude of specificities and lived realities. James Ferguson laments, "When we hear about 'Africa' today, it is usually in urgent and troubled tones. It is never just Africa, but always the crisis in Africa, the problems of Africa, the failure of Africa, the moral challenges of Africa to the 'international community,' even (in British Prime Minister Tony Blair's memorable phrase) Africa as 'a scar on the conscience of the world'" (2006, 2).

Africa thus remains a place defined by stereotypic imagery (Alcabes 2006). Into this laden, geopolitical space enters Oprah and her ilk, manufacturing images of Africa (usually featuring Oprah in the frame) for popular consumption. Celebrities are engaged in the work of constructing how Africa and its problems are perceived in the American imagination. Because each of Oprah's trips to Africa is meticulously documented for subsequent television episodes, her "philanthropic" work in Africa is seen by millions of viewers all over the world. Images of Africa become the geographic, political, and cultural background for Oprah's endeavors. We suggest that non-Africans become acquainted with Africa as documented and *strategically represented by* Oprah's camera crew.

Seeing Red (and Green)

Oprah and Bono recently helped launch the RED™ campaign, an example of the intersections of celebrity with philanthropy in the web of globalized capital. Here's how it works: from the website joinred.org, consumers purchase "red" products; these may be red in color, or not.[2] When a consumer good designated as RED™ is purchased, the company profiting will share a portion of its proceeds with The Global Fund to Fight AIDS, Tuberculosis, and Malaria. Already, millions of dollars have been distributed to African nations. The RED™ campaign embodies an alternative philanthropic strategy: rather than seeking money from donors, funds are instead raised through the power of capitalism. Consumers buy, and the needy (ostensibly) benefit.

Clearly, something interesting is happening in philanthropy, namely a shift from donation to consumption, and celebrities are in the thick of it. A recent *New York Times* article suggests, "Today, no well-heeled rock or movie star can ignore the lure of association with a good cause . . . But aid specialists are questioning whether the emphasis on celebrities and one-time hyper events does not do more harm than good, distracting attention from the *difficult, long-term problems*" (our emphasis; Cowell 2005, 3). On the face of it, tabloid coverage of celebrities and their charitable works is certainly an improvement over yet another spread of the hottest celebrity heiress exiting her limousine sans panties. But is the experience of consuming entertainment for good the same thing as being philanthropic?

We consume *causes* more than ever before. From the inexpensive, ubiquitous silicone bracelets in a range of colors signifying diseases and issues, to luxury purveyor Kiwi Collection's assertion that "philanthropy is the next big drive that luxury brands will need to catch up on," philanthropy *is* consumption unlike ever before (Dive 2008). Charity is not just about "doing good" these days but rather about buying goods, services, and experiences in the name of progress. But Fowler notes, "The sight of Bono and Oprah launching a $200 'RED' iPod as part of the eponymous campaign is a long way from the haunting image of a vulture near a bloated, starving child—images we saw back in the Ethiopian crises . . . Cause-related marketing can be great work by any standards of advertising, but the RED brand launch here in the U.S. comes across almost as if the brand, and identification with it, is greater than the cause" (Fowler).

Patricia Mooney Nickel and Angela Eikenberry describe this emergent phenomenon as *marketized philanthropy*. They argue, "philanthropy today is increasingly conflated with the mediums of consumption, profit, and media celebration as the basis for benevolent human relations. In its subordination of benevolence to the market, this [approach] stabilizes the very system that results in poverty, disease, and environmental destruction" (Nickel and Eikenberry, forthcoming). We prefer the term *philanthropic consumption* for these developments, as a way of emphasizing consumerist rather than charitable aspects. Such consumption is increasingly (and perhaps necessarily) global. Moreover, we suggest that philanthropic consumption is particularly amenable to the influence of celebrity spokespeople. As Gamson argues, "People in diverse industries have recognized the power of celebrity. The logic and nascent production arrangements of entertainment celebrity have spread rapidly, taking hold in arenas beyond entertainment: fashion, architecture, grass-roots social movements, literature, art, medicine, academia, and especially in electoral politics" (1994, 186). With the culture of celebrity and its economic reach comes the power of persuasion: if they endorse it, we will buy it.

Philanthropic causes and charity events have long employed entertainers to engage audience members with the aim of eliciting financial contributions. Increasingly, however, celebrities engage in what *Time Magazine* calls "charitainment"—high-profile, celebrity-studded philanthropic activities filmed and transmitted to the masses (Poniewozik 2005, 93–94). Charitainment is the intersection of celebrity worship with philanthropic consumption in a globalized, digital world. As superstars such as "Brangelina," Oprah, and Bono traffic around the globe—bearing witness, dirtying their hands, distributing large sums of money, and posing with the besieged—the omnipresent cameras record their every move. Back home in front of computer screens and televisions, viewers consume these celebrities and their favorite causes. We are compelled by emotions, including the desire to be just like our favorite celeb, to pay attention and to care. The private, embodied suffering of HIV/AIDS or hunger or genocide is magnified cinematically and subject to surveillance for our lasting entertainment. We are virtual tourists (or perhaps voyeurs?) of other people's lives and tragedies. And celebrities—with their hyper-exposure, international recognition, ease of travel, enormous sums of money, cultural capital, expedited passports, access to media, and flexible schedules—are ideally positioned to serve as tour guides on our digital journey to the land of philanthropic consumption.

Saving Africa, 50,000 Children at a Time

In 2005, just in time for the holiday season, *The Oprah Winfrey Show: 20ᵗʰ Anniversary DVD Collection* was released. The collection includes interviews with celebrities, Oprah "firsts" and "unforgettable moments," Oprah at Home, Behind the Scenes, Oprah's 50ᵗʰ Birthday Bash, Oprah's Weight, Wildest Dreams, Makeovers, and "Christmas Kindness" (hereafter, CK), which documents Oprah's trip to South Africa to deliver toys to children. In the DVD insert, Oprah writes, "I have been abundantly blessed and want to use the next 20 seasons of my life for what I know is my true calling—to be of service to women, children, and families in need around the world." While the Anniversary Collection most obviously serves as entertainment, Oprah's letter and inclusion of the CK segment mark the DVD as an artifact of philanthropic consumption.

Throughout CK, the venue shifts back and forth from Oprah "at home" in her television studio, to Oprah "on the road" in South Africa. Oprah reveals to the viewer months later what happened during the actual South Africa visit, using images filmed there. Oprah interprets the trip both while she is in South Africa and then back in Chicago, exposing multiple layers of (her) experience and reflection. This narrative, sometimes confusing, is obviously carefully edited and presented so as to elicit maximum emotional impact.

As the segment opens, a narrator promises that this is "an Oprah show like no other." Oprah remarks, "It was the single greatest experience of my life!" What could possibly top Oprah's list of best experiences *ever*? Before we even have time to guess, the narrator tells us—"Oprah in South Africa!"

From her Chicago studio, Oprah informs us, "This is more than a show . . . [it is] a journey that changed my life forever." She tells us she found herself wondering, "What can I do to make Christmas more meaningful?"

Oprah recounts what it was like on Christmas morning as a poor child. She anticipated the moment when other children would gather outside to tell each other what they had received for Christmas. "What will my story be?" Oprah recalls agonizing. What will she tell the other kids when she has received nothing on Christmas morning?

On Christmas Eve, three nuns arrive on her doorstep with a doll for her. But it is not just a toy that the nuns give Oprah. She recalls, "I mattered enough . . . They remembered me . . . To repay their kindness, I created that same experience for the children of South Africa."

Soon the scene changes from chic, composed Oprah in her studio to a landscape—the lush grasslands and rolling hills of South Africa. Oprah remarks over images of terrain, "I feel bonded to the land . . . When I first arrived here, it felt like I came home."

For Oprah, as for many African Americans, Africa *is* home. And to go "home," Oprah has gone natural. Rather than the styled coif that she sports for her talk show, in South Africa she wears cornrows. Oprah's own style marks the meeting of the global north and the global south—cornrows, pastel sweater sets, chinos, and glittering diamond studs.

Children fill the landscape. They sing, dance, run, and laugh for the cameras. "I saw myself in every child," Oprah tells us. *Every* child: Thousands of African children, many of them orphaned by AIDS. She is in South Africa for a reason—to hand-deliver presents to 50,000 children who, according to Oprah, have never received a single gift in their lives. This is a place where 1,700 people *daily* become afflicted with HIV and there are more than 14 million orphans (Karim and Karim 2005, 37). Oprah admits to the camera, "I knew we couldn't fix all that was wrong here, especially not in one trip." But she can and does bring jeans, shoes, sporting goods, school supplies, dolls, candy, and books to these beleaguered children.

The Oprah team (producers, cameramen, clowns, personal assistants, drivers, pilots, set crews, Stedman and Gayle) visits two regions—KwaZula-Natal and the Eastern Cape. The experience takes five months and over a hundred people to create and produce. It is all deemed to be "worth it." Oprah remarks, "For me, it would be the best Christmas I've ever known!"

But the experience comes with major challenges.

First, the plan is so ambitious, the Oprah team doesn't know if they can pull it off. Then the torrential rain begins, but by "some miracle" the rain ceases and the Oprah trucks roll on. The team erects a huge white tent at every stop, twelve times in two weeks. Children rush in and each receives a backpack stuffed with individual gifts. They walk miles in tattered shoes or no shoes at all to attend the celebration.

Nelson Mandela, South Africa's first democratically elected president and a man described by Oprah as one of her biggest heroes, flies to the celebration in a helicopter. Oprah and Mandela sit on an elevated stage watching the children sing and dance and clap below them on the grass.

Over the course of the entire trip, Oprah meets children from sixty-three different schools. These schools have broken windows and no pens and paper. But Oprah promises the children, "I grew up like many of you. No running water. No electricity, as a little girl. You can overcome poverty and despair in your life with an education. I am living proof of that."

To each crowd of children, Oprah declares, "Everybody here today will receive a present." And indeed, every girl gets a black doll, every boy a soccer ball. The children thank "Mama Oprah." Oprah tearfully states, "I would feel so lucky that I would get to do it all tomorrow."

Back in her Chicago studio, Oprah insists that the situations that many of the world's children live in are unacceptable. She remarks that if more of us *knew* about global issues, we would do something. She tells us that one in three South Africans is affected by HIV/AIDS, and children are abandoned, forced to survive on their own. There are so many children to be helped.

In Africa, she creates three huge Christmas parties for the kids hit hardest by poverty and HIV/AIDS. Christmas trees surrounded by wrapped presents fill the tent. The party has games, hot dogs, and Polaroids. This is the only picture that many of the children may ever have of themselves.

As the children unwrap the presents that Oprah's team hands out, Oprah begins to sob. She is so moved by witnessing the children's joy. She promises the children that people in the United States are thinking of them. She hugs the children and tells them that she loves them.

Again back in her studio, Oprah asks her at-home audience, "Have you ever known joy with a texture so thick you can physically feel it? I had a joy headache . . . These are my children . . . The spirit that burns alive in each of them does not die."

She tells of a girl named Esona whose mother lay dying of AIDS in a local clinic. Esona kept her mother's illness a secret for a long time because the disease is so stigmatized. Her mother is not able to receive any treatment because the clinic does not offer anti-retrovirals. The woman is treated for her symptoms, but she is left to die. The public policy, Oprah is told by clinicians, does not allow them to treat her for HIV.

As she discovers this, she begins to cry and repeats for the camera, "You do not have the drugs. That makes no sense to me." We see Oprah's emotion only. The dying woman is off camera. "I can see your spirit is strong," she tells a grieving Esona.

In Chicago, before Oprah breaks for a commercial, she promises, "When we come back, what you can do today! A child is orphaned by AIDS every fourteen seconds. So during this show 257 more children just like Esona will be left alone to fend for themselves."

Later she says, "My life was changed when I saw firsthand the devastation AIDS is having . . . As my friend Bono says, 'We have to help them right now.'" She describes Oprah's Angel Network and assures her audience: "It is my promise to you that your money will be spent to help a life that needs it . . . These children are just children. They're just like yours . . . They want to know that they matter . . . I promise you that the joy will be yours."

On camera, Oprah's entourage dutifully endorses what it feels like to help. One woman cries, "I wish I could take them all with me!" Another woman says, "What they have given to us is irreplaceable. It's something that money cannot buy." And yet ironically, massive amounts of money did buy it—whatever "it" is. A third staff member reports, "I've definitely been changed . . . It's never leaving our hearts." And a fourth rhapsodizes, "Over in America we read and study about it, but when you're here, it's beautiful." Which part is beautiful, a viewer might wonder: the devastation wrought by AIDS, the happiness in a child's face, or the rain-soaked African landscape?

As the segment concludes, laughing children run alongside the camera, waving and shouting to Oprah and her viewers. Back home in the studio, Oprah implores viewers to give to her foundation and tells us, "You, too, can have a joy headache."

The Politics of (Dis)Engagement

Surrounded by suffering children who are moved to laughter by cameras, gifts, and the presence of Mama Oprah herself, the CK narrative is nonetheless about Oprah. It is *Oprah's* quest for a meaningful (read *emotional*) Christmas that drives the team's adventure in South Africa. Camera shots and narrative strategically place Oprah qua celebrity at the center of the DVD segment. Children frolic in the background, but it is Oprah who sobs on close-up and tearfully questions the wisdom of the AIDS drug policy. It is Oprah who seems to be most affected by the ugly disease ravaging South Africa, not the stricken adults and orphaned children.

We are moved to care about the people of South Africa not because we witness with our own eyes the devastation wrought by AIDS and poverty (after all, we the viewers are not traveling in Africa), but because we see the devastation through Oprah's eyes, this celebrity with whom we are enamored and whose fame has claimed our allegiance (Gamson 1994). As philanthropic consumers and virtual tourists, we bear witness to *Oprah's* emotional journey. And in response, we open our checkbooks to save *her* South African homeland and *her* South African children, all fifty thousand of them.

And it should come as no surprise that viewers have responded generously to Oprah's causes, despite the fact that much of her audience has no prior connection to South African children. Oprah's relationship to her TV audience is one forged through consumption. Whether shopping for Oprah's favorite things or perusing *The Secret,* Oprah's audience buys, and buys into, whatever Oprah is selling. When Oprah promises viewers the possibility of a joy headache, she positions philanthropy as a pleasurable experience one can purchase through donating to the cause.

The success of "charitainment" is a testament to how powerfully celebrities such as Oprah mobilize feeling in the service of eliciting responses from their audiences. Oprah fosters momentary (and monetary) emotional responses from a largely American audience, but what she does not do is force her audience to ask themselves how the United States and its people are implicated in the problems she documents. By not locating Esona's mother's death in structural, cultural, and global webs of capital and politics, Oprah facilitates easy engagement while precluding the possibility of real social change.

For example, when Oprah asks why immunosuppressants are not dispensed at South African clinics, and she discovers that the clinics do not have any drugs, she cries, "I just don't understand." It is not that she, literally, does not understand; she is remarking on the absurdity of the situation. Why is it that drugs prolonging the lives of mothers and fathers exist, and yet these drugs are not accessible to the people that desperately need them? While Oprah asks the right questions, her interventions are never directed at the principle source of the suffering that she seeks to soothe. Her question implicates the pharmaceutical industry, global markets, capitalism, and foreign policy between "first" and "third" worlds. But rather than developing a critique of Big Pharma and asking her audience to boycott leading pharmaceutical firms, Oprah provides short-term material comfort to children who are suffering the devastation caused by the web of global political economies. And her audience is assured that they have done their part by purchasing their own joy headaches.

We ask: can structural change happen when "joy" is for the giver and not the recipient? If we position philanthropy as an effort aimed at promoting the common good and consumption as a means for satisfying individual need and desire, then philanthropy accomplished through consumption is more about the consumer than it is about who is supposed to be benefited by the charitable intervention. In the world of "charitainment," philanthropy serves as another mode of consumption aimed at self-improvement rather than geared toward structural and political change.

This is perhaps the most insidious consequence of philanthropic consumption mediated by celebrities. Active participation in celebrities' philanthropic work may raise funds, but it also principally fuels the production of celebrity. By lending support to charitable endeavors, consumers inevitably amplify a celebrity's popularity—and pocketbook. A celebrity with a successful charity is a well-regarded celebrity indeed. And it is precisely this celebrity culture and the industry that produces it that work *against* sustained social critique and corresponding long-term, thoughtful social action—no matter how many visits Oprah makes to Africa or how many conversations presidents have with Bono. By participating primarily through celebrity interventions such as Oprah's Angel Network or RED™, consumers inadvertently reproduce both a sense of helplessness *(How could I ever intervene on my own?)* and a limited understanding of issues that is simple and slick but pretends to be otherwise. In the end, we do more to advance celebrity careers and capitalism than we do to really save the world.

Change the World TV?

Unsurprisingly, in the spring of 2007, Oprah announced that she was adding to her media empire with a new reality television show, *Oprah's Big Give*. Participants competed against one another in philanthropic tasks. The participant who most creatively and successfully met each charitable challenge won a million-dollar prize. While we optimistically awaited its spring 2008 debut, hoping (though admittedly doubtful) that Oprah could facilitate the social engagement she appears so eager to incite, the show focused more on the personalities involved than the issues at hand. In the end, Oprah ultimately constructed another mode of philanthropic consumption aimed toward the audience's pleasure rather than lasting social change.

A more promising moment in Oprah history came in the late 1990s when Oprah posited a radically new television format she dubbed "Change Your Life TV." While critics slammed Oprah for supposing that daytime television could operate as anything other than a pacifying force, fans responded like never before. Oprah's popularity increased exponentially as audiences who many had written off as passive dupes organized book clubs, consciousness-raising groups, and weight-loss support systems. The change in format reimagined what TV could be and what it could elicit from its audience. We want to suggest that it is high time for another change in format. If there is any possibility of "Change the World TV," it will most certainly need to be produced by Oprah Winfrey. Few other celebrities have the power, clout, and political sensibilities to reshape an entire industry.

But what would life-changing and world-changing television look like? Rather than dismissing television or consumption of RED™ products altogether, we wonder about how television and shopping might be used innovatively. How would philanthropic consumption that effectively facilitated agency, cultural critique, and social action work? Could *The Oprah Winfrey Show*, and television generally, maximize the potential of its format by producing ongoing mini-series? Rather than limiting exploration of an issue to a single hour or, worse yet, a single segment, might television explore issues like AIDS in Africa, violence, and poverty over the course of multiple episodes? Such an approach might allow for examining the complexity of social problems, perhaps facilitating real interventions. Might RED™ products be sold with slickly designed booklets that describe the causes of the problems proceeds benefit, possible policy solutions, along with opportunities for ongoing participation in organizations aimed toward eradicating global health crises?

The biggest challenge for an Oprah-led "Change the World TV" and for philanthropic consumption more generally is to complicate the pleasure of consumption gained through philanthropic intervention. The problems of Africa that Oprah identifies require sustained, structural interventions and participation that extend beyond a charitable contribution. Oprah's audience cannot consume away the horror of untreated HIV/AIDS, the history of poverty, or the trauma of children routinely orphaned. To be the change that they seem to want to see in the world, Oprah's audience may have to be convinced that there is something to be gained—beyond a joy headache—from philanthropy and political engagement.

Notes

1. One hundred percent of the proceeds of the sale of the collection are directed to Oprah's Angel Network, a charitable foundation dedicated to education and advancement of women and children around the world. To date, Oprah's Angel network has raised $50 million, including $9 million in response to the televised coverage of the Christmas Kindness.

2. We are fascinated by the appropriation of the language and color of communism (and of blood) for this profit-making philanthropic enterprise. Bono (2007) has linked the color red to emergencies.

Works Cited

Alcabes, Philip. 2006. "Heart of Darkness: AIDS, Africa, and Race." *The Virginia Quarterly Review* 82, no. 1: 5–9.

Alexander, Mary. 2005. "Spirit and Hope in SA: Oprah." South Africa Info. June 13. http://www .southafrica.info/what_happening/news/oprah-130605.htm.

BBC News/Africa. "US Chat Show Host Could Be a Zulu," BBC News, http://news.bbc.co.uk/1/hi/ world/africa/4096706.stm

Bono. 2007. "Guest Editor's Letter: Message 2U." *Vanity Fair*, July, 32.

Cowell, Alan. 2005. "Celebrities' Embrace of Africa Has Critics." *New York Times*, July 1, 3.

Dive, Serge. 2008. "Luxury & Philanthropy," http://www.kiwicollection.com/around_world_detail/ ITEM=84/.

Ferguson, James. 2006. *Global Shadows: Africa in the Neoliberal World Order.* Durham, N.C.: Duke University Press.

Fowler, Ian. "The RED Campaign: Are We Really Feeling the Pain?," g-think, http://www.g-think .com/gt/articles/article/129.

Gamson, Joshua. 1994. *Claims to Fame: Celebrity in Contemporary America.* Berkeley: University of California Press.

Gates, Henry Louis, Jr. 2007. *Finding Oprah's Roots: Finding Your Own.* New York: Crown.

Karim, S.S. Abdool, and Q. Abdool Karim, eds. 2005. *HIV/AIDS in South Africa.* Cambridge, Eng.: Cambridge University Press.

Munnion, Christopher. 2005. "Oprah's Baffling Claim of Zulu Blood." *The Daily Telegraph.* June 14.

Nickel, Patricia Mooney, and Angela M. Eikenberry. Forthcoming. "A Critique of the Discourse of Marketized Philanthropy." *American Behavioral Scientist.*

The Oprah Winfrey Show: 20th Anniversary DVD Collection. 2005. Paramount Pictures.

Poniewozik, James. 2005. "The Year of Charitainment." *Time*, December 19, 93–94.

Sayers, Robin. 2006. "Countless Stars, One Campaign." *In Style*, September, 562.

Williams, Alex. 2006. "Into Africa," *New York Times*, August 13, 9.

Part III

The Oprahfication of Media

CHAPTER EIGHT

Oprah and the New News

KATHLEEN DIXON AND KACIE JOSSART

In March 2002, Matthew A. Baum reported in the *American Political Science Review* that increasing numbers of Americans were acquiring their news from so-called "soft" news sources. These sources, according to Baum, are primarily "daytime and late-night talk shows and entertainment and tabloid news programs." Citing Neilson ratings from 1999, Baum points out that *Winfrey*, with more than 6.4 million households viewing the program, was "watched by about as many households as the evening newscasts of the major networks" and had *seventeen times* as many viewers as CNN for the same six-month period (92). His argument is that media sources, by "repackaging" news stories within an entertainment medium, "create a dynamic that increases public awareness of political issues" (91).

The distinctions between "hard" and "soft" news, however, have become increasingly blurred over the past decades owing to late capitalism's consolidation of media ownership and technological innovations that arguably have had deleterious effects on television news. W. Lance Bennett, in *News: The Politics of Illusion*, for example, highlights the recent trend in "hard" news sources to increase the use of dramatic narratives in the ongoing battle for ratings and cites one "executive news producer of a major television network" as sending a memo to his editors and reporters that spelled out this trend: "Every news story should, without any sacrifice of probity or responsibility, display the attributes of fiction, of drama. It should have structure and conflict, problem and denouement, rising action and falling action, a beginning, middle, and an end. These are not only the essentials of drama; they are the essentials of narrative" (1988, 35).

The network news managers are forced to adopt these Winfrey-like practices to woo a fickle and fading audience (ibid.). But Winfrey has already achieved this seduction through a multitude of hybrid operations. To begin with, she gravitated to the talk show because it was a feminine, relatively undefined form. Bernard Timberg says, "The range of talk . . . has always been very wide" (2; see pp. 7–8 for a discussion of the afternoon talk show). But her rather masculine success as a businesswoman who owns her studio—only the third woman, after Mary Pickford and Lucille Ball, to do so—allows her to call the shots. If she wants to spend an entire hour on a story, as she has with several on the aftermath of Hurricanes Katrina and Rita or on global warming, she can. If she as host wants to morph from one role to another, she can. This creates the variety in her show that network news executives struggle to achieve, often failing in the process (note the hiring of Katie Couric to anchor *CBS Evening News*). And it is done in the service of Winfrey's didactic vision, described by Nancy Koehn in the following fashion: "Winfrey adopted a mission of helping her viewers live better lives through self-improvement and self-awareness. . . . According to its official mission statement, Harpo's goal was 'to be a catalyst for transformation in people's lives, to help them see themselves more clearly and to make the best choices they can using stories, real people's experiences, information and ideas'" (Koehn and Helms 2005, 16).

Winfrey's show is in some sense less a genre than a slice of life for her home audience. It moves from type to type and topic to topic as the need arises. This juggling act is what "women's work" has consisted of for millennia, one reason of many that Winfrey's audience "relates" to both her and the show. Depending upon how one codes the content, maybe only as much as 20 percent of the recent shows are in any way "political" or news-oriented. But they arguably pack a more powerful punch in their canny address to an audience that has shaped and been shaped by Winfrey. These newer shows demonstrate Winfrey's resourcefulness in remaining true to what we might say is the feminine source of her power while advancing into what has traditionally been more masculine territory.

Rhetoric and Melodrama

The terms "rhetoric" and "melodrama" historically denote different uses of language and gesture. Aristotle famously separated rhetoric from poetics. In what we have of the *Poetics*, he treats only drama, apparently according the highest honors to tragedy. Melodrama is often considered a modern and popular art form, but it does exhibit some of the magnitude of ancient Greek tragedy, with an emphasis on spectacle and a narrative line of peaks and valleys—perhaps eliciting Aristotle's terror and pity. In any case, melodrama may be what we moderns have instead of tragedy. Democracy, capitalism, and the scientific/ technological revolutions have combined to present the ordinary person a paradox: more than ever, power resides in the individual; more than ever, it does not. Even today, Third World people are "liberated" from manual agrarian labor only to find themselves without home or livelihood. First World college students, too, fear unemployment, or the cycle back to (this time, urban) manual labor in the "service sector." As Everywoman or man scans the cosmos for a moral order in these times of rapid, extreme, and impersonal change, melodrama is there to offer some clarity together with the necessity of emotional release and satisfaction (Brooks 1985, 42). Melodramas are meant to make us jeer at the vile villains and to weep at the suffering of virtuous victim-heroes[9] who, on the screen if nowhere else, are readily identifiable.

Melodrama is a modern development with roots in eighteenth-century Western European tragedy and sentimental drama. By the nineteenth century, it was forming out of a motley assortment of high and low cultural genres, "including Shakespearean tragedies, popular fiction (especially gothic), Romantic poetry, operatic libretti, newspaper and topical events, police journals and penny dreadfuls, paintings and etchings, popular songs and street ballads" (Gledhill 1987, 16–18). Silent films such as "The Perils of Pauline" are still recognized today in popular discourse as exemplary of the melodramatic narrative, featuring angelic young maidens in distress, victimized by moustache-twirling villains and rescued by bold and handsome heroes. The cliffhanger was sometimes literal (a type of peril) but came to refer to a break in the narrative that kept the audience "hanging": "To be continued." Television soap operas picked up this serial form, and also hewed to the same moral polarities; they, however, moved to a domestic setting. The afternoon television talk show of the 1980s and 1990s continued in the domestic vein, forging melodramatic narratives out of the testimonies of ordinary women, mainly, who were victims of abuse, discrimination, horrific accidents, and the like (Shattuc 1997, Grindstaff 2002). *The Oprah Winfrey Show* came to prominence purveying this type of melodrama.

And what of rhetoric? In Aristotle's formulation it differed from literary art in its specific address to the audience on topics of the day, rather than a performance expressing universal truths of human existence. Rhetoric aims to move its audience not primarily to an elevated and feeling contemplation, as art would do, but to belief or action in the public sphere. For Aristotle, rhetoric was not necessarily a suspect practice. It at least had the capacity for a balance among three kinds of appeals to the audience: logos (the appeal to reason), ethos (the appeal to character, especially that of the orator's), and pathos (the appeal to emotion). Modernity has issued many challenges to Aristotle's careful ordering of this triad—logos first, pathos last—but Western rationalist ideals have often governed *pro forma*, anyway, until very recently. The so-called hard news of Walter Cronkite's day appealed to reason through the use of factual evidence presented in lucid, organized fashion in direct, informal prose. Skeptical reporters who traded in literate wit and street cred, both masculine preserves, gathered "the facts." They built their ethos that way, like soldiers in a dirty war, but also relied upon the reflected avuncular authority of Cronkite, who at times, it seemed, became the voice of a nation. When he wiped a tear from his eye at the death of JFK, that was justifiable pathos and nurturing ethos.

Of the many changes that have transpired from that moment to this, one is clear: while rhetoric is shifting to pathos and ethos, melodrama as a mode—not always as rhetoric—has only increased its position. It holds sway on local, network, and cable news, on reality TV shows, in Hollywood blockbuster films and ESPN, on *People* magazine and *ET Tonight*. What used to be dismissed as a "feminine genre" can now be understood as everybody's "cultural mode" to use Linda Williams's phrase. Williams's notion is that the mode can morph, leaping from genre to genre, medium to medium; that's one reason that melodrama has cropped up everywhere. It may be well to remember, however, that rhetoric, in Plato's view, had something of the same plastic quality. A rhetorician plied the "art" of merely seeming truthful or knowledgeable on any topic whatsoever. Today's master rhetorician would do well to understand the mode of melodrama as an important contributor to the art of modern rhetoric and to know how it can operate effectively within a mediated world of rapidly swirling images, propelling and propelled by virtual capitalism.

So, both melodrama and rhetoric can expand, contract, transform, and move quickly, according to need. Both melodrama and rhetoric can and do involve drama and acting (in classical rhetoric, this references the fifth canon, delivery). Given the visual nature of modern media, rhetoric in the age of electronic, as opposed to print, media devolves to its origins as public performance (Barilli 1989, 125–29), something television news was slow to learn. But the big divide between melodrama and rhetoric—that the latter is more specifically instrumental—may be bridged by Linda Williams's concept of melodrama. For her, melodrama is a dialectic between strong pathos and action. The former is what most people associate with melodrama, and, as we have said, it is gendered feminine and easily dismissed. But action, especially "prolonged climactic action," is the byword of the Hollywood blockbuster, and even includes "classic" gangster and detective films (21). It is, of course, gendered masculine, and thereby earns the kind of respect that is rarely given to, say, *Oprah*. Nor must this action remain within the confines of fiction. Sentimental novels such as *Uncle Tom's Cabin* (treated in Williams's book) "painted metaphorical pictures of pathos and action that moved readers to strong emotion and occasionally even to action" (13). It is out of this fabric that Winfrey has fashioned a new rhetoric, a form of advocacy journalism that is expressed both on the set at Harpo Studios and on location via pre-filmed sequences.

Perhaps one of the best examples of Winfrey's use of the melodramatic aesthetic and appropriation of journalistic conventions is illustrated in a short excerpt that introduces her first "Town Hall" meeting, entitled, "Truth in America." (27 October 2006). The excerpt opens with a shot of Frank Rich's *The Greatest Story Ever Sold: The Decline and Fall of the Truth* highlighted on a shot of the *New York Times* Best-Seller list, while a deep, pounding, suspenseful soundtrack plays in the background. Winfrey's voice-over is simultaneously provocative and institutional, accompanied by a mix of melodramatic images and video clips that are directly related to her rhetoric: "This week, it's number two on the *New York Times* Best-Seller list. Frank Rich's new book, *The Greatest Story Ever Sold: The Decline and Fall of the Truth*, is a controversial and searing indictment of the Bush administration, challenging the reasons America went to war with Iraq."

The images flash by on the screen, some frozen, others highlighted by action: a fixed image of President Bush seated at a table surrounded by his advisors, all of them dressed in formal business attire, followed by action clips of American soldiers in Iraq, running down the street, shooting their weapons at unseen enemies while bombs explode nearby. The sounds of machine gun fire and explosions add to the drama, and the pounding music continues to crescendo, while Winfrey's voice-over continues: "First, Rich says, that in order to gain support for the war, the White House suggested there was connections [sic] between al-Qaeda and Saddam Hussein." A frozen shot of Bush speaking to the press is followed by photos of Osama bin Laden and Hussein, which are eventually placed side-by-side on the screen. Winfrey asserts: "Rich argues there was no such connections [sic]," as both images quickly vanish, replaced by an action clip of the Two Towers, fire and smoke billowing into the air. Photos of press conferences with Bush, who appears smiling and relaxed, follow, while Winfrey states, "Next, Rich takes the news media to task for not asking the hard questions in the aftermath of 9/11, even criticizing his own paper, the *New York Times*. And finally," Winfrey's voice continues, as the images blur in the background and the white, shadow words, "24/7," "Infotainment," and

"Critical Thinking" all slowly flash and then fade across the screen, "Frank Rich argues that our overheated, 24/7 infotainment culture, from cable news to the tabloids, has conditioned us to stop engaging in critical thinking. This is what he says."

More action-packed images of war and destruction follow, with American soldiers running for their lives as explosions occur all around them while Winfrey finishes: "According to Frank Rich, in this environment, where he says drama counts more than judicious journalism, the line between truth and fiction becomes blurred and that has made us a society that rarely questions what we are told and a society that is easily manipulated." During this final piece, frozen shots of the provoking "Mission Accomplished" sign and Jessica Lynch are followed with more shadow words that flash and fade across the screen: "Truth," "Rarely Questions," and "Easily Manipulated."

This particular excerpt is intriguing for a variety of reasons: first, it reflects the high quality of production that has become commonplace on *Oprah* and that helps to set it apart from other daytime talk shows. Second, it illustrates Winfrey's use of rational "hard" news conventions like an institutional tone and news footage of actual events, while remaining situated squarely within the sensational—swelling music, explosions, gunfire, and the pastiche of provocative images and words flashing and fading across the screen with dramatic speed. Finally, in spite of her skeptical institutional tone and careful language, Winfrey clearly intends this piece to be persuasive. While she *says*, "Frank Rich argues . . ." and "according to Rich . . . ," emulating the language and tone of objectivity one might hear from more "serious" or "hard" news sources, the melodramatic *images* that flash across the screen actually reinforce all of the claims that Winfrey attributes to Rich, belying this supposed neutrality and revealing the excerpt's persuasive intent.

This rhetoric also proposes action. The Rich episode is one of Winfrey's town hall programs that invite the studio audience to ask questions. The questioners seem to have been chosen before filming, for they leap up with alacrity, one at a time, before a roving microphone. Nonetheless, the questions seem genuine, and a dialogue between the audience member and Rich—initiated by Winfrey—does occur. Here is an example of the first exchange between the audience and guest.

WINFREY: Who here believes that we were not deliberately lied to [by the Bush administration about the reasons for going to war in Iraq]? Not? Yes? Hi.

UNIDENTIFIED WOMAN #5: I don't believe we were deliberately lied to. And if you look at the history in regards to all the intelligence, not only did President

Bush get the same intelligence, but so did President Clinton. And the bottom line is this: Saddam Hussein himself could have stopped this war. He did not comply with the UN. He did not comply with the weapons inspectors. What else were we to do as a nation?

RICH: Well, according to the Hans Blix report, Saddam was cooperating and what Blix told the UN was, "just give us a few more months. He's now opening up the sites to us. Let us go in." For whatever reason, we called it back and ended it, and ended that containment. On your first point, there was some intelligence that was good.

WOMAN #5: Right.

RICH: There was some intelligence saying there was no connection with 9/11. I guess the issue is, is it enough to go to war with Saddam if he wasn't planning to send a mushroom cloud our way? That's something you could debate. Take him out 'cause he's a horrible guy, a terrible dictator.

WOMAN #5: Right. Which he was.

RICH: That—which he definitely was. A horrible person in history.

WOMAN #5: Right.

RICH: But that wasn't the reason they gave us. That's the reason they talk about now. But before the war, it was all, a smoking gun will be a mushroom cloud, there could be a nuclear bomb in a major city. And there was no evidence to support that.

WOMAN #5: Did someone from the Bush administration directly say that Iraq was a link?

RICH: I'll let you be the judge. They never said Saddam Hussein ordered the attacks of 9/11.

WOMAN #5: Right.

RICH: Absolutely they never said that. But Dick Cheney, for instance, repeatedly said, "We know Mohamed Atta met with intelligence agents from the Saddam Hussein regime in the months before 9/11 in Prague." That meeting never happened.

WOMAN #5: Suggested that, yeah.

RICH: So it's the power of suggestion. So . . .

WINFREY: Well, let's ask this audience—let's ask this audience, before we went to war, were you under the impression that Saddam Hussein and Iraq had something to do with 9/11? Were you? Were you not? You did not think so? [pointing at an audience member] Yes, ma'am, you wanted to raise your hand? Hi.

UNIDENTIFIED WOMAN #6: I would like to say that one of the clearest ways to get your message through and be credible is by not saying it. It's by innuendo, it's by implication, it's by mindwashing.

The dialogue moves quickly because the show's production keeps the transitions between segments and speakers seamless, and yet, there is just enough questioning and hesitation (note Winfrey's questions before alighting on Woman #6) to maintain the feel of spontaneity. Even though these questioners were almost certainly chosen before the show, they do appear to be using their own language, and genuinely interacting with the guest and Winfrey. This is important, and less because of the treatment of the studio audience than that of the home audience, for they are being symbolically invoked. We in the home audience are treated to a dialogue that is rarely offered on any popular television show. Perhaps the reason that Winfrey has the courage to offer such fare—and during the "frivolous" afternoon hours, no less—is that she has a historic connection with her audience. She understands that they want to be entertained but she also seems to believe that they would like to be addressed as thinking adults—sometimes, at least. On this day, the home audience is meant to understand that they, too, are invited to be assertive, questioning citizens—within very definite bounds of civility (and the bounds of television production), enforced on stage by Winfrey herself. Whether the audience is invited to question Winfrey and the melodramatic production of her television program, however, is left unaddressed.

From Angel in the House to Angel Network

The masculine has enjoyed a longer presence in the public sphere and can be well represented in both melodrama and rhetoric; the feminine has been obliged to invent and adapt. In the West, women began to enter the public sphere in large numbers in the nineteenth century, and as they did so, they brought with them the values associated with that "other" sphere. Feminist film scholar Christine Gledhill describes the domestic or sentimental foundation of melodrama:

[M]elodrama's challenge lies not in confronting how things are, but rather in asserting how they ought to be. But since it operates within the frameworks of the present social order, melodrama conceives "the promise of human life" not as a revolutionary future, but rather as a return to a "golden past": less how things ought to be than how they should have been. The Edenic home and family, centring on the heroine as "angel in the house" and the rural community of an earlier generation, animate images of past psychic and social well-being as "moral touchstones" against which the instabilities of capitalist expansion and retraction could be judged and in which both labourer and middle-class citizen could confront the hostilities of the modern world. (1987, 21)

In almost every way, this quotation suits *Oprah*. The "family" on *The Oprah Winfrey Show* is complex and modern, but it functions also as a "moral touchtone." There are times on the show when one wonders whether the "golden past" on *Oprah* might be the 1960s of U.S. history. Quite obviously, the "angel in the house" morphs into the cyborgian woman who logs onto Winfrey's Angel Network website and uses her credit card to donate "an end table" (actually suggested on the site) to victims of Hurricane Katrina. Because the politics of *The Oprah Winfrey Show* are patently not "revolutionary," but mildly reformist, Winfrey will at times hide behind the vagueness of a golden past to avoid direct confrontations with powerful others (or even with the source of her own capitalist power). But though *The Oprah Winfrey Show* moves through Gledhill's melodramatic tradition, Winfrey does ultimately create out of it a melodramatic rhetoric of action in the present moment.

It begins by constituting a new modern space for the rhetorician as family member. We can see this at work in the episode "Living on the Minimum Wage," featuring guest Morgan Spurlock and his wife, Alex, who also appears as his latter-day hippie, vegan girlfriend in his film, *Supersize Me*, a kind of experiential expose of the risks to health posed by eating fast food. Spurlock now has a reality show on the cable channel FX that claims to document thirty days in the life of a person who agrees to live in a radically new social environment (such as a white bigot living with a black family); it is a show with definite liberal political overtones. On this *Winfrey* episode, Spurlock and Alex agree to live for a month on minimum-wage jobs.

The minimum-wage program features talk with Spurlock, Alex, and Winfrey on stage before the studio audience, interwoven with prefilmed segments that mimic the kind of reality TV Spurlock produces for FX. Moving back and forth between the two, Winfrey is able to question the guests and to emphasize key moments of experiential logos—the primary form of knowledge that the show offers, other than a few facts proffered in the opening monologue—and pathos from the filmed narrative. The whole builds an ethos of sincerity and concern on the part of both Winfrey and guests. These are modernist elements. As modern collage, the program is a combination of Spurlock's *30 Days* (itself quite hybridized) and *Oprah*. Winfrey has combined on her own show some trendy variety together with substantive "content" (as the media executives refer to it) at relatively little expense. She adapts Spurlock's show to the needs of her audience through framing devices, interrogative dialogue, and the addition of the kaffeeklatsch intimacy of Winfrey in the onstage "live" portion of the program. Finally, she has simultaneously promoted a show she presumably believes in that has lower ratings than hers.

Time and again the new *Oprah* creates a space of celebrity "family" that is promotional of a particular political idea or charity, of the specific celebrities and their products (recent films or CDs they've made), and of Winfrey and all of her products. But Winfrey is clearly the head of this capitalist and virtual family, and in this position she often revises the role of rhetorician to fit her feminine body. Time and again Winfrey reinvents herself on stage or in a prefilmed sequence as someone with authority who more or less governs the proceedings. Winfrey's privileged behind-the-scenes knowledge of the Spurlock film boosts her authoritative ethos as talk show host and newsmagazine anchor. On the global warming episode, Winfrey sits stationary on a stool while Al Gore strides the stage during and between video clips of his film, *An Inconvenient Truth*. Again she poses questions, but this time it is as though she is the professor hosting a guest lecturer. For the Hurricanes Katrina and Rita episodes, she is the "on location" news anchor, with celebrities like Julia Roberts and real CNN reporters Lisa Ling and Anderson Cooper acting as her correspondents. Nor does she forget her own television roots, we might say. She often positions herself as "girlfriend"—to take a term from Masciarotte (this is, after all, not a biological family; Winfrey herself is not even married). After Spurlock "confesses" (on the "Confession Camera") that he went hungry trying to live on the minimum wage, Winfrey responds naively: "Wow! I never thought of that." In this manner, she continues to court her audience, while offering them honorary membership in her "family" of mostly celebrities but occasionally also intellectuals and artists (especially in the Book Club episodes of recent years), liberal activists (like Spurlock), philanthropists, and liberal politicians.

The audience is also directly addressed on Oprah as mothers and daughters who are still subject to "the hostilities of the modern world" but who, on the new *Oprah*, are increasingly positioned as women of some privilege. At the beginning of the minimum wage show, the audience sees Winfrey first, dressed conservatively in dark colors, in medium shot with a video screen behind and to her right that projects the title of today's show. She looks into the camera and delivers the introduction. We will join mid-paragraph:

That's $8,000 less than what our government even considers poverty. The truth is that one out of every four workers earns even less than $8.70 an hour. Could you raise your children on that? Well, millions of people are. And why should you care? Because they are the very people that we all rely on each and every day. They are teacher's aides in your children's classroom, they are caring for your aging parents in a nursing home, they make sure that your hotel runs and your offices and schools are clean, security guards keeping buildings safe, paramedics who are there in your most desperate hour.

So our goal today is to open your eyes and hopefully your hearts to the millions of people around us who work thankless jobs for very little pay. (28 July 2006)

Early on, melodrama is implicit and/or lightly offered by means of intensifying words and Winfrey's own dramatic delivery ("what our *government even* considers poverty"). It then opens up with a long, five-clause compound sentence—the kind only spoken in conversation by someone who is passionate—and ends on an obviously melodramatic note of imagined suffering ("paramedics, who are there in your most *desperate* hour," emphasis Winfrey's). The explicit advocacy of the working poor, not something that television journalists sworn to objectivity are generally allowed to include in a news story even in these modern times, is the mark of Winfrey's new intimacy with her audience. Winfrey, who has shared personal heartache, bra style, and "my favorite things" with her audience, now shares her "goal" with them: "to open your eyes and hopefully your hearts."[1]

That the latter suggests audience action (digging into their pocketbooks and remembering social issues in the voting booth) can be deduced from a number of contextual clues. Viewers can at any time donate to the Angel Network, her charity organization (also linked to Winfrey's website and mentioned in her magazine, *O, The Oprah Magazine*); the audience was explicitly asked to do so during the shows on Hurricanes Katrina and Rita. Viewers are invoked as voters when the show features political guests (and increasingly the balance is in favor of liberals). A number of such guests appeared before the 2006 midterm election: Al Gore, Barack Obama, *New York Times* political reporter Frank Rich, and political commentator Bill O'Reilly, New Orleans mayor Ray Nagin. Winfrey herself finally made it clear whom she supported for president, Barack Obama (she endorsed him on the show). She adds this explicit political action to her already established philanthropic activities, for which she not only donates her own funds, but consciously acts as a role model before her viewers. Many of the celebrities who appear on her show are also positioned as philanthropic role models. Later in the program on the minimum wage, the invoking of the audience to action is continued by Spurlock's wife Alex, tearful over the generosity of a church organization in a poor neighborhood: "They have nothing and they give everything away that they have."

On September 6, 2005, Winfrey aired a program entitled "Winfrey on Location: Inside the Katrina Catastrophe." In this episode, she interviews New

Orleans Mayor Ray Nagin on the street in front of the Hyatt Hotel in New Orleans in the days following the hurricane and evacuation of hundreds of thousands of New Orleans residents. He describes the horrific conditions experienced by Katrina survivors during the five days they spent inside the Superdome awaiting federal intervention in the way of essential resources like water and food, and recounts examples of various atrocities experienced by women and children victims during this time, such as rape and murder. After Nagin becomes visibly choked up and walks away from the interview, Winfrey first faces her crew and then looks directly into the camera, declaring through tears as she stamps her feet and waves a fist in the air, "This makes me so mad! This makes me so mad. This should not have happened. This should not have happened."

In this episode, Winfrey does not attempt to lay blame at the feet of any particular individual or institution, instead focusing on *how things should have been*: she is clear in articulating the tragedy through the lens of moral responsibility, and in delivering a synergistic appeal to her predominantly middle-class female audience to help her set things right. She begins and ends in the space of innocence, portraying Katrina survivors as "virtuous victims" and the bureaucrats who prevented them from receiving timely assistance as the potential villains of this particular melodrama, while managing to distance herself from a political position that would alienate members of her audience who consider themselves politically conservative. There are veiled references to "the feds" and to the lack of response as being "about politics," but Winfrey is careful to avoid a specific political affiliation or clear accusations against specific persons or entities.

Further, rather than emphasizing the potential role of race or class in the lack of prompt federal response, Winfrey encourages others, like Nagin, to broach the issue, allowing her to appear to inhabit a neutral, objective position that enhances her ethos. Bennett points out that "journalists play their gatekeeper role (or, if you prefer, exercise their power) in a low-key way that seems to avoid taking sides" (15), and Winfrey's approach in these episodes reflects her awareness of the idealized role the American journalist is supposed to play under such circumstances. She is no stranger to the conventions of news: she was a ten-year veteran of local television news when she took over as anchor for *A.M. Chicago*, the program that eventually became nationally syndicated as *The Oprah Winfrey Show*. A former black beauty queen who was often disparaged for her looks on white-owned television shows (Manga 2003, 28), she also knows the limits of objectivity. It would be difficult, indeed, to believe that she does not know how her black female body "reads" to her mainstream audience, or how Nagin's would. Here is a visual version of ethos. That it should go unheralded does lend an added gravitas.

Communications scholar John Corner is interested in the hybridization of news, "the mixing of elements from what were previously distinct conventions, thus breaking down some of the older genres, including those dividing 'higher' from 'lower' forms or demarcating the 'serious' from the 'entertaining'" (90). Certainly the new *Oprah* shows demonstrate this. On the episode aired on the Katrina disaster, for instance, the program opens not within the traditional studio set employed by *The Oprah Winfrey Show* but with a head-and-shoulders shot of Winfrey seated at a desk, directly addressing her viewing audience. Her hair is pulled back tightly, and she is wearing a conservative, button-down, pale blue blouse. Behind her is a backdrop of a shot of post-Katrina New Orleans. News anchor Winfrey uses the serious tone and reporting style of the evening news: "With the city underwater and under siege, we found Mayor Ray Nagin, who refused to evacuate." The cameras cut immediately to an excerpt providing graphic images of the catastrophic destruction of downtown New Orleans, complete with melodramatic background music, and Winfrey, performing as both news anchor and reporter, narrates as the footage plays: "All week long, Mayor Ray Nagin never left his city. I found him at his command post, at the Hyatt Hotel." What follows is the prerecorded interview footage mentioned earlier, originally filmed using handheld cameras, a move that simultaneously reinforces Winfrey's ethos and pathos: the sense of immediacy transmitted by footage that appears to be less edited and produced than the excerpts between which it is sandwiched. The use of text at the bottom of the screen, "Winfrey: Live on Location in New Orleans," appears throughout the program; that, and the institutional manner in which the footage is introduced, mimic the conventions of "hard" or "serious" news sources, which lends the episode the ethos that is both consciously and unconsciously associated with hard news, while simultaneously blurring the boundaries between the "serious" and the "entertaining." The dramatic interview with Nagin, during which both he and Winfrey are moved to tears and anger over the unnecessary suffering of the hurricane victims, makes a candid appeal to the viewer's emotions.

But what most distinguishes the new Winfrey is that, as she says in the minimum wage episode, she has "a goal." And it is not simply to make more money (Koehn and Helms 2005, 18). Winfrey does endorse products and engages in product giveaways, sometimes in a showy fashion. Her programs contain plenty of commercials. She charges television stations top dollar to air her syndicated show (7–9). This distance between the rich and the poor the show does sometimes deliberately thematize, including in the episodes on Hurricanes Katrina and Rita. A rare television silence accompanies before-and-after stills or moving images of people's homes, and even bodies. Shiny new

FEMA trailers are repeatedly juxtaposed with muddy tents. Winfrey sometimes speaks, apparently frankly, about what it means to be rich and to have a conscience.

The Angel Network, according to the Oprah website, has raised more than $50 million since its inception in 1998 in its efforts to "help underserved people rise to their own potential" (www.oprah.com). The Network provides funds for scholarships to Boys and Girls Clubs of America; for Habitat for Humanity, which builds homes for the poor; to build schools in rural areas in ten different countries; and to help provide food, clothes, and education to children in South Africa, among many others. Winfrey reinforces her already well-established ethos through her own personal philanthropy: by paying 100 percent of the operating and fundraising costs out of her own pocket for the Network, she assures her viewers that their entire donation will be used for charitable purposes (www.oprah.com). We should observe, in the body of our text rather than in a footnote, that Winfrey's Angel Network has received the highest rating possible by Charity Navigator, an organization that examines the forms that charities use to report their income to the government.

Perhaps Winfrey's use of melodrama reinstates the "suffering" victor as the virtuous victim, as Williams says often happens in popular melodramatic texts. Perhaps the gift of an end table salves the viewer's conscience. But it may be that the real power of the new *Oprah* lies not in the money that it raises but in the influence it is having on mainstream politics. Centrists and liberals cast wide but not deep. In the end, it is impossible to know how or whether the new *Oprah* does more harm than good in its inculcation of a hyper-capitalist and consumerist ethos side-by-side that of a virtual "caring" family—a family that votes and performs good deeds. What we do see is that, given the right conditions and the resources—including, in this case, a talent for melodramatic rhetoric—the public sphere is capable of some kind of reconstitution. The show provides firm evidence that such a thing is indeed occurring.

Notes

1. Interesting, too, that she addresses the audience with the assumption that her viewers are not those employed in these positions (as teacher's aide, nursing home assistant, or paramedic, for example)—that her audience, in this specific spiel, doesn't *include* women she would categorize as the "working poor" (they are the object here, instead)—even while we know that they do, indeed, make up a portion of her audience.

Works Cited

Aristotle. 1926. *The "Art" of Rhetoric*. Tr. John Henry Freese. Cambridge, Mass.: Harvard University Press, 1991.

Baum, Matthew. 2002. "Sex, Lies, and War: How Soft News Brings Foreign Policy to the Inattentive Public." *American Political Science Review* 96: 91–109.

Barilli, Renato. 1989. *Rhetoric*. Minneapolis: University of Minneapolis Press.

Bennett, W. Lance. 1988. *News: The Politics of Illusion*. New York: Longman.

Brooks, Peter. 1985. *The Melodramatic Imagination*. New York: Columbia University Press.

Corner, John. 1998. *Studying Media: Problems of Theory and Method*. Edinburgh: Edinburgh University Press.

Gledhill, Christine. 1987. "'The Melodramatic Field: An Investigation." In *Home is Where the Heart Is*. London: British Film Institute.

Grindstaff, Laura. 2002. *The Money Shot: Trash, Class, and The Making of TV Talk Shows*. Chicago: University of Chicago Press.

Koehn, Nancy F., and Erica Helms. 2005. *Oprah Winfrey*. Cambridge: Harvard Business School.

Manga, Julie. 2003. *Talking Trash: The Cultural Politics of Daytime TV Talk Shows*. New York: New York University Press.

Oprah.com. "Angel Network." http://www.oprah.com/uyl/angel/uyl_angelabout.jhtml

Shattuc, Jane M. 1997. *The Talking Cure: TV Talk Shows and Women*. New York and London: Routledge.

Timberg, Bernard M. 2002. *Television Talk: A History of the TV Talk Show*. Austin: University of Texas Press.

Williams, Linda. 2001. *Playing the Race Card: Melodramas of Black and White from Uncle Tom to O.J. Simpson*. Princeton: Princeton University Press.

The Oprahfication of 9/11

September 11, the War in Iraq, and The Oprah Winfrey Show

JAAP KOOIJMAN

On September 11 and 12, 2001, for the first time in its fifteen-year run, *The Oprah Winfrey Show* was cancelled. The talk show resumed its daily broadcast on September 13 with an episode aptly entitled "America Under Attack," which was repeated the next day. The cancellation of *Oprah* fit the state of confusion that American television immediately found itself in right after the terrorist attacks. On the one hand, 9/11 was a television event. From the moment the first plane hit the Twin Towers, millions of viewers around the world stayed glued to their television sets to capture the latest news and to relive the moment again and again. Yet, on the other hand, the flow of American television had been interrupted, as its regular programming was replaced by nonstop commercial-free news coverage and other "appropriate" content. As Lynn Spigel has shown, American television needed just a little time to regain its balance between public service and commercial interest, quickly returning to the programming that "channeled the nation back to normalcy—or at least to the normal flows of television and commercial culture" (Spigel 2004, 239). Within two weeks after 9/11, *Oprah* too returned to normalcy, with an episode of "Oprah's Book Club" (24 September 2001) and, four days later, an episode on "What Parents Should Know About Ecstasy" (28 September 2001).

In this chapter, I will discuss how *The Oprah Winfrey Show* presented the aftermath of 9/11 and the pending war in Iraq in its episodes. These episodes are relevant, as they show how political issues as international terrorism and warfare can be translated into a personal experience of the political, thereby adding to the American public debate a range of perspectives that conventionally are not included within the political discourse. Moreover, *Oprah* is broadcast daily in 134 countries around the world, making Oprah Winfrey arguably one of the most influential Americans in global media culture (Illouz 2003a, 2–3). In this way, these episodes help to shape the way non-Americans view "America," including the way in which the United States responds to the tragedy of 9/11, the War on Terror, and the war in Iraq.

9/11 on *The Oprah Winfrey Show*

During the first two weeks after 9/11, almost all of the episodes of *The Oprah Winfrey Show* focused on the terrorist attacks and the way American citizens should respond to such a tragedy: "America Under Attack: Where Do We Stand Now?" (17 September 2001), "How to Talk to Children about America Under Attack" (18 September 2001), "Dr. Phil Helps Grieving Americans, Part 1 and 2" (19 and 25 September 2001), "Tribute to Loved Ones Lost" (20 September 2001), "Music to Heal Our Hearts," starring Sam Harris singing "You'll Never Walk Alone" (21 September 2001), "What Really Matters Now?" (26 September 2001), and "Americans Take Action" (27 September 2001). In the months that followed, *The Oprah Winfrey Show* continued to devote regular attention to 9/11 and its aftermath, specifically showing how American viewers should cope with the threat of terrorism within their daily lives, educating the American viewers about Islam within an international context, providing a forum for both experts and viewers to discuss international politics, and, most significantly, restoring the faith in America and its ideals of freedom and democracy.

In her excellent essay on American television after 9/11, Lynn Spigel has criticized the way *The Oprah Winfrey Show* tends to personalize and dramatize 9/11 as an event that needs therapeutic counseling rather than an understanding of international politics. Spigel specifically focuses on an episode that features a pregnant widow whose husband has died in the September 11 attacks and who has not only lost her husband but her voice as well. According to Spigel, "the program implicitly asks viewers to identify with this woman as the moral and innocent victim of *chance*," and thus "any casual agent (or any sense that her suffering is actually the result of complex political histories) is reduced to the 'twist of fate' narrative fortunes of the daytime soap" (Spigel 2004, 247, emphasis in original).[1] Although *The Oprah Winfrey Show* indeed depoliticizes 9/11 by turning it into an individual personal experience, thereby oversimplifying the sociopolitical context, the talk show does emphasize personal agency, suggesting that its guests and viewers are not innocent victims of their circumstances but capable of making changes if they choose to do so. In this specific episode, the voiceless widow is advised by *The Oprah Winfrey Show*'s regular therapist Dr. Phil (in his infamous quick-fix psychology style) to take back control over her own life. Similarly, in all 9/11 episodes, the viewers are challenged to "see what you can do at home" to make sense of the terrorist attacks, thereby actively turning the political into the personal. To describe such a process, Jane Shattuc borrows from the mainstream press the term "Oprahfication," which originally was used to denounce American television's sensationalism. As Shattuc explains, talk shows such as *The Oprah Winfrey Show* not only connect the private to the public sphere by including the perspectives of ordinary people in the public debate (which traditionally tends to be dominated by certified and mostly male experts) but also "translate politics into the everyday experience of the political" (Shattuc 1999, 177).

This process of Oprahfication, a characteristic of the talk show genre in general, can be viewed as having both a positive and a negative impact on the public debate on television. Positively, Oprahfication has resulted in a more open and diverse debate, enabling voices to be heard that previously were often excluded, including those of women, ethnic minorities, and gays and lesbians (Gamson 1998). Yet, negatively, Oprahfication often has resulted in oversimplification, trivialization, and sensationalism, as serious issues tend to be reduced to confessions of personal scandal and sexual lifestyle meant to entertain rather than to inform the public. Both the positive and negative sides of Oprahfication run parallel to the Americanization debate. The talk show, often considered to be originally an American television genre, presents characteristics that traditionally are associated with American commercial television in contrast to European public service television. In such a comparison, American television is perceived as popular entertainment, while European television is considered to be part of the bourgeois public sphere. European television, historically rooted in public broadcasting, addresses its viewers as citizens ("audience-as-public") who need to be informed to enable a public debate based on rational argumentation, resulting in political consensus. Commercial American television, on the contrary, addresses its viewers as consumers ("audience-as-market") who need to be kept entertained, thereby placing a strong emphasis on emotional argumentation and personal choice, resulting in sensationalist conflict (Ang 1991, 24–32; Murdock 2000; Ouellette and Lewis 2004). Several scholars, including Ien Ang, Graham Murdock, and Laurie Ouellette, have rightfully argued that such a distinction is much too rigid, as there are many examples, both in the United States and in Europe, that show that the two traditions are present in the media cultures on both sides of the Atlantic. Moreover, the distinction tends to become strongly gendered,

reinforcing the rationality of the public sphere as masculine and the emotionality of the private sphere as feminine. However problematic, recognizing this
distinction remains significant, if only to show how it is being challenged by
The Oprah Winfrey Show, which actually merges the two traditions.

On *The Oprah Winfrey Show*, and particularly the 9/11 episodes, Oprah
Winfrey often explicitly addresses her viewers as citizens who have a right to
be informed in order to decide for themselves about important political and
social issues. Noteworthy, and perhaps rather surprisingly, in spite of her large
global audience (which actually might outnumber her American one), Winfrey
tends to identify her viewers as *American* citizens, whose undeniable rights are
identified as being fundamentally American as well. In addition, *The Oprah
Winfrey Show* provides ordinary Americans with a forum to discuss current
affairs, not only as featured guests, but also through audience participation and
discussion boards made available on the show's website. *The Oprah Winfrey
Show* is also a heavily sponsored program, however, targeting its viewers as
consumers constituting a large market for a wide variety of commodities to be
sold, ranging from fashion, film, and pop music, to furniture, food, and literature. Products that are featured on *Oprah* (including Oprah as a trademarked
commodity herself) often become instant bestsellers, a commercial impact
that became highly visible with the success of Oprah's Book Club (Farr 2004).
Moreover, the effective combination of American citizenship with consumerism is heavily invested with American ideology. Oprah Winfrey herself, as a
formerly overweight African American woman who became one of the most
powerful individuals in the American media industry, embodies an American
success story, whose star myth (Oprah's American Dream) is reinforced by each
episode of her talk show. As Eva Illouz has shown, Oprah Winfrey uses her
life biography, including her personal history of sexual abuse, poverty, racism,
and being overweight, to make a connection with her audience and to help
them to make the political personal (Illouz 2003a, 37–43).[2] In addition to using
Winfrey's star myth, *The Oprah Winfrey Show* regularly employs American
celebrities, who appear on the show to promote themselves and their recent
products by revealing a glimpse of their personal lives, suggesting that they
too are just ordinary people, encountering the same problems as the *Oprah*
viewers do.[3] This use of the star myth is not limited to the celebrities of the
entertainment industry. During the presidential elections of 2000, both the
Democratic candidate Al Gore and the Republican candidate George W. Bush
visited *Oprah* (respectively, 11 and 19 September 2000). Although the interviews
include "serious" political topics, most attention is paid to the "person" behind
the candidate. Al Gore recalls how the priorities in his life shifted drastically
after his youngest child was seriously injured in a car accident, whereas George

Bush, in his turn, discusses his ongoing battle with alcoholism, revealing that he decided to quit drinking while he was jogging. In this way, reaffirming the American Dream, *The Oprah Winfrey Show* combines citizenship with consumerism, politics with entertainment, and public issues with private affairs, all in one commercially profitable television show.

Although more severe than most of the talk show's regular topics, 9/11 does fit easily within the format of *The Oprah Winfrey Show*. Similar to the way *Oprah* approaches other traumatic experiences, 9/11 is treated first as an issue that can be dealt with pragmatically. Practical questions are addressed, such as "How to Control Your Fears" (18 and 25 October 2001), "When Will You Fly Again?" and "Will You Fly This Holiday Season?" (12 October and 16 November 2001), "What Does High Alert Mean?" (2 November 2001), and "Living with Terrorism" (9 November 2001), the latter episode consisting of pretaped interviews with women living in Northern Ireland and Israel. In the twice-broadcast episode "America Under Attack" (13 and 14 September 2001), Dr. Phil tells the audience that "it is not a weakness to hurt and feel and cry" and that giving blood and displaying the American flag might help to cope with the pain: "We do need to give ourselves permission to grieve." The episode "How to Talk to Children About America Under Attack" (18 September 2001) features First Lady Laura Bush as guest, who explains that 9/11 has made her realize that "the people we love, [and] our country" are the most important. Answering Oprah Winfrey's question if the president is still able to sleep at night, Laura Bush answers: "Yes, we're both sleeping. . . . He's so proud of America. . . . We've never been so unified. It strengthens him and it strengthens me when we see how people are handling it all over the country." Like Dr. Phil, Laura Bush emphasizes the therapeutic quality of loving each other and honoring America, as she suggests that, to deal with the fear and anxiety brought on by 9/11, American children can "write letters to their own firefighters and policemen in their neighborhood to thank them in honor of those that were lost." By transforming possible feelings of fear, anger, anxiety, and grief into acts of explicit American patriotism, *The Oprah Winfrey Show* translates 9/11 into a personal yet collective experience of the political, albeit with little room for political questioning or dissent.

In addition, *The Oprah Winfrey Show* provides its viewers with background information on international affairs, specifically on the history of Afghanistan and Islam, in the episodes "Is War the Only Answer?" (1 October 2001), "Islam 101" (5 October 2001), and "Inside the Taliban" (11 October 2001). Although the role of the United States as nation state is mentioned, most notably the "billions of dollars in weapons supplied by the United States" to Afghanistan in its war with the Soviet Union, the emphasis is placed on the distinction between

Muslim fundamentalism and the peaceful character of Islam. That the 9/11 terrorists do not represent the majority of Muslims, either worldwide or within the United States, is the talk show's most repeated message. In the episode "Where Do We Stand Now?" (17 September 2001), Oprah Winfrey's question "Why do they hate us?" is answered by Judith Miller, a reporter for the *New York Times,* specializing in the Middle East: "I find that most Middle Easterners admire and envy America. There is only a small minority that hates us and resent us for our power and what they perceive as our arrogance." The episode "Islam 101" (5 October 2001) features portraits of two "normal and modern" American Muslim women, Manal and Noreen, who explain that their practice of Islam, including wearing the hijab veil, is an example of the American freedoms of religion and choice, rather than an example of religious oppression. "We're just leading our lives, practicing our faith, doing everything else that normal America does." Different than in the later episodes that question whether or not the United States should invade Iraq (which will be discussed further on in this chapter), there is little room for dissenting voices, as the talk show's focus is primarily on promoting unity and human universalism, suggesting that, in spite of religious and cultural differences, ultimately all people are the same. Thus, although *Oprah* touches upon the political reality of American foreign policy, the talk show does so uncritically by presenting America as the embodiment of freedom and democracy, thereby reinforcing rather than questioning the dominant role the United States plays in international politics.

Here the double bind of Americanness and self-acclaimed universalism comes to the foreground. In an essay written before (but published after) 9/11, Eva Illouz argues that *The Oprah Winfrey Show* exports an American conception of suffering around the world, one that "is individual, is located in the private sphere, has a psychic character and concerns the self." By making a distinction between "imported suffering" (images of anonymous non-Western suffering as shown on the Western news) and "exported suffering" (narratives of suffering by individuals as presented on the globally mediated American talk shows), Illouz suggests that "the first is a daily and perhaps by now routinized reminder of the inequality in the distribution of collective resources across the globe, [whereas] the second is more democratic in that it includes all and invites all of us [both Americans and non-Americans] to join in the community of sufferers" (Illouz 2003b, 196). In other words, American suffering is individualized and personalized in such a way that it becomes widely (even globally) accessible as a universal human experience. This notion is made visible by the 9/11 episodes of *The Oprah Winfrey Show,* which present 9/11 not only as a tragedy that happened specifically to the United States but also as a collective traumatic suffering that can be shared universally, across national and cultural boundaries. The *Oprah* episodes "Music to Heal Our Hearts" (21 September 2001), "Dr. Phil on Deciding What's Important Now" (9 October 2001), and "Photos That Define Us" (5 November 2001) use artistic expressions, such as poetry, gospel music, photography, and prayers, as inspirational sources for collective healing. Even "Martha Stewart's Comforts of Home" (8 November 2001), featuring the latest trends in home decoration, is presented as part of this 9/11 healing process, suggesting that "staying home is offering a new sense of comfort." By focusing on the belief that the love for one's family and home is a universally shared ideal, *The Oprah Winfrey Show* suggests that cultural differences can be overcome by celebrating a universal multiculturalism, thereby mystifying the socioeconomic realities of international politics.

This perspective of American exceptionalism as universal ideal is reinforced by the way *The Oprah Winfrey Show* repeats the conventional depiction of an imagined America as the Beacon of Freedom and Opportunity, which provides a safe haven for refugees coming from all around the world. The episode "Why I Came To America" (31 October 2001) features pretaped interviews with former and recent immigrants who describe how they found "freedom" in America after they escaped from oppressive regimes, including Nazi Germany, the Cambodian Khmer Rouge, and the Taliban of Afghanistan. The "before America" segments are shown in black-and-white, with gloomy music as soundtrack. When the immigrants begin talking about their arrival in the United States, however, the screen returns to color, while the camera zooms in and the soundtrack plays upbeat music, clearly an attempt to invoke the clichéd metaphor of light triumphing over darkness. The episode's main guest is Mawi Asgedom, who, as a young child, immigrated to the United States with his family. A pretaped video segment describes the family's "escape" from "their war-torn country of Ethiopia after spending years in a refugee camp and trekking through the brutal deserts of Africa." As Winfrey's voice-over states: "Mawi has taken full advantage of what America has to offer. . . . [He] received a scholarship to Harvard and was chosen by his class to give the commencement speech at graduation." Although, in the pretaped segment, Asgedom mentions the racism and inhospitality that he and his family encountered in the United States, in the following studio interview, Winfrey exclusively focuses on him being an American success story. Asgedom confirms Winfrey's view by exclaiming: "Where else but America can someone have no money, not know the language, grow up, work hard, respect other people, and end up getting a scholarship to go to college? That's only possible in America. That's the American Dream that people have been dreaming about for years." In the thread "What kinds of opportunities does America offer that might not be found elsewhere?" on the talk show's digital message board (www.oprah.com), this claim of American exceptionalism prompted some disagreement. Canadian viewers point out that in Canada immigrants can also live in a free society and make their dreams come true. One viewer, being herself an immigrant from Ethiopia living in the United States, explains that Mawi Asgedom is the exception, not the rule. Most Ethiopian immigrants work in low-paid jobs, do not have the money to go to college (let alone Harvard), and encounter structural racism in their daily lives. Such dissenting voices, however, are not included in the talk show's broadcast, perhaps because they do not fit within *Oprah's* presentation of America as the Beacon of Freedom and Opportunity.

By using Mawi Asgedom's American success story, thereby emphasizing the values of meritocracy such as individual agency and self-reliance, *The Oprah Winfrey Show* not only claims that freedom is exceptionally American but also uncritically assumes that the American conception of these values is universally shared. Subsequently, the talk show explicitly connects the American Dream to 9/11, albeit in a subtle way. One of the pretaped interviews features Thida Mam, a refugee from Cambodia who, as Winfrey's voice-over tells us, "walked hundreds of miles to reach freedom in the United States." Freedom is often taken for granted, Thida Mam explains, except by those who do not live in freedom, adding: "After September 11, we, as Americans, need to protect [our American freedom] because there is no other America to go to." One could, of course, easily dismiss *The Oprah Winfrey Show* as an example of hollow American rhetoric, continuously repeating outworn clichés of "America" mixed with the therapeutic jargon of self-help psychology. Such a perspective, however, would ignore how *The Oprah Winfrey Show* effectively makes individual stories of the American Dream visible. Not only Oprah Winfrey herself but also her featured guests (both celebrities and ordinary Americans) again and again are presented as living examples that the American conception of meritocracy, including its values of freedom, individualism, and self-reliance, is attainable and also—allegedly—universally shared.

Iraq on *The Oprah Winfrey Show*

During the year following 9/11, *The Oprah Winfrey Show* continued to pay attention to the aftermath of the terrorist attacks with episodes focusing on personal experiences, such as "Lauren Manning's World Trade Center Survival Story" (11 March 2002), and episodes remembering the victims of 9/11, such as "A Tribute to the Mothers of September 11" (10 May 2002) and "A Tribute to the Fathers of September 11" (14 May 2002). But *The Oprah Winfrey Show* also addressed the political debate, specifically, during the end of 2002 and the beginning of 2003, questioning whether or not the United States should invade Iraq, including episodes such as "Is War the Only Answer?" (22 October 2002), "Should the U.S. Attack Iraq?" (6 February 2003), "What You Should Know About Iraq" (6 March 2003), and "Anti-Americanism: Why Do So Many Dislike the U.S.?" (18 March 2003). These episodes received an ambiguous response. While proponents of the war have criticized Oprah Winfrey for allowing "nonpatriotic" and "anti-Bush" views to be expressed on national television, opponents of the war have criticized Winfrey for using her talk show to "market the war" to a mass audience and for conforming to the "propaganda" of the Bush administration.[4] Once the United States had invaded Iraq, Winfrey did follow-up shows, such as "Reporters on the Front Lines in Iraq" (27 March 2003) and "War Stories" (15 April 2003).

Similar to the 9/11 episodes, the Iraq episodes fit within the regular format of *The Oprah Winfrey Show*. Winfrey talks with both experts and the studio audience about the necessity of an American attack on Iraq, the political position of the United States in the world, and the personal consequences for Americans in the military and their families left back home. Expert studio guests include Daniel Benjamin, coauthor of *The Age of Sacred Terror* (22 October 2002), Fawaz Gerges, author of *America and Political Islam* (6 and 18 March 2003), and Kenneth Pollack, author of *The Threatening Storm: The Case for Invading Iraq* (22 October 2002 and 6 March 2003), who all use *The Oprah Winfrey Show* not only to inform the viewers about their expertise and political standpoints but also to promote their books. In addition, *The Oprah Winfrey Show* features pretaped segments featuring well-known opinion makers and politicians, ranging from documentary maker Michael Moore explaining how American military actions in the past have resulted in a growing anti-Americanism around the world (18 March 2003) to Condoleezza Rice, introduced by Oprah Winfrey as "our cool, collected national security advisor," who justifies an American invasion of Iraq by stating that the United States is "helping to free the Iraqi people" (15 April 2003).

Conventionally, the public debate on war and foreign policy tends to be dominated by (mostly male) experts who use technical and military jargon. *The Oprah Winfrey Show* breaks with this mode by including "others" (both male and female laymen) within the debate. The invited experts are encouraged by Winfrey to translate the debate into terms that can be understood by the average viewer at home. Moreover, as the implied viewers of *The Oprah Winfrey Show* are female (more specifically, as Oprah Winfrey often points out in her show, housewives and mothers), other voices are included within the traditionally masculine debate on warfare. In other words, by including the "housewife" within the discussion, the distinction between the (masculine) public and (feminine) private sphere is bridged. By combining political and personal arguments, *Oprah* shows the potential for a more broad and inclusive debate. A wide range of arguments are voiced by the audience members, both proponing and opposing the war in Iraq, using both "rational" and "emotional" arguments, ranging from "we are only involved in Iraq because of the oil and the economic interests of big business" to "I don't want my son to go to war." The debate continues in the "After the Show" segment, which is not broadcast on national television but can be viewed on the Oprah.com website and the Oxygen cable network. Moreover, on the website, viewers are invited to send in comments.

The episode "Is War the Only Answer?" (22 October 2002) is telling in the way in which gender plays a significant role in changing the political into a personal experience of the political. The aforementioned Daniel Benjamin and Kenneth Pollack are the experts present in the studio. Both see the (then still pending) war in Iraq as a necessary evil. Saddam Hussein needs to be disarmed to guarantee American national security. While Benjamin and Pollack are being interviewed in the studio, their comments are alternated by pretaped interviews with two female experts, Helen Caldicott and Jody Williams, who, unlike Benjamin and Pollack, oppose the war. Caldicott fears that a war in Iraq will lead to nuclear war; Williams warns that "preemptive self defense" will set a dangerous precedent. Different than the studio interviews, the pretaped segments are melodramatically edited through the use of close-ups, Winfrey's voice-over, added archival clips, and a swelling soundtrack. Whether or not intentionally, the juxtaposition of the male studio experts and the female pre-taped experts suggests a gender divide between male proponents and female opponents of the war, which is emphasized by the melodramatic editing of the "feminine" argument (even though both female experts use the conventional masculine jargon to question the necessity of war). This gender divide is challenged by the pretaped—and again melodramatically edited—interview that follows. Peggy Noonan, journalist of the *Wall Street Journal* and former speechwriter of President Ronald Reagan, emphasizes the distinction between a male and female perspective on warfare. In principle, Noonan claims, women are against war, as they pass on life; however, women are also caring and want to protect their children. At the moment when "children are being threatened" (thus not something abstract like "national security"), women "naturally" will support the war. As Noonan continues:

Is war the only answer? I am not completely convinced at this point that it is in America's interest to move the war to Iraq and remove Saddam Hussein. As a mother, you do not want your kids to go to war, and you don't want your kids to live in wartime. You want your kids to live in peace. . . . My big question is: Do we have to go to war now to make ourselves safe? Is moving on Iraq going to make the world safer? War is brutal. It is full of waste. It is full of cruelty. Inevitably, children and civilians are harmed. But it is not the worst thing. Sometimes wars have to be fought to protect people, and to protect the world. Not protecting the world is the worst thing.

With her argument, Noonan personalizes the debate by addressing the audience as mothers, playing on their assumed emotions of "maternal instinct" in stark contrast to the "rational" arguments by the other (male and female) experts. Noonan cleverly appropriates the anti-war stance to eventually present a pro-war position, justified not by the conventional masculine jargon of warfare but by evoking the image of a mother protecting her children.

As shown by the contradictory reactions of both the proponents and the opponents of the war in Iraq, accusing Oprah Winfrey of either opposing or promoting the war effort, the Iraq episodes of *The Oprah Winfrey Show* can be perceived in different ways. On the one hand, the talk show has broadened the public debate by including both supporting and opposing arguments, made by both experts and ordinary audience members. Moreover, *Oprah* has enabled the inclusion of personal "emotional" arguments that tend to be excluded from the political "rational" debate, thereby bridging the gap between the public and the private sphere. On the other hand, by turning the political into a personal experience of the political, *The Oprah Winfrey Show* seems to suggest that political positions are predominantly an individual and personal choice, thereby mystifying the way *Oprah* structures the debate through its choice of guests and the way their contributions are edited, as is shown by the segment of Peggy Noonan. In addition, the emphasis on individual and personal choice tends to hide other social-economic and political interests, including (but not limited to) Oprah Winfrey's own economic interest as a commercial television maker.

On her twentieth-anniversary *The Oprah Winfrey Show* DVD box set, Oprah Winfrey singles out 9/11 as a pivotal moment in history, enabling her to present her 9/11 episodes as important contributions to American society. Although one could easily dismiss the talk show's rhetoric of American exceptionalism, presenting the exceptionally American experience as a universal one, *The Oprah Winfrey Show* does succeed in translating an event of international terrorism into a personal yet collective experience of the political, thereby enabling ordinary viewers at home to make sense of international politics within their own lives. While the 9/11 episodes leave little room for dissenting perspectives, the

Iraq episodes of *The Oprah Winfrey Show* do provide a forum for critical voices. In this way, *The Oprah Winfrey Show* functions in an ambiguous fashion: on the one hand, the talk show enables a more diverse public debate, enabling the enunciation of voices that tend to be excluded in the conventional discourse, while on the other, these perspectives are framed within a format that tends to reduce citizens to consumers and political positions to personal choices. Moreover, eventually, *The Oprah Winfrey Show* tends to reinforce rather than challenge the dominance of the United States within global politics and culture.

Notes

This article is based on parts of chapter 2 of Jaap Kooijman, *Fabricating the Absolute Fake: America in Contemporary Pop Culture* (Amsterdam: Amsterdam University Press, 2008).

1. Although Spigel does not name a specific episode of *The Oprah Winfrey Show*, she is most likely referring to "Dr. Phil Helps Grieving Wives" (2 October 2001).
2. See also Howard, "Beginnings with O," in this volume for further elucidation of Oprah's biographical strategies.
3. For example, actress Brooke Shields talked openly on *The Oprah Winfrey Show* about her suffering from postpartum depression after the birth of her daughter, using the opportunity to promote her recent book on the same topic, *Down Came the Rain* (4 May 2005). Two weeks later, actress Kristie Alley discussed her continuous battle with being overweight, while also promoting her book *How to Lose Your Ass and Regain Your Life* and her fictionalized reality television show *Fat Actress*, starring herself (16 May 2005).
4. As example of Winfrey as anti-war, see Ben Shapiro, "The Oprah schnook club," *Townhall.com* (19 March 2003): http://www.townhall.com/columnists/BenShapiro/2003/03/19/the_oprah_schnook_club, accessed 23 July 2008; as example of Winfrey as pro-war, see Fedwa Wazwaz, "Oprah Winfrey: Warmonger?" *CounterPunch* (5 November 2002): http://www.counterpunch.org/wazwaz1105.html, accessed 23 July 2008.

Works Cited

Ang, Ien. 1991. *Desperately Seeking the Audience*. London/New York: Routledge.

Farr, Cecilia Konchar. 2004. *Reading Oprah: How Oprah's Book Club Changed the Way America Reads*. Albany: State University of New York Press.

Gamson, Joshua. 1998. *Freaks Talk Back: Tabloid Talk Shows and Sexual Nonconformity*. Chicago: University of Chicago Press.

Illouz, Eva. 2003a. *Oprah Winfrey and the Glamour of Misery: An Essay on Popular Culture*. New York: Columbia University Press.

———. 2003b. From the Lisbon Disaster to Oprah Winfrey: Suffering as Identity in the Era of Globalization. In *Global America? The Cultural Consequences of Globalization*, ed. Ulrich Beck, Natan Sznaider, and Rainer Winter, 189–205. Liverpool: Liverpool University Press.

Murdock, Graham. 2000. Talk Shows: Democratic Debates and Tabloid Tales. In *Television Across Europe: A Comparative Introduction*, ed. Jan Wieten, Graham Murdock, and Peter Dahlgren, 198–220. London: Sage.

Ouellette, Laurie, and Justin Lewis. 2004. Moving Beyond the "Vast Wasteland": Cultural Policy and Television in the United States. In *The Television Studies Reader*, ed. Robert C. Allen and Annette Hill 52–65. London/New York: Routledge.

Shattuc, Jane M. 1999. The Oprahfication of America: Talk Shows and the Public Sphere. In *Television, History, and American Culture: Feminist Critical Essays*, ed. Mary Beth Haralovich and Lauren Rabinovitz, 168–80. Durham/London: Duke University Press.

Spigel, Lynn. 2004. Entertainment Wars: Television Culture after 9/11. *American Quarterly* 56, no. 2: 235–70.

CHAPTER TEN

From the Nobel to Oprah

Toni Morrison, Body Politics, and Oprah's Book Club

EDITH FRAMPTON

In *The Nobel Lecture in Literature* of 1993, Toni Morrison indicts "the faux language of mindless media," which, along with other dehumanizing discourses, she says, "must be rejected, altered, and exposed," in its relentless perpetuation of the "bottomed-out mind" (16). Given this statement, it might at first seem paradoxical that Morrison has been a highly visible participant in one of the most notable phenomena in the history of television, Oprah's Book Club. This literary enterprise of Oprah Winfrey has been criticized alternately as lowbrow, hyper-commercialized, or patronizing of viewer/readers. But exploration of the Book Club's engagement with the novel *Song of Solomon*, which initiated Morrison's public relationship with Winfrey and her reading group, offers a different understanding of both Oprah's Book Club and Morrison's fiction. This treatment shows that Winfrey's literary project is an unusually women-centered and politicized market force that, its detractors notwithstanding, deserves closer scrutiny from feminists focusing on women writers championed by the Book Club.[1] This was the realization that Morrison made herself, in the course of her first encounter with this television phenomenon. It was an encounter that was mutually enlightening for Morrison, Winfrey, and the members of the Book Club.

History of the Book Club

In 1996 Winfrey inaugurated Oprah's Book Club on *The Oprah Winfrey Show*, which has been the highest rated daytime talk show since its initial season in

1986. It enjoys a daily viewing audience that ranges between fifteen and thirty-three million people on almost 350 channels worldwide (Farr 2005, 1–15; Illouz 2003, 243; Peck 2000, 229; Squire 1997, 98). With this audience base from which to draw for its membership, Oprah's Book Club is easily the largest and most publicized reading group in U.S. history.

Winfrey attests that the Book Club component of the show began very modestly, at the suggestion of her friend and senior producer, Alice McGee, with whom Winfrey had enjoyed a longstanding relationship as "book buddies" (Winfrey 1999, 1). In the club's original phase, a book selection was announced on air once per month. The extraordinary success of the venture took Winfrey, her staff, and the publishing world completely by surprise. After each monthly announcement of a Book Club selection, sales of the chosen book skyrocketed, as devoted club members, eager to participate in this community of primarily female, middle- and working-class readers, purchased their copies and waited for the episode in which the book was being discussed.[2] Subsequently, a taped discussion with the writer, Winfrey, and a few club members, over an intimate dinner, would be televised, along with a carefully edited profile and an interview of the writer in front of a live studio audience.

The second selection for the club was Toni Morrison's complex third novel of 1977, *Song of Solomon*. After it was announced, print sales of *Song of Solomon* quadrupled to 1.2 million, turning a critically acclaimed book into a popular bestseller overnight (Maryles 1997, 18; Hall 2003, 647). This is an astonishing display of market force by a community of female readers. As Morrison herself acknowledged on the air, "To give [*Song of Solomon*] a new life that is larger than its original life is a revolution" ("How'd They Do That" 1996, 4).

Literature, Gender, and Politics

Not all authors have approved of Winfrey's selection of their work for the Book Club or the ways in which she treats literature on the talk show. Jonathan Franzen, for example, publicly admitted to cringing in response to Winfrey's selection of his 2001 novel, *The Corrections*. Franzen's subsequent attempts to downplay his negative comments only further highlight the prevalence of cultural phobia and gendered prejudice in some perspectives on Oprah's Book Club. In a National Public Radio interview with Terry Gross, aired on October 15, 2001, Franzen said that he had hoped that he would attract an elusive male readership from "golfing or watching football on TV or, you know, playing with their flight simulator or whatever" (*Fresh Air 2001*, 2). He expressed fear that Oprah's selection of *The Corrections* would mark it as a "woman's" book and thus detract from its appeal to the very audience he was attempting to attract. Identifying himself with the masculine-gendered arena of New York intellectuals, Franzen disassociates himself from what he perceives as the low-brow antics of daytime television talk shows. But what his fumbling attempts to mitigate his initial comments reinforce is precisely the degree to which the domestic continues to be linked with women and conceptually segregated from "the high-art literary tradition"—the phrase that Franzen used himself to describe the niche to which he aspires (Campbell 2002, 1). In spite of the fact that the esteemed Nobel Laureate Toni Morrison had preceded him, the author of *The Corrections* was less than enthusiastic about his book's selection for Oprah's Book Club.

Others have raised similar questions about Winfrey's literary enterprise, expressing doubt about the ability of her primarily female, daytime-television viewers to comprehend fully, for example, the political message underlying the plot of a novel such as *Song of Solomon*. Referring to "the lowest common denominator of daytime TV discourse," literary scholar John Young complains that "Winfrey's discussion of *Song of Solomon*, for example, reads the characters entirely within the rubric of talk show topics. 'It's about 10 OPRAH shows rolled into one book,' Winfrey told her audience when announcing the selection." However, it is in fact only by demoting the novel's important feminist politics in relation to its racial concerns that Young is able to conclude that "[w]ithin this framework *Song of Solomon* loses its vital political subtext, as the Book Club's discussion ignores the critique of American racial history" (2001, 182).

Related to claims about the alleged depoliticization of Book Club selections is the argument that discussions also reduce readers to passive consumers, who are disciplined into "correct" reading regimens. Supporting this position is cultural sociologist Eva Illouz's observation that "Oprah Winfrey does more than select books; she actively shapes their meaning by interpreting them for and with her readers" (Illouz 2003, 110). More emphatically, media critic Janice Peck stresses that, despite *The Oprah Winfrey Show*'s veneer of an "inclusive, participatory, and democratic" discussion that incorporates "the voices and experiences of social groups historically banished from media representation" (2000, 233), Oprah's Book Club, by sharp contrast,

is clearly implicated in maintaining and perpetuating high/low culture distinc-tions, in disciplining viewers into authoritatively legitimized modes of reading and correct interpretations, in upholding the binary of reading books versus watching television and in narrowing viewers' freedom to exercise their own cultural choices, given that Winfrey selects all of the books. . . . Oprah's Book Club [can] be seen as authoritarian, antidemocratic, and elitist. (240–41)

In order to bolster this claim, she implies that Toni Morrison is complicit in the depoliticized universalization that Peck attributes to Winfrey's Book Club. To illustrate her argument, Peck takes Morrison's description of *Song of Solomon*, which the author provided at the televised dinner discussion, out of context. According to her, Morrison's depiction of the novel as being "about the ways in which we discover, all of us, who and what we are" demonstrates a typical Book Club tendency to define reading reductively, as a quest for self-knowledge or self-improvement (*The Oprah Winfrey Show 20th Anniversary Collection* 2000, Disc 5; Peck 2000, 239). Ignored by Peck, however, are Morrison's additional points: that the novel cannot be reduced to a single sentence and that it is "about a man who learns to fly and all that that means"—comments that precisely underscore the irreducible complexity of literature that resists singular or monistic interpretations ("How'd They Do That?" 1996, 6).

While claims about the depoliticization of Oprah's Book Club are instructive, they are born out of limited conceptions of the political. Close analysis of the transcripts of the Book Club discussion of *Song of Solomon* reveals a very different literary engagement from that suggested by Franzen, Young, Peck, and Illouz. The four Book Club members who participated in the discussion with Morrison at Winfrey's Chicago home contribute a collaborative analysis of *Song of Solomon* that is acutely cognizant of, and brings to light, the rich feminist politics of the novel. While their group discourse does not contain the codified language of academic feminism and unfolds in more conversational modes, it is nonetheless both political and feminist in terms of the women's issues that it foregrounds and its dialogic analytical approach. In particular, these club members provide a critical dimension that is lacking in much of the scholarship on this novel, by focusing on the empowerment and pleasure of motherhood, and specifically breastfeeding. Furthermore, the informal, collaborative nature of their analysis, situated in the domestic sphere of Winfrey's home, represents an anti-authoritarian critical approach that subverts traditional, monologic, patriarchal critical discourse. In order to appreciate the political charge of the Book Club's engagement with *Song of Solomon*, it is helpful to consider it in relation to the feminist politics of difference that emerged in the 1970s.

Feminist Politics of Difference

While feminism has historically emphasized equality between men and women, a major strand of the feminist movement since the mid-1970s has involved a dominant, albeit fiercely contested, focus on women's differences from men and a valorization of these differences, which have been seen by some as "potential sources of strength and power for women, and, more broadly, of a new blueprint for social change" (Eisenstein 1983, xii). The shifting emphasis onto and celebration of women's differences began to influence both creative writing and scholarship in a wide range of disciplines in the second half of the twentieth century. As a partial result of this, widespread interdisciplinary and artistic interest emerged in motherhood as a significant component of many women's lives worldwide. Maternity and mothering practices began to be understood as potentially empowering rather than simply oppressive for women. Ellen Ross articulates the reasons for this interest in the maternal, in her 1995 essay "New Thoughts on 'the Oldest Vocation': Mothers and Motherhood in Recent Feminist Scholarship":

Looking at mothers as "subjects" means learning about the details of their daily material work; and the quality of their feelings for their children; about changes mothering brings in relationships with jobs, men, friends, and lovers; about the public activities and political positions stimulated by women's experiences as caretakers of children; . . . about styles of child care and the meaning of mothering and fathering in different regions, cultures, and communities . . . Without full recognition of the phenomenology of mothering the ability of feminist scholarship to comprehend the scope of women's lives today is much diminished. (398–99)

Through their attention to Toni Morrison's representation of domesticity, motherhood, and female embodiment in *Song of Solomon*, the members of Oprah's Book Club participate in and contribute to ongoing feminist debates about the role of parenting and the transformative somatic aspects of maternity in many women's lives.

The group's televised discussion highlights the novel's engagement with the embodied maternal practice of breastfeeding, which has been a continuously contested cultural practice in relation both to feminism and to popular culture. Valorizations of breastfeeding have often been accused of a conservative and biologically essentialist reduction of women to their reproductive capacities or, on the other hand, as insignificant in relation to larger issues facing women today. To critics, an emphasis on maternal nursing can be seen to ignore the needs and struggles of many people, including lesbian, gay, and adoptive parents, and the vast number of women who must work full-time outside of the home. From this perspective, a privileging of the maternal or of time-intensive mothering practices such as breastfeeding is understood as ideologically disabling of women's fullest participation in the public sphere or as simply impossible under constrained economic and social situations. These issues are particularly acute in relation to people of severely impoverished communities.

However, the vital emphases on material conditions, economic equity, and political agency in different women's lives—long primarily associated with Anglo-American modes of feminist thought—have been consistently countered by "French feminism." Within this tradition, social transformation is effected, in part, through interventions at the level of language, the symbolic, and the aesthetic, since revolution occurs in part by means of discourse that subverts hegemony and the status quo. Furthermore, for Julia Kristeva and others aligned with her thinking, our conception of the "political" should not be framed solely within capitalist discourses of economic production that exploit the body in time, marginalizing the pleasures of the body insofar as these cannot be recruited into economically rewarding processes. A "refusal to equate work with life" is an alternative stance, posited by Toni Morrison herself, which has served as a meaningful caveat for some feminists—one that resonates with post-Lacanian valorizations of *jouissance* (Morrison 1981, 166). To the extent that parenting and its attendant practices, such as breastfeeding, are articulated as pleasurable and valorized as such, they are politically subversive of hegemonic economic, consumerist models of social relations.

The Breastfeeding Subject of *Song of Solomon*

In keeping with second-wave feminist emphases on feminine "difference," Toni Morrison consistently foregrounds the female body as a discursive, racialized construct but also as it is experienced phenomenologically by individual characters. As I have argued elsewhere, one component of this preoccupation is an emphasis on maternal and, more specifically, breastfeeding subjectivities, through multiple Morrison novels.[3] Paradoxically, this emphasis is at odds with and subverts an approach to female embodiment valorized by some theorists of African diasporic experiences and literatures, for whom a frequent refrain celebrates the distancing of women from their overdetermined embodiment.

Morrison's work, on the other hand, refuses to deny the body, choosing subversive reappropriation over rejection. This reappropriation was a key focus of the Book Club's incisive feminist analysis of *Song of Solomon*, a novel set in the violent decades preceding the civil rights movement in the United States. In a narrative as preoccupied as this one is with the processes of naming, the names of characters are especially significant. The protagonist Milkman's own nickname signifies and bears witness to the breastfeeding relationship that he shared with his mother, Ruth, for over five years. While this relationship has been neglected, for the most part, in critical readings of the novel that focus on issues of masculinity, African American heritage, and race relations, it marks both the protagonist's particular identity and Morrison's text generally. The repetition of Milkman's name throughout the novel perpetually recalls the moment of weaning early in the book, when mother and five-year-old son are discovered breastfeeding and the little boy named Macon Dead III is "rechristened with a name he was never able to shake":

In late afternoon, before her husband closed his office and came home, she called her son to her. When he came into the little room she unbuttoned her blouse and smiled. He was too young to be dazzled by her nipples, but he was old enough to be bored by the flat taste of mother's milk, so he came reluctantly, as to a chore, and lay as he had at least once each day of his life in his mother's arms, and tried to pull the thin, faintly sweet milk from her flesh without hurting her with his teeth.

She felt him. His restraint, his courtesy, his indifference, all of which pushed her into fantasy. She had the distinct impression that his lips were pulling from her a thread of light. It was as though she were a cauldron issuing spinning gold. Like the miller's daughter—the one who sat at night in a straw-filled room, thrilled with the secret power Rumpelstiltskin had given her: to see golden thread stream from her very own shuttle. And that was . . . a pleasure she hated to give up. So when Freddie the janitor . . . looked in the window past the evergreen, the terror that sprang to Ruth's eyes came from the quick realization that she was to lose fully half of what made her daily life bearable. (1977, 15, 13–14)

In contrast to the Book Club's engagement with the novel, scholarly readings of *Song of Solomon* tend to mimic Freddie's astonishment at discovering that "Miss Rufie" still breastfeeds her five-year-old son. While the embarrassment and revulsion of numerous critics are revealed by their minimal engagement with this significant narrative moment, Freddie is more generous and contextualizes his surprise, as he says, "you don't see it up here [in the North] much." Freddie associates extended nursing with the traditions of the South and muses: "Used to be a lot of womenfolk nurse they kids a long time down South. Lot of 'em. But you don't see it much no more" (14).

Given, as critic Valerie Smith argues, that within the ethos of the novel, the South is privileged as an ancestral home, in which "communal and mythical values prevail over individualism and materialism," an association with southern traditions is a positive one (Smith 1995, 12). From this perspective, the novel represents the interdependency of the breastfeeding relationship as a valuable holdover from an earlier time in the cultural history of African

Americans, a link to a rapidly disappearing past. By means of her breastfeeding, Ruth forges a link with ancestral epistemologies, despite her subjugation to western ideologies of the nuclear family. Her extended nursing constitutes a fleeting yet powerful resistance to being interpolated completely within hegemonic discourses of middle-class womanhood. This resistance to patriarchal standards is something that emerges as especially significant in the Book Club discussion of the novel.

In addition, breastfeeding signifies an empowerment specifically situated in the female body. By means of lactation, Ruth experiences the possession of a "secret power" that is as valuable as the ability to spin "golden thread." This is in sharp contrast to women's value under male rule. With her own body, "her very own shuttle," she is able to create a seemingly magical substance. Her sense of empowerment, such an excruciatingly tenuous commodity within her life, is a profound "pleasure she hated to give up." This pleasure and power that Ruth accrues through the materiality of breastfeeding is also linked by Morrison to knowledge since, like the protagonist of the "Rumpelstiltskin" story with whom Ruth identifies, she saves herself and is able to keep her child through her unique knowledge and quick wits (Hirsch 1995, 79).

However, what complicates Morrison's nursing scenario here is the representation of the little boy's response. He is described as bored, reluctant, restrained, courteous, and indifferent to this daily interaction with his mother. More pointedly, in keeping with the standards and prejudices of the middle-class culture to which he has been subjected, he had "begun to suspect . . . that these afternoons were strange and wrong" (14). The cost of Ruth's "balm," the "gentle touch or nuzzling" that she requires in order "to get from sunup to sundown," is her son's tedium and embarrassment (13). Added to these is Milkman's disgust when, as an adult, he is eventually able to extract the story of the origin of his nickname. On the other hand, Milkman's eventual epiphany (decades later in the woods at night) can be read as casting a more positive light on his experience of the childhood scene of nursing. These subsequent nocturnal revelations retroactively reinflect his formative breastfeeding experience with positive value at the novel's close.

In short, *Song of Solomon* projects a range of meanings and values onto the nursing relationship. One aspect of the novel's engagement with this relationship is the evocation of a resonant breastfeeding subjectivity in Milkman. Remarkably, that subjectivity exists on a public, communal plane, rather than on a personal, intimate, domestic one. Furthermore, it is a cross-gendered subjectivity. Milkman is thus the mature male who remains the breastfeeding subject, an identity inscribed in his name. In spite of his masculinity, he is perpetually linked to his mother's milk. Hence, Marianne Hirsch is able to argue that "Ruth unwittingly renames Milkman through her act of nursing, repossessing him from the symbolic, connecting him to her with a stream of milk, an alternative to the ink the fathers, white and black, use to write their children's names" (1995, 85).

To argue that Milkman's connection to his mother and his broader maternal heritage is founded upon the embodied interaction of breastfeeding is consistent with the worldview of his wise and eccentric paternal aunt, Pilate, who has received far more critical attention than Ruth. Prominent among her many eccentricities is Pilate's decision to carry a bag of human bones with her through much of her life travels, because, as the narrative persistently reiterates, "[y]ou just can't fly on off and leave a body" (147, 208, 332). The somatic, *Song of Solomon* insists, cannot be rejected, ignored, forgotten, or merely reduced to its symbolic value.

While Morrison foregrounds a male-gendered nursing subjectivity, she more radically creates an intersubjective positionality, which includes both Milkman *and* Ruth. The novel privileges the breastfeeding relationship as an exemplary space between subjects, serving as a bridge that dissolves individuality in favor of mutuality, connection, and interdependence.

Oprah's Book Club Meets Morrison

Morrison's privileging of intersubjectivity and interrelationality over autonomy and separation resonates with the readers who gathered for the dinner discussion of *Song of Solomon* with Oprah and Morrison, as recorded in the show's transcripts. During the dinner party, one club member, Celeste Messer, testifies that she "could connect" with Ruth's pleasure in her embodied difference and, specifically, her reluctance to renounce breastfeeding, as a heightened experience of embodied difference. Referring to her professional life, Messer recalls that, "the one time people saw that I was a woman was when I was pregnant or pumping in the rest room" ("Behind the Scenes at Oprah's Dinner Party" 1996, 13). In keeping with second-wave feminist valorizations of the feminine, she expresses appreciation for the rare recognition that she is not only a member of the workforce but also a woman.

Furthermore, she implicitly reveals the degree to which the female embodied difference that she here celebrates, signified by the lactating maternal breast, has been rendered abject—consigned as it was in her case to the public restroom at her place of work. In order to save up milk for her child and stimulate her breasts to continue lactating, Messer needed to pump at the office; however, this evidence of her maternity was not sanctioned within the public sphere of work. She was therefore expected to hide her lactation among the toilet stalls, where women are often driven not just to pump but to breastfeed their babies. By subsequently bringing her covert maternity into the public discourse of *The Oprah Winfrey Show,* Messer makes a feminist political gesture, subverting the abjection of the closeted lactating body. Her intentional exposure of her nursing practices, and the producers' decision to air this segment, can be understood as conceptually revising Freddie the janitor's forced exposure of Ruth's secret breastfeeding in *Song of Solomon.* Fictional, lived, and televised experience thus mirror and transform one another as part of the Book Club discussion.

Messer's ensuing revelations and the responses to them capture the flavor of an early-second-wave feminist women's consciousness-raising group, in which participants confessionally relate their personal experiences in an intimate setting to other group members. The tone of their discussion is informal, reflective, and supportive, as participants testify and bear witness to each other's experiences. Note, for instance, the continual interjection as Messer reveals her breast-pumping experience:

MS. MORRISON: Mm-hmm.

MS. MESSER: I mean, I got to know more women in that restroom pumping . . .

MS. MORRISON: Mm-hmm.

MS. MESSER: . . . and I hope that's cut out.

WINFREY: That would be the very thing left in.

MS. FOYES: Right.

WINFREY: I got to know more women pumping in the restroom.

MS. MESSER: But it was like, I–I—at night—in the middle of the night, I'd sit there in the dark with my babies . . .

WINFREY: Did you relate to Ruth at all?

MS. MESSER: Ruth is where I connected, with the breastfeeding, because she . . .

WINFREY: Mm-hmmm.

MS. MESSER: . . . with the Milkman connection.

MS. MORRISON: Right. Right.

MS. MESSER: That I didn't want to let it go, because that's the one time I felt I–I connected to all of mankind.

WINFREY: Right.

MS. NEAL: Right.

MS. MORRISON: Right.

MS. MESSER: And I was a woman. And as soon as the pregnancy's gone and the breast-feeding's gone . . .

WINFREY: Whoa.

MS. FOYES: You're back on your own.

MS. MESSER: . . . I'm kind of back in the man's world. ("Behind the Scenes at Oprah's Dinner Party" 1996, 13–14)

Messer articulates not only her pleasure in feminine difference but, more specifically, the embodied practice of breastfeeding, by means of which she experiences a rare and valuable sense of human interconnection. It is an experience that she disassociates from the male-dominated public sphere of alienated labor and sociality, with its valorization of autonomy and separation, which structures much of her daily life. Breastfeeding, by contrast, takes place, as she says, "in the middle of the night . . . in the dark."

Song of Solomon's significant engagement with breastfeeding, overlooked within most criticism on the text, thus emerges as a particularly important aspect of the novel for Messer and the other members of the group. Since to speak is to claim a certain agency, the Book Club discussion of breastfeeding in Morrison's novel involves issues of voice, action, and power for women in their largely devalorized and silenced roles as mothers. However, in addition to the transformative impact of articulating the silenced voices of mothers, there is an intrinsically revelatory value to excavating narratives of the sensual, playful, nurturant, and sometimes painful relationship between infants and their parents that inhere in breastfeeding. Such narratives illuminate a potentially rich and meaningful experience and relationship available to people, which has, in various ways, been ignored, undervalued, demonized, rendered impracticable, sanitized, or monumentalized in various discourses that circulate around the mother and the maternal in our patriarchal culture. Morrison's narrative of Ruth and Milkman, in *Song of Solomon*, incites Messer to come out of the closet (or out from among the toilet stalls) and relate her own personal narrative of breastfeeding. At a broader and more radical level, the Book Club discussion of the intensely intimate corporeal and affective experience of breastfeeding contributes to subverting the cultural hegemony of the heterosexual dyad. The pleasures of embodied interaction are lent multiplicity and diversity, highlighting the polymorphousness of experience not only for the child but for the adult as well, in keeping with French feminist theorizations of Freudian insights.

The emphasis on interrelationality in the group's discussion is also reflected in the metatextual format of their analysis. The conversational, interactive, polyphonic discourse of the Book Club members, with its repeated interjections, confirmations, challenges, and encouragements, is an interrelational mode that stands in direct opposition to the singular, monologic discourse of the individual, authoritatively sanctioned scholar. This polyphonic discursive mode engaged by Winfrey, Morrison, and the Book Club members not only mirrors the polyphony that theorist Mikhail Bakhtin has attributed to the novel genre generally, it also constitutes a political positionality, according to which collectivity, collaboration, and interdependence are privileged over the hegemonic ideology of individualism. In contrast to Peck's allegations, that Winfrey "shapes" the meaning of her club selections, in this case Messer and the other club members collaboratively construct meaning.

Other critics have similarly noted the experiential, identificatory, communal aspect of the club's reading practice, which in no way detracts from the feminist political charge of its analysis. Sarah Robbins, for instance, observes that "the original Book Club took a highly gendered and populist approach to the act of reading, emphasizing affect over intellect, pleasure over highbrow study, and shared, life-related meaning making over decontextualized aesthetic analysis" (2007, 230). Claims that the Book Club ignores racial issues are also countered by Robbins's metatextual analysis, in which she argues that "Winfrey worked to build a cross-racial community of readers, approximating the kind of antiracist solidarity that [bell] hooks had called on feminists to promote" (235). Out of the four club members selected for the dinner discussion with Morrison, only Messer is white, and Winfrey highlights this racial difference, at one point jokingly referring to her as the "Little Miss White Lady Celeste" who gained new insight into race and class through her engagement with *Song of Solomon.*

Winfrey has emerged as a significant champion of Toni Morrison's work, selecting three additional Morrison titles for her club—more than any other author. In fact, in a subsequent televised club discussion of *Sula*, Winfrey claims that without Morrison there never would have been a Book Club on her show (*The Oprah Winfrey Show 20th Anniversary Collection* 2005, Disc 5). Thus, while literature, the literary marketplace, and traditional literary prizes such as the Nobel continue to be sites of gender struggle, a new literary prize could be said to have emerged from an unexpected sphere. Much as Milkman is reclaimed by his mothers, Oprah's Book Club repossesses a piece of the literary sphere for middle- and working-class women by creating its own analytic mode and alternative literary prize, in which the domestic and maternal—including the intercorporeal breastfeeding relationship—are valued as worthy of critical study. Oprah's Book Club offers both immense material rewards to its selected authors and a meaningful literary community to a widespread, diverse female readership. Given the latter, it is perhaps not surprising that the club has been mocked, disparaged, or ignored by some members of the literary elite. It is a politically oriented, women-centered enterprise that, in the face of its detractors, deserves admiration from feminists and women writers alike.

Morrison's encounter with the Book Club was as instructive for her as it was for the Book Club. Toward the end of the evening, she admits that, before having attended the dinner-discussion, she had entertained a somewhat patronizing attitude toward Oprah's Book Club, not unlike that of Jonathan Franzen:

WINFREY: . . . I think the evening surprised even Miss Toni Morrison. We're saying goodbye now. What a happy time we had. It was a delight. It was an evening we will always remember.

MS. MORRISON: Very much so . . . . I told them I thought, oh, well, it might be sort of sweet and stupid. But I had no idea . . .

WINFREY: Really?

MS. MORRISON: . . . that they would be such interesting women—such difference, complicated, you know. How could you tell? . . . I could have written a nice little essay and showed up . . . But this was a really—a truly memorable dinner. ("Behind the Scenes" 1996, 18–19)

In *The Nobel Lecture in Literature* Morrison alludes to the "indecent" discourse of the "made-for-television script" and the "sound bite" (1993, 26); however, in her subsequent encounter with the daytime-TV phenomenon of Oprah's Book Club, she discovered not only an untapped marketplace for her fiction but, perhaps even more surprisingly, a complex feminist politics, manifested in both the metatextual format of the group's unscripted, interactive dinner discussions and also the textual analysis of the collective, riveted to some of the most pressing cultural issues in contemporary women's lives, including the dilemmas and delights of maternal embodiment and the practice of breastfeeding.

Notes

Special thanks to Mary Eagleton, Lucie Armitt, and the Contemporary Women's Writing Network, at whose conference at the University of Wales, Bangor an earlier version of this essay was first presented.

1. According to Audrey Dentith and Roberta F. Hammett, "[l]ike the audience of *The Oprah Winfrey Show* and the heroines of the book club selections, the original book club participants were usually women. Female authors outnumbered males by approximately three to one, and almost all of the novels' protagonists were female" (2007, 213).

2. In a poll of viewers of *The Oprah Winfrey Show*, conducted by the *New York Times* and posted on Oprah.com, 35 percent identified themselves as working class and 42 percent identified themselves as middle class. By contrast, in an online poll conducted by Oprah.com, 52 percent of participants identified themselves, in one question, as working class and 65 percent identified themselves, in a separate question, as middle class ("How Do You Feel About Class"). Accord-

ing to Linda Kay, "[i]n 2001 the audience for *The Oprah Winfrey Show* consisted of 72 percent women, a figure that has remained fairly consistent since the show started in syndication in 1986" (2007, 53).

3. The discussion of *Song of Solomon* in this section draws on my previous work on Morrison's novel (Frampton 2005a, 2005b).

Works Cited

"Behind the Scenes at Oprah's Dinner Party." 1996. Transcript of *The Oprah Winfrey Show*, December 3. Harpo Productions, Inc.

Campbell, James. 2002. "When Popular Culture Meets Grand Literary Tradition: The Case of Jonathan Franzen." In *The Boston Review: A Political and Literary Forum*, April/May. http://www.bostonreview.net/BR27.2/campbell.html (accessed June 19, 2006).

Dentith, Audrey, and Roberta F. Hammett. 2007. "Some Lessons Before Dying: Gender, Morality, and the Missing Critical Discourse in Oprah's Book Club." In *The Oprah Phenomenon*, ed. by Jennifer Harris and Elwood Watson, 207–26. Lexington: University Press of Kentucky.

Eisenstein, Hester. 1983. *Contemporary Feminist Thought*. Boston: G. K. Hall.

Farr, Cecilia Konchar. 2004. *Reading Oprah: How Oprah's Book Club Changed the Way America Reads*. Albany: State University of New York Press.

Frampton, Edith. 2005a. *Writing in "White Ink": Twentieth-Century Narratives of Breastfeeding*, unpublished PhD thesis, University of London.

Frampton, Edith. 2005b. "'You just can't fly on off and leave a body': The Intercorporeal Breastfeeding Subject of Toni Morrison's Fiction." *Women: A Cultural Review* 16, no. 2: 141–63.

Fresh Air. 2001. Transcript of WHYY, National Public Radio, October 15.

Hall, R. Mark. 2003. "The 'Oprahfication' of Literacy: Reading 'Oprah's Book Club.'" In *College English*, 65:6, July: 647.

Hirsch, Marianne. 1995. "Knowing Their Names: Toni Morrison's *Song of Solomon*." In *New Essays on Song of Solomon*, ed. by Valerie Smith, 69–92. Cambridge, Eng.: Cambridge University Press.

"How Do You Feel About Class?" Undated. Class in America. *The Oprah Winfrey Show*, Oprah.com, http://www.oprah.com/cgi-bin/poll0826_new.cgi (accessed July 17, 2007).

"How'd They Do That." November 18, 1996. Transcript of *The Oprah Winfrey Show*. Harpo Productions, Inc.

Illouz, Eva. 2003. *Oprah Winfrey and the Glamour of Misery: An Essay on Popular Culture*. New York: Columbia University Press.

Kay, Linda. 2007. "My Mom and Oprah Winfrey: Her Appeal to White Women." In *The Oprah Phenomenon*, ed. by Jennifer Harris and Elwood Watson, 51–64. Lexington: University Press of Kentucky.

Maryles, Daisy. 1997. "The Oprah Scorecard," In *Publishers Weekly*, 244:16, April 21: 18.

Morrison, Toni. 1977. *Song of Solomon*. London: Vintage, 1998.

———. 1981. *Tar Baby*. New York: Alfred A. Knopf.

———. 1993. *The Nobel Lecture in Literature*. London: Random House.

Peck, Janice. 2000. "Literacy, Seriousness, and the Oprah Winfrey Book Club." In *Tabloid Tales: Global Debates Over Media Standards*, ed. by Colin Sparks and John Tulloch, 229–50. New York: Rowman & Littlefield.

Robbins, Sarah. 2007. "Making Corrections to Oprah's Book Club: Reclaiming Literary Power for Gendered Literacy Management." In *The Oprah Phenomenon*, ed. by Jennifer Harris and Elwood Watson, 227–58. Lexington: University Press of Kentucky.

Ross, Ellen. 1995. "New Thoughts on 'the Oldest Vocation': Mothers and Motherhood in Recent Feminist Scholarship." *Signs: Journal of Women in Culture and Society* 20, no. 2: 398–99.

Smith, Valerie. 1995. Introduction to *New Essays on Song of Solomon*, ed. by Valerie Smith, 1–18. Cambridge, Eng.: Cambridge University Press.

Squire, Corinne. 1997. "Empowering Women?: The *Oprah Winfrey Show*," In *Feminist Television Criticism: A Reader*, ed. by Charlotte Brunsdon, Julie D'Acci, and Lynn Spigel, 98–113. Oxford: Oxford University.

The Oprah Winfrey Show 20th Anniversary Collection, 1985–2005. 2005. Harpo, Inc. Disc 5.

Winfrey, Oprah. 1999. "National Book Award Acceptance Speech." National Book Award Acceptance Speeches: Oprah Winfrey, 50th Anniversary Gold Medal Recipient. The National Book Foundation. http://www.nationalbook.org/nbaacceptspeech_owinfrey.html (accessed July 3, 2006).

Young, John. 2001. "Toni Morrison, Oprah Winfrey, and Postmodern Popular Audiences," *African American Review* 35, no. 2: 181–204.

CHAPTER ELEVEN

Lost in Translation

Irony and Contradiction in Harpo's Production of Zora Neale Hurston's Their Eyes Were Watching God

TRYSTAN T. COTTEN

On March 6, 2005, at 9 P.M. ABC network aired the movie *Their Eyes Were Watching God*, a screen adaptation of Zora Neale Hurston's 1937 novel (by the same name) produced by Oprah Winfrey's media production company, Harpo, Inc. Hurston's novel was adapted to screenplay by playwright Suzan-Lori Parks and writers/producers Misan Sagay and Bobby Smith Jr., who have a long list of awards and achievements in both Hollywood and foreign cinema. It is not clear what role Oprah Winfrey played in the film's production, but it seems safe to say (at the very least) that she had a heavy stake in the movie's focus on romance in the novel and approved of the director's final cut.

The film focuses on and celebrates a young black woman's desire to explore the larger world beyond her grandmother's farm and to find true love in a passionate and caring man. Rural cinematography, dialogic conflict, and seasoned Hollywood actors draw viewers into the cinematic narrative. Like the novel, the film begins where it will end with Janie (played by actor Halle Berry) returning from the Everglades to Eatonville after running away with and eventually killing her third love, Tea Cake. The filmic narrative unfolds in Janie retelling her story to her best friend, Phoebe (played by actor Nicki Micheaux), in a pastoral scene of idyllic countryside. This scene of nature and many others encompassing the infamous pear tree of *Their Eyes*, which recurs at key moments throughout the movie similar to its *tropic* function in the novel, mark Janie's budding sexuality and potential fecundity.

In comparison to the novel's rich and complexly structured narrative that engages a range of diverse issues among blacks (sexual norms, black folk expression, color hierarchies, patriarchy, and so forth) the filmic narrative focuses almost exclusively on Janie's three marriages and her search for romantic love. Especially disturbing about this focus is the film's obvious omission of vital portions of the novel dealing with race, racism, and an entrenched male chauvinism informed by racism, which muted Hurston's eloquent rendering of how interlocking systems of oppression complicate black women's pursuit of financial security, romantic love, and personal happiness. There is a brief moment of signifying race early in the film when Janie is returning from the Everglades to Eatonville and passes a sign identifying the town as the first black town to be incorporated in America, which immediately signals the importance of race and the African American struggle for economic and political self-determination. Yet, the many important scenes dealing with racial subjects in the novel are left out of the movie altogether. The book's portrayal of rural folk life in black southern communities is also downplayed to a large extent, moreover, including some of its less savory aspects like color hierarchies among some African Americans. Hurston bypasses conventional representations of black women as figures of tragedy, objects of scorn, and mediators of male heroism, moreover, casting Janie, for example, as strong-willed, persevering, *and* romantic, but this was lost in actor Halle Berry's one-dimensional rendering of Janie's character. Hurston's exploration of black women's powerlessness at the hands of African American patriarchy is reduced to an issue of miscommunication between the sexes. In translating the novel into screenplay, Harpo producers overemphasize the novel's romantic elements and steer clear of its more controversial scenes and dialogues.

It is with some irony that Harpo remade Huston's novel as a romance and erased all references to race and racism, because Hurston chose this genre for *Their Eyes* precisely to challenge racial caricatures of African Americans in American literature and to present plots that show blacks as a more complex and humane people not unlike other racial and ethnic groups in America. Romance allowed Hurston to treat "the higher emotions and love life" of African Americans and cast them as "the average, struggling, non-morbid Negro[s]" (Hurston 1950, 170, 173). While the genre is not conducive for social protest, Hurston navigates its codes strategically to convey a love story about black female desire and the underlying race, class, and gender politics that trouble the course of its fulfillment. She does not sacrifice politics to aesthetics but adroitly balances both in a web of uneasy tensions to show how the intersectional nature of multiple, interlocking oppressions shape every aspect of black women's lives, including their pursuit of something so seemingly nonpolitical as romantic love. This balancing act by Hurston was a missed opportunity for Harpo producers to capture on screen what she so skillfully expressed in literary form.

Cracks and Fissures

One effective strategy that Harpo producers use to neutralize the novel's social commentary is the overemphasis of its romantic elements. Janie's quest to find her own voice and live by her own values in the novel is reduced to getting hitched in the movie, which reduces and refocuses Hurston's critique of the very social and political injustices that complicate and undermine black women's attainment of personal happiness. Harpo's choice is effective because romances tend to preclude exploration of social and political issues, although, as noted earlier, Hurston adeptly weaves a piercing political voice throughout *Their Eyes* that seems to be lost on the screenwriters and producers. Before the film begins, viewers encounter Winfrey's face and voice, which preface the movie with the following:

I remember when I first read this book. I fell in love with the story. It was one of the most beautiful, poignant love stories I have ever read. This is a story about a woman allowing herself to be a full woman and not subjected to the definition or identity that others have carved out for her. The first time Tea Cake kisses Janie reinvents the whole idea and notion of kissing. I would have to say [that] if you can get a kiss like that you can die a happy woman. When this movie airs, Zora Neale Hurston, wherever she is, is gonna give a shout.

Winfrey's preface hones viewers' attention more narrowly to the movie's romantic themes and encourages audiences toward a *romantic* totalization of Janie's story. The screenplay flattens the three-dimensionality of Hurston's portraiture of African American women's struggle into a form that is more familiar and agreeable to Oprah's viewers—mixing romance and rag-to-riches ascension, which the preface merely reinforces. Viewers who do not read the novel are unaware of how Hurston skillfully appropriates and transforms a largely apolitical genre (romance) in order to render a politicized portrait of the racial, gender, and class realities that converge and complicate black women's struggle for something so seemingly simple as love. Audiences certainly would not know that Janie battles an entrenched black patriarchy or that Hurston satirically dissects black people's internalization of white supremacist attitudes in their own communities. Nor would viewers be aware that Harpo producers go to great lengths to whitewash their adaptation of any racial controversies.

The first screenplay distortion of Hurston's novel is a significant one, as it involves the omission of Nanny's testimony about the burdens of black womanhood and of black women being relegated to the bottom rung of multiple hierarchies (racial, gender, and class) as "mules of de world." This occurs when Nanny (played by Ruby Dee) voices concern about Janie's future but excludes the racial references in Nanny's speech in the novel. In the novel Nanny tells her own story of struggling against racial and class oppression and counsels Janie: "Honey, de white man is de ruler of everything as fur as Ah been able tuh find out . . . So the white man throw down de load and tell de nigger man tuh pick it up. He pick it up because he have to, but he don't tote it. He hand it to his womenfolks. De nigger woman is de mule so far as I can see" (14). Most of Nanny's mother-wit about the severity of interlocking systems of oppression for black women is stricken from Harpo's screenplay and shortened to "Honey, women are the mule of the world."

Hurston's positioning of Nanny's story in the first few pages of the novel is narratively strategic and significant, because it frames the trajectory of Janie's quest for love in the story's unfolding. Nanny follows this observation up with examples from her own bondage in the novel, which provides a historical context for understanding her haste to find a husband for Janie and explains why it is so difficult for Janie to feel romantically fulfilled. Nanny describes having been ensnared in a web of insidious contradictions of being raped by the slaveholder and then later being beaten by the slaveholder's wife for being raped. Adding another layer of absurdity to this contradiction, Nanny describes the circumstances of Janie's birth and how her mother (Leafy) had been raped by a black schoolteacher. These elaborations are important because they illustrate how black women have historically been relegated to the lowest rung of American society, shouldering burdens and abuses on many fronts, including many white women and black men whose own tormented oppressions have turned them to be tyrants rather than allies of black women. Nanny's testimony also underscores how the intersection of these burdens shapes the choices available to them, guaranteeing them neither pedestal nor protection in a sea of contradictions, absurdities, and erasures that are destined to navigate without ever fully transcending them. Hurston adroitly weaves this politicized history and subjectivity into the narrative codes of romance fiction, but, in Harpo's version, the producers meticulously and comprehensively delete it from the screenplay.

Harpo's version of *Their Eyes* follows the narrative trajectory of Nanny getting old and searching for a husband for Janie. But because the bulk of Nanny's testimony is omitted and replaced instead by images of Janie flirting with strangers and journeymen who are passing through the neighborhood, the movie insinuates that Janie needs a husband because she is on a fast track to becoming a single (teenage) mother. Such a reductive sexualization of Hurston's representation of Janie's struggle is part of Harpo's overemphasis on the novel's romantic elements in producing the movie. But in the novel, Nanny wants to find Janie a husband not simply because of Janie's sexual awakening but also for financial security. Nanny is old and will die soon, and she is aware that the farm will not be enough to support Janie: "Ah raked and scraped and bought this piece uh land so you wouldn't have to stay in de white folks' yard and tuck yo' head befo' other chillin at school. Dat was all right when you was little. But when you got big enough to understand things in yo' face. And Ah can't die easy thinkin' maybe de menfolks white or black is makin' a spit cup outa you" (Hurston 1937, 19). This is why Nanny urges Janie to settle down with the old man, Logan Killicks, who has sixty acres of land (14).

Nanny's testimony in the novel also recalls the strength and dignity with which black women have historically resisted oppression. It signifies the struggles of bondswomen like Harriet Tubman, Harriet Jacobs, Harriet Wilson, and Sojourner Truth: rape by slave owners and battling the jealous wife; the perils of a women escaping slavery while worrying about their children's safety; and their courage to risk their lives for freedom for themselves and others. Harpo producers' elision of race and racism from the movie, however, disconnects Janie's journey from these women's struggle. Abstracted out of historical inequalities of race and class, Janie's life in the film is treated as being interchangeable with all other women, which gives the impression that systemic inequalities make little substantive difference in the quality of women's lives and their pursuit of happiness and prosperity. While female bonding and support constitute an important staple of Winfrey's talk show, Hurston does not sentimentalize sisterhood between black and white women as free from racial and class tensions. But in the novel, Nanny's testimony illustrates how white women have treated black women with both compassion and contempt. The slave mistress's sadistic vindictiveness toward Nanny illustrates the latter, while the white woman who gives her and Leafy shelter and work after the Civil War exemplifies the former. Hurston presents both sides of white and black women's relationships and the sociopolitical forces complicating them, but Harpo overlays this complexity with the image of uncomplicated sisterhood that is presumed and touted on *The Oprah Winfrey Show* (*TOWS*).

Nanny's story frames Janie's journey and helps sew threads of historical continuity to previous generations of women who contended and fought valiantly against several fronts of oppression. Unfortunately, Harpo's bleaching of Nanny's testimony deracializes Janie's journey in the movie and makes it difficult for viewers to understand and appreciate the unique challenges that she (and most other black women) face against multiple levels of oppression in their search for the good and happy life. Janie's character in the movie might be played by Halle Berry, but the movie does not come across as uniquely an *African American* woman's story.

Hurston's ability to celebrate and render vividly the texture of African American rural experience is also largely absent in Harpo's rendition of *Their Eyes*. As a writer, poet, and anthropologist, Hurston documented, analyzed, and sought especially to preserve the rural folk customs of African Americans for posterity. But the Harpo screenplay alters the lyrical cadence, rhythm, and rhetorical creativity of the black folk idiom in the novel to fit the more mainstream version of English. This is unfortunate because Hurston's anthropological and literary works have helped readers appreciate the creativity and play of black vernacular, including its grammatical-syntactical overhaul of standard English, signifying ingenuity, and *folk* sensibility. Hurston wanted to present the lives of "average struggling, non-morbid Negroes," and eschewed the dictates of protest literature and racial stereotyping of mainstream publishers. Her work is devoted to presenting the human being-ness of black life in both its simplicity and complexity.

Producers at Harpo alter the novel's dialogue and use high-profile, award-winning celebrities (Halle Berry, Ruby Dee, Ruben Santiago-Hudsen, Terrence Howard, Micheal Ealy), which change the working-class, *folk* texture of the narrative and make it difficult for viewers to appreciate Hurston's celebration of rural African American life. The cast's fame, wealth, and social status add bourgeois polish and an air of cosmopolitanism to characters whose culture is mainly rural, working class, and seasonally migrant in the novel. Using Hollywood celebrities tends to undercut any translations of Hurston's appreciation for rural Negro life to the screen. This Hollywood gloss highlights and contributes to another contradiction between the film and novel in which the characters in the movie enjoy a higher socioeconomic standing (middle class) than those in the novel, who are rural farmers and laborers. Hurston's characters are not even proletarians in the novel, let alone middle-class professionals and skilled artisans. In the novel, Nanny is a freedwoman who has survived slavery and other hardships, but Harpo producers change her occupation and social class to educated schoolteacher in the film and whitewash her triumphs over racism. Most of the wealth in the novel is centralized in the figure of Joe Starks who owns Eatonville's only general store and most of the land that he rents to the townspeople. Everyone else in the novel is poor.

Only a few scenes in the movie delve into the rich texture of African American folk culture. The first two appear early in the movie and are brief, passing images that show Janie's grandmother laundering and Killicks and Janie plowing the farm. These scenes help convey both the hard work and toil performed by black agricultural labor and Oprah's message (an ideological pillar of *TOWS*) that self-initiative and hard work bring success. The images appear in a montage that begins with Janie's humble class origins and progresses to her leaving Killicks for Joe Starks, a proactive decision of self-love that delivers her from poverty.

In chapter 6 of the novel, the townspeople taunt and mock a mule, which showcases the creative ingenuity of the folk vernacular, but this does not make it into the movie. Other characters tease the mule's owner, Matt Bonner, and elaborate endlessly on its misfortunes and misery: "Yeah, Matt, dat mule so skinny till de women is usin' his rib bones fuh uh rub-board, and hangin' things out on his hock-bones tuh dry" (49). This rhetorical play and creativity, called "playing the dozens" in the black vernacular tradition, involves quick-witted retorts, a sharp, caustic tongue, and call-and-response. The main objective is demonstrating verbal ingenuity and dexterity between two interlocutors who are sparring in a war of words, encouraged by a chorus of onlookers laughing and cheering the action along. The game ends when one player stumbles or stutters in her/his response, runs out of responses altogether, or gets angry. Hurston captures this verbal ingenuity of the dozens in chapter 6:

Out in the swamp they made a great ceremony over the mule. They mocked everything human in death. Starks led off with a great eulogy on our departed citizen, our most distinguished citizen and the grief he left behind him, and the people loved the speech . . . [T]hey hoisted Sam up and he talked about the mule as a school teacher first . . . He spoke of the joys of mule-heaven to which the dear departed brother had departed this valley of sorrow; the mule-angels flying around; the miles of green corn and cool water, a pasture of pure bran with a river of molasses running through it; and most glorious of all, *No* Matt Bonner with plow lines and halters to come in and corrupt. Up there, mule-angels would have people to ride on and from his place beside the glittering thrown, the dear departed brother would look down into hell and see the devil plowing Matt Bonner all day long in a hell-hot sun and laying the raw-hide to his back.

With that the sisters got mock-happy and shouted and had to be held up by the menfolks. Everybody enjoyed themselves to the highest and then finally the mule was left to the already impatient buzzards. (Hurston 1937, 57)

This excerpt is one of the many entertaining scenes of rural black culture in Hurston's novel, illustrating some of the rhetorical ingenuity and linguistic prowess of using rich metaphors, onomatopoeias, irony, hyperbole, topsy-turvy inversions, satire, and call-and-response signifying repetitions of the vernacular tradition. Eulogizing the mule reflects (among other things) black folks' ability effortlessly to transform misfortune and tragedy into amusement and laughter, which incorporates the blues aesthetic of turning suffering and oppression into meaningful manna for the weary. The mule's funeral mocks religion lightheartedly, moreover, not to deconstruct but to bring comic relief to the institutionalization of religion and remind readers of its communal origins in the folk gathering together, witnessing, and testifying about their trials for spiritual release. These linguistic and rhetorical ingenuities of the folk vernacular in the novel, which were central to Hurston's work of preserving rural folk culture for posterity, are missing from Harpo's version of *Their Eyes*.

Producers at Harpo hacked away other important elements from the novel, including some of the more entertaining moments, like Hurston's satirical deconstruction of racism perpetuated by blacks against each other as a (black) minstrel parody of white supremacy. As part of her design to show blacks in their *human* complexity and simplicity, at their best and their worse, Hurston explores internalized racism among blacks. Chapter 16 is taken up with one of Janie's neighbors, Mrs. Turner, whose main function in the novel is to parody blacks who worship white and European skin color and physiognomy over African features. Mrs. Turner is a "milky sort of a woman" who hates dark-complected African Americans: "Ah jus' couldn't see mahself married to no black man. It's too many black folks already. We oughta lighten up the race. . . . And they makes me tired. Always laughn'! Dey laughs too much and dey laughs too loud. Always singin' ol' nigger songs! Always cuttin' de monkey for white folks. If it wuzn't for so many black folks it wouldn't be no race problem. De white folks would take us wid dem. De black ones is holdn' us back" (Hurston 1937, 134–35).

Mrs. Turner's character is a blackface caricature of white supremacy. Her racism is extreme, so radically beyond the pale that it surpasses the Ku Klux Klan: "Look at me! Ah ain't got no flat nose and liver lips. Ah'm a featured woman. Ah got white folks features in my face. Still and all Ah got to be lumped in wid all de rest. It ain't fair." The hyperbole of Mrs. Turner's character satirizes America's obsession with race, racial difference and separation, turning it into an absurd spectacle of illogical gibberish. As the dialogue progresses, she becomes more clownish and increasingly nonsensical. Hearing this deterioration of logic, Janie begins to back away and wonder about Mrs. Turner in a moment in the conversation that casts anti-black racism as an obsessive-compulsive anxiety disorder: "Mrs. Turner was almost screaming in fanatical eagerness by now. Janie was dumb and bewildered . . . It was so evident that Mrs. Turner took black folk as a personal affront to herself " (136). Hurston could be more didactic in her treatment of this subject, but she chooses a more subtle tool of ridicule instead, satire, to deconstruct it and push the boundaries of romance fiction while simultaneously steering clear of the protest soapbox. Harpo producers lost an opportunity to highlight Hurston's ingenuity by excluding Mrs. Turner's character from the movie screenplay along with other scenes from the novel.

There are more joyful scenes of communal festivity in the movie that come closer to approximating Hurston's appreciation for rural black folk life. After moving to the Everglades and settling in with the "permanent transients," Tea Cake teaches Janie how to fish, hunt, and enjoy the local blues. In the movie, these scenes function to build the romantic tension and plot between Tea Cake and Janie, as they appear in a larger sequence of images focused on their budding love. In addition to the jook joint scene, the movie briefly showcases the African American blues tradition in faithful adherence to Hurston's description of the rural folk culture. This is one of only a handful of scenes in the movie that animates the black folk cultural expression of Hurston's novel and shows the work-hard/play-hard motto of black migrant culture. Although Tea Cake picks the guitar in Hurston's novel, Michael Ealy (who plays his character in the film) pounds the piano with physically expressive body language that conveys the raucous amusement of communal merriment of blues culture.

Changing the Message

Harpo producers also overemphasize romance by downplaying patriarchy and Hurston's clever dissection of the racial underpinnings of some black men's abuse of women. To be sure, the movie acknowledges male abuse and neglect of women in Janie's second marriage to Jody. But it does so in ways that isolate his behavior as incidental and disconnected from the larger entrenchment of black patriarchy. Jody and Janie's marriage begins with romantic bliss and unfolds alongside the town's development, as he is the common agent driving both of their trajectories forward. A sequence of images showing the hustle and bustle of blacks working together erecting buildings, street lamps, and applying for federal recognition honors Hurston's project of representing blacks outside dominant representational modes and presents a refreshing contrast to screenplays that rely on caricatures of blacks as brutes and clowns to entertain audiences.

As Jody becomes more powerful as the town mayor, however, their marriage begins to turn sour. He exerts increasing control over Janie in paternalistic ways that eventually lead to physical abuse and her realization that she must become a small or lesser presence in relation to him, dispassionate and dispirited in order to be the mayor's wife. Harpo producers skillfully navigate the ideological minefield of representing abuse by black men. The film relies on one explicit scene of Jody slapping Janie to convey the eventual downslide of her loss of self and neglect over the course of their twenty-year relationship, and any abuse and neglect after that is insinuated rather than made explicit, thereby avoiding the black brute's demonization of black men. This characterization is also avoided by the portrayal of Jody as an entrepreneur and politician, an aspirant to the bourgeoisie, which tends to counter representations of the brute anchored in class and racial biases. The film also effectively conveys Janie's gradual loss of self in the marriage and its connection to Jody's increasing power in the town. But the movie stops short of contextualizing Jody's abuse and neglect in a larger patriarchal prerogative of beating women in order to counter feelings of racial inferiority wrought by white supremacy. The racial logic that underpins (and explains) African American patriarchy offered by Hurston in the novel is deleted from key moments in the film's dialogue, giving viewers the impression that Janie's three marriages dissolve for three individual, totally unrelated reasons.

Janie's first marriage to Killicks fails in the movie because she is repelled by his age, hygiene, and lack of attractiveness, which is conveyed by dialogues between her and Nanny initially and later between her and Killicks in bed. This is a fairly accurate representation of their relationship in the novel, but there is an important reference to Killicks's own internalized racial inferiority in relation to Janie's light skin complexion that exacerbates their other differences (generational, gender, work ethic and values, and property) and drives a wedge of mistrust between them that Harpo producers leave out of the film. Without trust, the marriage between Janie and Killicks cannot survive because it lacks a foundation on which to build and bridge the many other divisions separating them. Killicks does not bend to or recognize Janie's need to be pampered like a princess in the novel because he believes that, because of her light skin, she sees herself as above or better than him and other darker skin blacks (29). Racial anxiety is a recurring motif throughout the novel. It fuels Killicks's insistence that Janie plow the fields and do traditional men's work, because the labor-intensive farm work masculinizes her and brings her down from the (racialized and class-inflected) pedestal of "lady" typically reserved for middle-class white women. The bedroom scene and dialogue that reveal his racial anxieties in the novel are edited out of Killicks's lines in the movie. When Janie asks Killicks to clarify his mumbling in the film's bedroom scene comparable to the novel, he expresses the resignation of a man who is too tired by field work to argue with her rather than the righteous indignation of being scorned because of racial prejudice. In the novel, however, he is more expressive.

The latter half of the movie is devoted to Tea Cake's and Janie's relationship. Tea Cake is Janie's true beloved (and third relationship) who sweeps her away from a lonely widowhood and promises love, tenderness, and adventure. He awakens a deep longing within Janie, lulling her with sweet promises, coy glances, and a simple journey-man's charm. Several scenes play up the sexual tension between Janie and Tea Cake during their initial meeting in the store. But he is also a dysfunctional, shiftless hustler who steals Janie's money for drinking and gambling. Occasionally, he also slaps her around, which enhances his own sense of manhood and self-respect: "It relieved that awful fear inside of him. Being able to whip her reassured her in possession. No brutal beating at all. He just slapped her around a bit to show who was boss" (140). Tea Cake would be the perfect love, if it were not for these problems.

Despite what Oprah suggests in the film's preface, Janie's relationship with Tea Cake is not all romantic bliss. While their bond resembles the kind of romantic love that Janie idealizes, it is nonetheless wrought with problems of irresponsibility, manipulation, addiction, codependency, and abuse—problems explored repeatedly on *TOWS*. Although Tea Cake brings Janie more happiness than Jody or Killicks, all the men in her life are abusive or manipulative in some way. Jody and Killicks are emotionally distant and exert dominance physically and through emotional intimidation and neglect and occasionally physical abuse. Tea Cake's gradual encroachment on Janie's autonomy mimics the classic profile of domestic violence, and because her love is blind, she is the perfect prey. Janie's neighbors observe how Tea Cake lulls Janie into isolation, encouraging her to cut ties with friends and the church for a life of youthful abandon. When they move to the Everglades and away from Janie's social support system, Tea Cake begins to change and their relationship deteriorates. The filmic version includes him stealing her money for gambling and then later sweet-talking his way back to her. Tea Cake's control over Janie is more insidious than Jody's because he preys on her desire for love and adventure in order to gain her trust. Tea Cake's abuse of Janie is important for understanding why Janie kills him in the novel. But in the movie his abuse is never mentioned, and the doctor's disclaimer about Tea Cake's dementia insinuates that he attacks Janie because of insanity. In the novel, Janie instinctively surmises that Tea Cake's impending mental breakdown could have dire consequences for her, because she is a battered woman who has learned to track abusers' moods and behavioral patterns in order to survive.

In all three relationships, Hurston critiques black men's mistreatment of black women as patriarchal compensation for internalized white supremacy, making the connection among racism, sexism, and misogyny. The occasion for this insight in the novel occurs when Mrs. Turner attempts to introduce Janie to her brother as a more desirable suitor for Janie than Tea Cake because "[Mrs. Turner] didn't forgive her for marrying a man as dark as Tea Cake, but she felt that she could remedy that. That was what her brother was born for" (134). Tea Cake's darkness makes him less in Mrs. Turner's worldview, a racial snub that he translates into a (gendered) threat to his manhood, which ignites envy, jealousy, anger, and possessiveness. Rather than confront the Turners about their (internalized) white supremacy and the other would-be suitor, Mrs. Turner's brother, Tea Cake displaces his anger onto a safer target, Janie, beating her and boasting to other men around town that "Janie is wherever Ah wants tuh be. Dats de kind uh wife she is" (141). His bragging takes place in a chorus of male characters trading stories and strategies about how to control women, and white supremacy is not far from the narrative surface as an underlying motive. Another character chimes in: "Tea Cake you sho is a lucky man . . . Uh person can see every place you hit her. Ah bet she never raised her hand to tuh hit yuh bah, neither. Take some uh dese l' rusty black women and dey would fight yuh all night long and nest day nobody couldn't tell you ever hit 'em. Dat's the reason Ah done quit beatin' mah woman. You can't make no mark on 'em at all" (140–41). Even as the men are talking about controlling women, race (and skin color) emerges nonetheless to illustrate how racism, sexism, and misogyny are inextricably intertwined in black patriarchy. The subtle reference to skin tone in this dialogic excerpt shows how white supremacy guts black men's (gendered) self-esteem as providers and protectors and connects domestic violence in black families and communities to such racial demoralization. Hurston illustrates how race and racism are inextricably intertwined with the domination of black women and how this domination, moreover, is not an isolatable event of marital discord or miscommunication between the sexes but rather is constituted by a network of collusions, directives, and rationales that institutionalize dominance and control as necessary, normative, and normal.[1]

Conclusion

As a tragic romance, *Their Eyes* tells the story of how a young black woman learns to maneuver through a cultural and social minefield of racism, poverty, and dysfunctional men to avoid new enslavements and validate her own voice and values. Winfrey's description of the novel as "a story about a woman allowing herself to be a full woman and not subjected to the definition or identity that others have carved out for her" captures an element of Hurston's design for *Their Eyes*. But Harpo's overemphasis on the novel's romance as a "beautiful, poignant love story" leads producers to delete vital portions of the novel that help explain Janie's journey—its complicated twists and turns—as something other than a quest to get hitched.

It is with some irony that Harpo's version of *Their Eyes* focuses mainly on the novel's romance, excluding its lessons and insights about race/racism and its impact on African American women's lives. Such concentration contradicts Hurston's life work of celebrating the aesthetic creativity of rural black folk, of articulating black women's desires (and pains), including exposing the social and cultural forces informing them, and of cleverly transgressing and transforming genres to convey such complexities. On one hand, Harpo's version of *Their Eyes* contributes to a progressive agenda of offering more interesting, complex portraitures of African Americans, as it avoids the familiar racist, sexist stereotypes of Mammies and Jezebels, Toms, Coons, and Tragic Mulattos, and offers uplifting images of blacks as ordinary people working hard and sacrificing to pursue dreams and aspirations shared by other races and ethnicities. This is no small accomplishment in a culture that conditions us to accept racist caricatures as normative representations of blacks and reject more complex, uplifting portraits as unrealistic. *Their Eyes* recalls other movies, like *Love Jones* (1997), *Love and Basketball* (2000), and *How She Move* (2007), and offers contrasting relief to the hypersexualization of black women in films like *Monster's Ball* (2001), *Booty Call* (1997), and *Waiting to Exhale* (1995). But, whereas romance was a gateway for Hurston to delve into the psychosocial complexities of African American life and defy racial stereotyping in mainstream American literature, ironically, it is used as a tool by Harpo to edit out Hurston's treatment of race, racism, and racialized patriarchy in black families and communities.

Harpo's deracialization of *Their Eyes* was not lost on some viewers who felt that producers "inaccurately portrayed the characters and the reasons for their actions, thus misleading viewers about the book."[2] One high school student was especially keen about Harpo's failure to translate Hurston's creative genius on screen:

I expected the film to portray the novel. Unfortunelty [sic], the film focused too much on Janies [sic] passion and sexual life, as opposed to focusing on Hurstons [sic] intended topic. This book is supposed to portray the struggles a young black woman endured in order to find true happiness. The film really did not focus on the pear tree, it was only showed one near the beginning. Though in the novel the pear tree isn't mentioned, we, as the reader understand the symbolims [sic] of the pear tree and how it is carried throught [sic] the novel. Another important scene left out was when the town men of Eatonville patronized [sic] a poor yellow mule. The mule symbolizes Janie, and how she is taunted and embarresed [sic] by Joe Starks. Alot [sic] of parts were left out . . .[3]

How might the contradictions between Harpo's movie and Hurston's novel be explained? Why would Harpo producers avoid all contents and references to race and racism in a novel whose generic codes Hurston managed skillfully to navigate *in order to* address these issues? Is it difficult to translate the novel's interweaving of romance and race (social commentary) to the screen? Could a middle ground have been struck that allowed for some inclusion of racial contents in the film? Is this pattern of minimizing the aesthetic merits and social critique of literature reproduced elsewhere in the Oprah Industry?

Several scholars pointed out that Oprah minimizes discussions on the social message and aesthetic merits of literature selected for her Book Club. Kathleen Rooney observes that Winfrey's general treatment of literature glosses over questions of artistic construction and treats books as "stepping stones to a better life" or self-help manuals (2005, 142). Roberta F. Hammett and Audrey Dentith concur that Oprah's literary discussions on *TOWS* "work to minimize the social implications of cultural identities, including gender, race, and social class, and thwart a deeper understanding of social politics in the contemporary world, . . . reifying a culture of individualism while subverting the importance of gender, race, and class identity" (2007, 215). On novels dealing explicitly with racial issues, like Toni Morrison's *The Bluest Eye*, they found that Oprah's "comments on race remained superficial, failing to make explicit and problematic the multiple differences within African American life and their relation to whiteness and its continuing privileges. Even talk of slavery was silenced because it makes people feel guilty. . . . On many occasions, she even distorted the spoken words of others in ways that avoided or circumvented forms of social and cultural critique, a maneuver that indicates her ultimate attention to popularity polls and television ratings" (224, 220).[4]

Given these observations, I want to suggest that Harpo producers played up the romance of *Their Eyes* and excluded the racial issues because they did not want to alienate the largest demographic of Winfrey's followers—white women between eighteen and fifty-five years old. Producers may have reasoned that the novel's romantic elements would appeal to all (heterosexual) women (regardless of their racial and class differences) and that including its deeper expositions of slavery and Jim Crow might alienate a significant portion of this audience. But what about African American viewers? To represent race from a *black* perspective raises a familiar question about the signifying limits of black textual practices observed by Houston Baker and other scholars: how black texts can be introduced to racially bipolar audiences without destroying their central message and integrity. If black viewers had been consulted, would they have wanted *all* of the novel's references to race and racism left out of the movie? Did Harpo think that African Americans would not notice the omissions? Or was it assumed that blacks would not care and that watching an all-black cast on television would suffice to placate them?

Normative procedure for resolving potential racial conflicts in Hollywood cinema is to tailor productions to the preferences of white viewers, many of whom do not want to address contemporary issues of race or be reminded of America's sordid history. When race/racism is treated, it is typically for the purpose of celebrating it as a problem of the past and idealizing white moral conscience for helping the Negro struggle for social justice. Films like *To Kill a Mockingbird* (1962), *Mississippi Burning* (1988), *Amistad* (1995), *Ghosts of Mississippi* (1996), *A Time to Kill* (1996), and *Finding Forrester* (2000) are illustrative. What African American viewers may think or feel about the ways in which a black text or story is told or the industry's assault on their character are rarely considered. Harpo's adaptation of *Their Eyes* to the screen was anything but a modern minstrel Muppet show. The movie treated blacks and African American culture as normative and ordinary and refused typical Hollywood patterns of casting blacks and blackness in comic relief or tragic modes. On another ironic level, Harpo, Inc., accomplishes what Hurston intented: to present a complex portrait of "the higher emotions and love life" of African Americans and "destroy many illusions and romantic traditions which America probably likes to have around" about black people (Hurston 1950, 173). Yet, it does so by whitewashing most of the novel's black folk cultural expression and almost all of its references to race, racism, and the (racialized) sexism of black women.

What is the worst that could have happened if producers at Harpo had compromised and included Nanny's speech, Mrs. Turner's character, and the mule's funeral? These concessions might have showcased Hurston's creative genius at telling a specifically *black* female story, showing how race and racism are present in so many layers of African American life, even in something so seemingly simple as romantic love, without putting race at the narrative center. At the very least, Nanny's speech might have given viewers some appreciation for the people (especially women) whose lives, liberty, and happiness were sacrificed to make America into the empire that it is today. A more accurate representation of Tea Cake's character might have provided a more nuanced understanding of the complex motivating factors that determine domestic abuse in some black households and communities.

It is difficult to know whether a more authentic rendering of Hurston's novel would have hurt the movie's or Oprah's Nielsen ratings. Winfrey's popularity among women declined when she publicly endorsed Senator Barack Obama for president in fall 2007, which may offer some insight into the delicate balance of telling an explicitly *black* story to a predominantly white audience. When Oprah endorsed Obama, she made her race salient in a way that it had not been before, as a political force in the public sphere, and not simply as a performance prop requiring careful manipulation and control. (See Howard's and Crowley's essays in this collection for further analysis of how Winfrey manages race to her advantage in auto/biographies and on *TOWS*.) Gallup polls show that Oprah's favorability ratings went from 74 to 66 percent and her unfavorability increased 50 percent from 17 to 26 (Malcolm). The poll does not break this statistic down into further categories of racial and ethnic difference, but other polls by CNN and MSNBC showed that black women supported Obama by an eight to two margin over Hillary Clinton during the party primaries, suggesting that the majority of fans disagreeing with her endorsement were white viewers. Decline for Winfrey could also have resulted from other factors, including a downward trend in Winfrey's ratings that had already begun two years earlier (Malcolm), or disaffected Republican fans upset by her endorsement of a Democrat. Other followers were outspoken and dismayed by her choice to back a man over a woman candidate, implicitly identifying her gender for alliance while simultaneously eliding her racial identity as an equally legitimate basis.

Winfrey's ratings have since improved and Obama's landslide victory in the election seems to have vindicated her among fans. On election night, Winfrey was interviewed by a reporter about her endorsement. She talked about the importance of taking a chance, of going out on a limb to honor principle, and acknowledged the impact of her actions on her popularity: "I knew that this was the right moment for me to stand up, regardless of what others would think or say. I knew that this was the right thing to do." If principle is important, then why did Oprah allow Harpo producers to bleach *Their Eyes Were Watching God* free of all its most central racialized dialogues, motifs, and subplots to spare white viewers and insure safe Nielsen scores? While Oprah was not present on the production set during the entire time of the film's shooting and editing, she most likely had a definitive say in how the final cut turned out. Heavy editing of the novel's more explicit racial themes seems to have been guided more by (market) concerns not to ruffle the feathers of white viewers. When Harpo produces a biography about Obama's life—and there will be one, given her fondness for him, their personal relationship, and Oprah's penchant for making movies about blacks—one hopes that producers will be guided by his message of *change* (over profit) and produce something more faithful to the president's vision and journey than their adaptation of Hurston's novel to the screen.

Notes

1. In a subtle, nuanced manner and again avoiding explicit protest of Jim Crowism, Hurston reveals the threads connecting gender and racial domination in black families and communities to show how racism emasculates black men, who, in turn, lash out at black women in an attempt to regain some modicum of manhood. The chorus of patriarchs tragically illustrate and reiterate Nanny's earlier point that women are "mules of de world," that black patriarchy makes black women bear "de load" of socioeconomic and psychological burdens of white supremacy. The lighthearted jocularity of the men's discussions on battering tips for controlling their wives satirizes and caricatures black male domination as a feeble attempt to mask underlying feelings of inadequacy and insecurity resulting from racism. Such insight by Hurston and her brilliant use of hyperbole and irony to deconstruct it are lost to movie viewers because Harpo producers excluded these scenes and dialogues from the movie.
2. www.bizrate.com/dramadvds_videos/their-eyes-were-watching-god-dvd--pid338755485/com pareprices.html
3. www.bizrate.com/dramadvds_videos/their-eyes-were-watching-god-dvd--pid338755485/com pareprices.html
4. John Young also finds a pattern of downplaying politics in the marketing strategies of Book Club selections that resonates with other scholars' observations. He analyzes reprint editions of books marketed with the Oprah Book Club seal and shows how the original book jacket of an unequivocally racially charged text like Toni Morrison's *The Bluest Eye* is altered to capitalize on Morrison's literary achievements and celebrity status and erase the novel's obvious racial references. The original cover for Morrison's novel reads: "This is a love story— / except there isn't much love in it. //It's also a fairy tale— / except only the fondest nightmares come true. //It's a murder story— / except the victim lives. //It's not only a black story, / it's a very dark one." The original is replaced by the following *Times'* description on the book cover of "Oprah's" edition: "Toni Morrison's *The Bluest Eye* is an inquiry into the reasons why beauty gets wasted in this country. The beauty in this case is black." This sounds like an opening sound bite for an *The Oprah Winfrey Show* episode. The hint of bitter ironies in the African American human (and especially black women's) condition, is lost in this second marketing strategy. The latter profile reduces the novel to superficial market concerns and rarefies notions of race and racism as merely incidental to more fundamental issues (beauty).

Bibliography

Collins, Patricia Hill. 2004. *Black Sexual Politics: African Americans, Gender, and the New Racism.* New York: Routledge, 2004.

Davies, Carol Boyce. 1994. *Black Women, Writing and Identity: Migrations of the Subject.* New York: Routledge.

Hammett, Roberta F., and Audrey Dentith. 2007. "Some Lessons Before Dying: Gender, Morality, and the Missing Critical Discourse in Oprah's Book Club." In *The Oprah Phenomenon* ed. Jennifer Harris and Elwood Watson. Lexington: University Press of Kentucky.

Harris, Jennifer, and Elwood Watson. Eds. 2007. *The Oprah Phenomenon.* Lexington: University Press of Kentucky.

Hefferman, Virgina. 2005. *New York Times*. clk.atdmt.com/VWV/go/cllcaworo120000114vwv/direct/01/" target="_blank">&ltimg view.atdmt.com/VWV/view/cllcaworo120000114vwv/direct/01/"/a>

Hurston, Zora Neale. 1937 (1990). *Their Eyes Were Watching God*. New York: Harper & Row.

———. 1950 (1979). "What White Publishers Won't Print." In Alice Walker, ed., *I Love Myself When I am Laughing . . . and Then Again When I am Looking Mean and Impressive a Zora Neale Hurston Reader*. Westbury, N.Y.: Feminist Press.

Malcolm, Andrew. 2008. "As Obama Delegate Numbers Climb, Oprah's Ratings Tumble" *Los Angeles Times* http://latimesblogs.latimes.com/washington/2008/05/oprah_obama.html

Rooney, Kathryn. 2005. *Reading with Oprah: The Book Club That Changed America*. Fayetteville: University of Arkansas Press.

Contributors

MONICA J. CASPER is Associate Professor of Sociology and Director of Women's and Gender Studies at Vanderbilt University. Her research and teaching interests center on women's health, sociology of health and medicine, bodies and sexualities, feminist science and technology studies, cultural studies, bioethics, and trauma studies. Dr. Casper is author of *The Making of the Unborn Patient: a Social Anatomy of Fetal Surgery* (Rutgers University Press, 1998), which won the 1998 C. Wright Mills Award from the Society for the Study of Social Problems and the Distinguished Book Award from the Sex and Gender Section of the American Sociological Association. She is editor of *Synthetic Planet: Chemical Politics and the Hazards of Modern Life* (Routledge, 2003). She has written numerous articles on fetal surgery, ethical aspects of prenatal diagnosis and treatment, intersex issues, and breast and cervical cancer.

TRYSTAN T. COTTEN is Assistant Professor of African American Studies in the Department of Ethnic and Gender Studies at California State University, Stanislaus. His areas of scholarship and teaching are globalization and post/colonialism, queer/transgender studies, feminist theory, African Diaspora, and indigenous American literatures. He is the co-editor of *Cultural Sites of Critical Insight* and *Unmaking Race, Remaking Soul.*

KARLYN CROWLEY is Director of Women's and Gender Studies and Assistant Professor of English at St. Norbert College. A recent article from her current project, *When Spirits Take Over: Gender and American New Age Culture,* includes "New Age Feminism? Reading the Woman's 'New Age' Nonfiction Bestseller in the United States" and appears in *Religion and the Culture of Print in Modern America,* ed. Charles Cohen and Paul Boyer, University of Wisconsin Press, 2008.

KATHLEEN DIXON, Professor of English at the University of North Dakota, is the author of a forthcoming book on television talk shows, *Revisiting the Global Village: Three Nations, Three Talk Shows* (Peter Lang). She has also published two books of rhetorical analysis, *Making Relationships: Gender in the Forming of Academic Community* (Peter Lang 1997) and *Outbursts in Academe: Multiculturalism and Other Sources of Conflict* (Heinemann 1998). Most recently, she has published individually- and co-authored essays on the rhetoric of television talk shows in the *Journal of Popular Culture* and the *European Journal of Women's Studies*.

EDITH FRAMPTON is Lecturer in the Department of English and Comparative Literature at San Diego State University, in California. She is the author of *Michèle Roberts*, forthcoming in the Northcote House series, Writers and Their Work. Dr. Frampton's essays on contemporary women writers, Kleinian psychoanalytic theory, and maternal embodiment have appeared in the *Textual Practice, Women: A Cultural Review*, and *Australian Feminist Studies*.

KATHERINE GREGORY is a Health Media Researcher for a government agency in New York City. As an interdisciplinary scholar, ethnographer, and media practitioner focusing on identity, cultural production, and resistance in marginalized social groups, she has taught on such subjects in divergent disciplinary programs at numerous universities in the United States. Her recent book, *The Everyday Lives of Sex Workers in the Netherlands*, addresses working conditions, cultural practices, and social agency of transgendered and migrant sex workers.

JOHN HOWARD is Professor of American Studies at King's College London. He is the author of *Concentration Camps on the Home Front: Japanese Americans in the House of Jim Crow* (2008) and *Men Like That: A Southern Queer History* (1999), both from the University of Chicago Press. He is the editor of three volumes in social and literary history. His work has been translated for publication into German and Japanese.

KACIE JOSSART is a doctoral candidate in the English Department at the University of North Dakota. Her master's thesis, "Transforming the Fairytale: A Diachronic Study of the Utopias of Popular Romance," earned the university's Distinguished Thesis award.

ADRIANA KATZEW is Assistant Professor of Art Education and Director of the Art Education Program at the University of Vermont. Her research focuses on the intersections among Chicana/os, Latina/os, art, education, and activism. She is an artist working in photography and mixed media and has taught photography and creative writing to immigrant children from Puerto Rico and the Dominican Republic.

LILIA DE KATZEW is an Associate Professor of Chicana and Chicano Studies and Chair of Ethnic and Gender Studies Department at California State University, Stanislaus. Currently, she is engaged in interdisciplinary research about different emergent identity constructs experienced by Chicanas and Chicanos and has published articles and book chapters on the pedagogical spaces of Ethnic Studies and Chicana/o Studies, Chicanas/os in education, Chicana/o identity construct, and on the Chicana/o language. She has also worked in numerous Chicana/o community related projects and research programs about Chicanas/os' sociocultural identity construct, health, and education.

JAAP KOOIJMAN is Assistant Professor at the Media and Culture Department at the Universiteit van Amsterdam. His specializations include American popular culture within a global context and Americanization. His most recent book, *Fabricating the Absolute Fake: "America" in Contemporary Pop Culture* (Amsterdam University Press, 2007) examines how images of "America" are appropriated in contemporary Dutch pop culture. His essays on American politics and popular culture have been published in the *Presidential Studies Quarterly*, the *Velvet Light Trap*, *Post Script*, the *European Journal of Cultural Studies*, *GLQ: A Journal of Lesbian and Gay Studies*, and several essay collections, including *Impossible to Hold: Women and Culture in the 1960s* (New York University Press, 2005) and *Popular Music and Film* (2003).

JENNIFER L. REXROAT is a doctoral candidate in the Department of Political Science at the University of Illinois at Chicago with a concentration in the Gender and Women's Studies Program. Her dissertation, "Race, Class, and Feminist Identification," examines the existence of de facto feminism among women of low socioeconomic status and women of color. Her major fields of teaching and research interest include American politics, public policy analysis, and gender and politics.

SHERRA SCHICK teaches in the Department of Communication and Theatre at DePauw University. She specializes in the various ways that media contributes to the construction of race, gender, class, and nationality, and how we might understand this process through the close analysis of media texts and institutions.

KIMBERLY SPRINGER is Senior Lecturer in the American Studies Department at King's College London. She is co-editor of *Stories of Oprah*, as well as *Still Lifting, Still Climbing: African American Women's Contemporary Activism* (New York University Press, 1999). She is the author of *Living for the Revolution: Black Feminist Organizations, 1968–1980* (Duke University Press, 2005). Her writings on black feminism, gender, race, sexuality, and culture have been published and reprinted in a number of monographs, including *Yes Means Yes: Visions of Female Sexual Power and a World Without Rape* (Seal Press, 2008), *Cambridge Companion to W.E.B. DuBois* (Cambridge University Press, 2008), *Interrogating Postfeminism: Gender and the Politics of Contemporary Culture* (Duke University Press, 2007), *Feminist Television Reader: A Reader* (Oxford Television Studies, 2007), *Black Power Studies: Rethinking the Civil Rights and Black Power Eras* (Routledge, 2006), *When Race Becomes Real: Black and White Writers Confront their Personal Histories* (Chicago Review Press, 2002), and *Reel Knockouts: Violent Women in Film* (University of Texas Press, 2001).

HEATHER LAINE TALLEY is a doctoral candidate in the Department of Sociology at Vanderbilt University. Her research and teaching interests focus on sociology of the body, disability studies, science and technology studies, gender and sexuality, and cultural studies. Her dissertation research articulates the sociology of facial "disfigurement" via four case studies of sites wherein "disfigured" faces are remade. She has written on the political implications of images of disability in popular culture, feminist disability studies, and contemporary queer political discourse. She lives a block away from where Oprah's father cuts hair in East Nashville and dreams of inheriting Oprah's show.

Index

abstinence, xvi, 85–86, 90, 92, 97
Abstinence Only Movement, 90, 92, 96
Abt, Vicki, 43
Adams, Oleta, 36
Adams, Yolanda, 36
advocacy journalism, xvii, 119
Afghanistan, 135, 137
Africa, 99–100, 101, 104–7; Ethiopia, 137–38;
    Ethiopian crisis, 103; South Africa, xi, 24, 36,
    101, 104, 107
agency, xv, xvii, 21, 35, 54–55, 58, 61, 110, 138; and
    motherhood, 148–50, 155; personal, 41, 46,
    132; sexual, 91, 93; social, 85
A.M. Chicago, 126
American Dream, xii, xiv, 4, 11, 15, 71, 134–36;
    and exceptionalism, xvii, 137–38, 141; and
    patriotism, xvii, 135
ancestral epistemologies, 152
Ang, Ien, 63n2, 133
Angel Network, viii, xiv, 36, 101, 107–9, 110n1,
    122–23, 125, 128
Angelou, Maya, 11, 36
anti-Americanism, 139
antipoverty, 99
Anzaldúa, Gloria, 78
archetypes, 44–45
Aristotle, 116–18
Asgedom, Mawi, 137–38
atonement, 87, 93
Attala County, Mississippi, 4–7
authentic power, 39–40, 53, 56

Bakhtin, Mikhail, 156
Bakker, Jim and Tammy Faye, 13

Ball, Lucille, 116
Beloved, 15
Benjamin, Daniel, 139–40
Berry, Halle, 161
Bin Laden, Osama, 119
Black Brute, 170
black patriarchy, 163, 169–72, 177n1
black vernacular, 35, 38, 166–67
blues, 167
Blues aesthetic, 168
Bono, 99–100, 102–4, 109, 110n2
Boys and Girls Clubs of America, 128
Bryan, John, 5
Buffalo United Methodist Church, 6, 7
Bush, George W., ix, 134–35
Bush, Laura, 135
Bush administration, 119–21, 139. *See also* Bush,
    George W.

cable news, 118, 120
California State University (Stanislaus), 66
Camp Sister Spirit, 14
cancer, 53, 72
capitalism, xiii, 8, 87, 115–18; and celebrities,
    108–9; and philanthropic consumption,
    100–2
CBS Evening News, 116
Central Valley, California, 65, 67–68, 77, 80,
    81n8
"Change Your Life TV," 36, 52–53, 88, 109
Charitainment, 103, 108–9
Charity Navigator, 128
Chicana/o civil rights movement, 66, 72, 75. See
    also *Movimiento*

church, 5–8, 34–39, 42, 45, 71, 125, 171–72
citizen(s), 77, 122–23, 132–35
citizenship and consumerism, 135
civil rights movement, viii, xiv, 10, 12, 24, 27,
    72, 150
Clinton, President Bill, xi, 100, 121
Clinton, Hillary, 176
Cloud, Dana L., 11, 28
CNN, ix, 115, 124, 176
CNN Larry King Live, ix. *See also* King, Larry
Color Purple, The, xi, 15
Colored Museum, The, 12
commodity culture, 86
confession, xvi, 20, 35, 71, 77, 85, 87, 133, 154;
    confessional, 69, 89, 92
consciousness-raising, 20, 26, 110, 154
consumer(s), xi–xiii, 16, 79, 86, 92, 100, 102–3,
    108–9; citizens as, 133–34; consumerism, 128,
    134–35, 142
contradiction(s), xv, xviii, 19, 28–30, 164, 166, 174
Cooper, Anderson, 124
Corner, John, 127
Cosby, Bill, 12
Cotroneo, Gina, 40–41
Couric, Katie, 116
Cracker Barrel Restaurants, 15
Cronkite, Walter, 118

Danticat, Edwidge, 37
De Certeau, Michel, 52
de facto feminism, 21–22
Decker, Jeffrey Louis, 71
Dee, Ruby, 164
DeGeneres, Ellen, 13, 22. See also *Ellen*
Democracy, 117, 132, 136; and capitalism, 117
diet, xi, 23, 86
domestic violence, 171
Donahue, x
Donahue, Phil, 10, 13, 20, 35. See also *Donahue*
Dr. Phil, 132–35, 137
Driedger, June Mears, 42, 45

education, 24, 66–68, 71–73, 76–79, 80
Ellen, x, 13, 22
empowerment, 6, 20, 25, 27, 30, 31n5, 41, 42–43,
    51, 52, 56, 61, 62, 66, 68, 70, 71, 77, 148, 152

episodes: "Americans Take Action," 132;
    "America Under Attack: Where Do We
    Stand Now?," 132, 135; "Anti-Americanism:
    Why Do So Many Dislike the U.S.?," 139;
    "Christmas Kindness," xvi, 100, 104; "Dr.
    Phil Helps Grieving Americans, Part 1
    and 2," 132; "Dr. Phil on Deciding What's
    Important Now," 137; "Give Away," 35; "How
    to Control Your Fears," 135; "How to Talk
    to Children about America Under Attack,"
    132, 135; "Inside the Taliban," 136; "Islam
    101," 74, 136; "Is War the Only Answer?,"
    136, 139, 140–41; "Is Your Child Leading
    a Double Life?," 91; "Lauren Manning's
    World Trade Center Survival Story," 138;
    "Letters to Oprah's Book Club," 37; "Living
    on the Minimum Wage," 123; "Living with
    Terrorism," 135; "Martha Stewart's Comforts
    of Home," 137; "Music to Heal Our Hearts,"
    132, 137; "On Discovering Why You Are
    Here," 44; "On How to Get Your Power
    Back," 40; "Oprah Goes to Africa," xvi;
    "Oprah's Book Club," 131; "Photos That
    Define Us," 137; "Reporters on the Front
    Lines in Iraq," 139; "The Secret Lives of
    Teen-age Girls," 93; "Should the U.S. Attack
    Iraq?," 139; "Suburban Teens: The New
    Prostitutes," 92; "Teenagers and Dating:
    When's the Right Time?," 95; "Tribute to
    Loved Ones Lost," 132; "A Tribute to the
    Fathers of September 11," 138 "A Tribute to
    the Mothers of September 11," 138; "Truth
    in America," 119; "War Stories," 139; "What
    Does High Alert Mean?," 135; "What Parents
    Should Know about Ecstasy," 131; "What
    Really Matters Now," 132; "What You Should
    Know About Iraq," 139; "When Will You
    Fly Again?," 135; "Where Do We Stand
    Now?," 136; "Why I Came to America," 137;
    "Will You Fly This Holiday Season?," 135;
    "Winfrey on Location: Inside the Katrina
    Catastrophe," 125–26
Epstein, Debbie, 20
ESPN, 118
ET Tonight, 118
ethos, 118, 123–24, 126–28

European television, 133
"exported suffering," 136

familialism, 74, 77
FEMA, 128
Ferguson, James, 102
Fiske, John, 55
folk vernacular, 168
Foucault, Michel, 87
Franklin, Kirk, 36
Franzen, Jonathan, viii, xviii, 146–48, 157
Freston, Kathy, 36

Gates, Bill, 99
Gates, Henry Louis, 101
Gates, Melinda, 99–100
gender, 133, 140, 146–47, 152–53, 156, 162–64, 170,
    172, 174, 176, 177n1
Gerges, Fawaz, 139
Gledhill, Christine, 122
global audience, 89, 134
global markets, 108
global media culture, 132
global warming, 116, 124
Gore, Al, ix, 124–25, 134. See also *Inconvenient
    Truth*
Graham, Stedman, xi, 14, 23, 46n1, 105
Greene, Bob, vii. *See also* diet; weight
Gross, Terry, 146

Haag, Laurie, 35
Habitat for Humanity, 16n4, 128
Hall, Stuart, 52
Hamer, Fannie Lou, 11
Hans Blix Report, 121
Hansberry, Lorraine, 13
Haraway, Donna, 55
Harris, Sam, 132
Harrison, Barbara Grizzuti, 38
hegemony, hegemonic culture, 87
Henson, Brenda and Wanda, 14
HIV/AIDS, 99–100, 101, 104, 106, 110
Hirsch, Marianne, 152
Hollywood, 99, 118, 161, 166, 175
Houston, Whitney, 28. *See also* "I'm Every
    Woman"

Huerta, Dolores, 72
human universalism, 136
Hurricane Katrina, xvii, 116, 123
Hurricane Rita, 116
Hurston, Zora Neale, 161
Hussein, Saddam, 119, 121, 140

"I'm Every Woman" (theme song), 28, 36, 65
"imported suffering," 136
Imus, Don, 74, 82n18
In Style, 99
Inconvenient Truth, 125
individualism, xiv, 6, 11, 72, 73, 76
"Infotainment," 119–20
Iraq, 119, 132, 136, 138–42
Irony, 162, 168, 173, 177n1
Islam, 132, 135–36

Jacobs, Harriet, 165
Jenkins, Henry, 55
Johnson, Richard, 56
Johnson, Tammy, 39
Jouissance, 150
Joyrich, Lynn, 55

Kaffeeklatsch, 124
Kennedy, Adrienne, 13
King, Larry, ix, 23, 24. See also *CNN Larry King
    Live*
Kinsey reports, 88
Kristeva, Julia, 150

Latino, 65, 67, 78–81, 89
Lee, Hattie Mae (grandmother), 4–7
Lee, Vernita (mother), 4
Lesser, Elizabeth, 34
Ling, Lisa, 124
LivingOprah.com, vii. *See also* Okrant, Robin
Lofton, Kathryn, 37, 74–76, 87
logos, 117–18, 123
Look to the Stars, 99
Lynch, Jessica, 120

Mammy, 12, 13, 39
Mandela, Nelson, 106
Marketized philanthropy, 103

marriage, 23–24, 45, 46n1, 78, 79, 88, 162, 169–70
Martin, Steve, 15
Masciarotte, Gloria-Jean, 19, 20, 30, 124
McDonald, Katrina Bell, 65
medical intuitive, 44
melodrama, xvii, 116, 117–18, 122–23, 126–28, 140
Meyer, Joyce, 13
Miller, Judith, 136
Mirande, Alfredo, 73, 77
Misciagno, Patricia, 19, 211
Miss Black America, 10
Miss Black Nashville, 10
Miss Black Tennessee, 10
Moore, Michael, 139
Moorti, Sujata, 19, 20
moral instruction, 89; panic, xvi, 87, 91
Morehouse College, 11
Morrison, Toni, xvii, 11, 100, 145–57, 174, 177n4
motherhood, 148–49
Movimiento, 75–76. *See also* Chicana/o civil
    rights movement
MSNBC, 30, 176
Murdock, Graham, 133
Musto, Michael, 101
Myss, Caroline, 44–45

Nagin, Ray, 125
National Child Protection Act, ix, 36. *See also*
    Oprah's Bill; sexual abuse
National Organization of Women (NOW),
    60–61
National Public Radio, vii, ix, 146
National Research Council, 78
Native Son, xi, 15
Naylor, Gloria, 11
Neilson ratings, 115
Nelson, Joshua, 36
networking model, 55
*New Earth: Awakening to Your Life's Potential,
    A*, 33
New York Times, 5, 59, 101–2, 125, 136; Best-Seller
    List, 119
9/11, xii, 119, 121; and Islam, 136; Oprahfication
    of, 131–41; questioning, 120–21
Noonan, Peggy, 140–41
Nudelman, Franny, 43

O, the Oprah Magazine, x, xi, xii, 24, 25, 37, 86,
    91, 125
O at Home, x
Obama, Barack, ix, xi, xixn3, 125, 176
Okrant, Robin, vii–viii. *See also* LivingOprah.
    com
One Campaign, 99
Oprah & Friends, x
Oprah Culture Industry (TOCI), xii–xvii
Oprah website, 86, 88, 128
Oprah Winfrey Leadership Academy for Girls
    South Africa, 24–25, 36, 101. *See also* school
Oprah Winfrey Network (OWN), x
Oprah Winfrey Show, The (TOWS), ix–x, xiii–xv,
    xvii, 11, 12, 14, 19–21, 22–23, 26, 27–28, 30,
    34–36, 38, 39–40, 44–45, 51, 53, 55, 65, 66–67,
    68–69, 70–72, 74–75, 76–78, 85–97, 115–28,
    167, 171, 174
Oprah.com, vii, x, xv, 40, 53, 61, 140
Oprah's Big Give, viii, 109
Oprah's Bill, ix. *See also* National Child
    Protection Act
Oprah's Child Predator Watch List, 9
Oprah's Favorite Things, vii, ix, xv, 38, 108, 145
*Oprah's Roots: An African American Lives
    Special*, 38, 101
Ouellette, Laurie, 133
Oxygen Media, x, 24, 140

Parks, Lori, 161
pathos, 118–19, 123, 127
Paz, Octavio, 79
Peck, Janice, ix, xii, 71, 76, 147–48, 156
People magazine, 118
philanthropic consumption, 99, 102–3; and
    consumers, 108–10
philanthropy, 100
Pickford, Mary, 116
Piney Woods School, 11
Pinkett Smith, Jada, 92–93
Pinsky, Dr., 95
Planned Parenthood, 90
Plant, Sadie, 55
Plato, 118
political (dis)engagement, 99–100

politics, ix, xi, xvi, xvii, 20, 26–27, 29, 56, 87, 103, 108, 123, 126, 128, 132–33, 135, 136, 141–42, 147, 148, 157, 162, 163, 174, 157n4
Pollack, Kenneth, 139–40
popular culture, xi–xii, 62, 100, 149
promiscuity, xvi, 85
Prose, Francine, 59
Public sphere, 20, 45, 117; and debate, 133; and gender, 122, 128, 149; and private sphere, 141–42; rape, 9, 40–43, 126, 164, 165; rapport, 4, 20, 35, 42; "sister sensibility," 33, 36, 41, 44

RED Campaign, xvi, 102
Rice, Condoleezza, 139
Rich, Frank, 119–20, 125
Riera, Dr. Mike, 95
Rivera, Geraldo, 35
Rhetoric, xvii, 88, 116, 128, 138, 141; abstinence-only, 96; feminist, 24–25; and melodrama, 116–19, 122–23, 128
Rhetorical creativity, 35, 42, 45, 166–68
Rhetorical tropes, 6
Robbins, Bruce, 40
Robbins, Sarah, 156
Roberts, Julia, 124
Robertson, Pat, 13
romance, 161–64, 169, 172–73
Ross, Ellen, 149

Sacred Contracts: Awakening Your Divine Potential, 44. See also Myss, Caroline
Sagay, Misan, 161
Sandoval, Gloria, 72
Sara Lee Corporation, 5
Sawyer, Diane, 25
school, xiii, 5, 6, 8, 9–11, 16n2, 44, 36, 101, 106, 128. See also education; Oprah Winfrey Leadership Academy for Girls South Africa
Seat of the Soul, The, 39, 42. See also Tolle, Eckart
Secret, The, 108
Seesholtz, Mel, 43
Seiter, Ellen, 55
self-help, 1, 6, 8, 11, 35–36, 100, 138, 174
self-improvement, 36, 77, 88, 100–1, 109, 116, 148
sensationalism, 133
sexual abuse, ix, xiv, xv, 22, 37, 38, 40, 70, 134

Shange, Ntozake, 13
Shattuc, Jane, 37, 55, 63n2, 133
Smith, Bobby, Jr., 161
Smith, Dr. Robin, 36, 92, 93
Smith, Valerie, 151
Social Security Act, Title V, 96
Soul Series (radio), 36
Soul Stories (message boards), 52, 53–57, 59–62
Spigel, Lynn, 131–32
spirituality: changes in, 88; "new," 34; "old," 34; overtones of, 87; principles of, 52, 87
Springer, Jerry, 13
Spurlock, Morgan, 123
Squire, Corinne, 20–21, 35
Steinberg, Deborah Lynn, 20
Steinem, Gloria, 22
Stern, Howard, 91
Summerville, Cheryl, 15
Supersize Me, 123
Swaggart, Jimmy, 13

Tannen, Deborah, 20
teen pregnancy, 14, 88, 89, 90, 97
Tennessee State University, 10, 11
terrorism, xvii, 131, 132, 135, 141
theme song. See Houston, Whitney; "I'm Every Woman"
therapeutic discourse, 71–72, 74
Time Magazine, viii, 99, 103
Tolle, Eckart, 33
Tolstoy, Leo, 100
"Town Hall" meeting, 119
tragedy, 89, 116–17, 126, 132, 136, 162, 168
transcendence: race, 11, 21; spiritual, 51, 52, 56, 61
Travolta, John, 100
Truth, Sojourner, 22, 25, 165
Tubman, Harriet, 22, 165
Twentieth Anniversary DVD Collection, 100, 104
Twin Towers, 131

universal woman, xvi, 73, 74, 78
universalism, xvii, 136

Village Voice, 101
voters, 125
voting, 25, 125, 128

Wakeford, Nina, 54–55
Walker, Madame C. J., 22
Wall Street Journal, 140
Walters, Barbara, 15, 23
War on Terror, 132
weaving model, 55
weight loss, 12, 37, 38, 70, 110, 134
Weiss, Richard, 8
Wells, Ida B., 22
Wilbur, Shawn P., 54, 62
Williams, Linda, 118
Williams, Serena, 92–93
Williams, Venus, 93
Wilson, Harriet, 165
Wilson, Sherryl, 70

Winans, BeBe and CeCe, 36
Winfrey, Oprah: de facto feminism, 21–22,
    27–28; and lesbian rumors, 13, 14, 22–23;
    personal as political, 141–42; rape, 9
Winfrey, Vernon (father), 4
Wolfe, George C., 12
Women of Brewster Place, The, xi, 15
women's movement, viii, ix, xiv, 19–20, 21, 27
women's work, 55, 116; and war, 140–41
WVOL, 11

Young, John, 147, 177

Zukav, Gary, 39–43, 45, 51, 53, 56. See also *Seat of
    the Soul*; *Soul Stories, The*